A Musicology for
Landscape

Drawing conceptually and directly on music notation, this book investigates landscape architecture's inherent temporality. It argues that the rich history of notating time in music provides a critical model for this under-researched and under-theorised aspect of landscape architecture, while also ennobling sound in the sensory appreciation of landscape.

A Musicology for Landscape makes available to a wider landscape architecture and urban design audience the works of three influential composers – Morton Feldman, György Ligeti and Michael Finnissy – presenting a critical evaluation of their work within music, as well as a means in which it might be used in design research. Each of the musical scores is juxtaposed with design representations by Kevin Appleyard, Bernard Tschumi and William Kent, before the author examines four landscape spaces through the development of new landscape architectural notations. In doing so, this work offers valuable insights into the methods used by landscape architects for the benefit of musicians, and by bringing together musical composition and landscape architecture through notation, it affords a focused and sensitive exploration of temporality and sound in both fields.

Dr David Nicholas Buck is founder of his eponymous design practice and is a landscape architect and educator with a special interest in the temporality of landscape. He has designed projects in Asia and the UK and has published widely on a range of design topics.

Design Research in Architecture

Series Editors:

Professor Murray Fraser
Bartlett School of Architecture, UCL, UK,

Professor Jonathan Hill
Bartlett School of Architecture, UCL, UK

Professor Jane Rendell
Bartlett School of Architecture, UCL, UK

and

Professor Teddy Cruz
Department of Architecture, University of California at San Diego, USA

Bridging a range of positions between practice and academia, this Routledge series seeks to present the best proponents of architectural design research from around the world. Each author combines innovative historical and theoretical research with creative propositions as a symbiotic interplay. In offering a variety of key exemplars, the book series situates itself at the forefront of design research investigation in architecture.

Other titles in the series

Marcel Duchamp and the Architecture of Desire
Penelope Haralambidou
ISBN 978 1 4094 4345 2

Digital Poetics
An Open Theory of Design-Research in Architecture
Marjan Colletti
ISBN 978 1 4094 4523 4

Transitions: Concepts + Drawings + Buildings
Christine Hawley
ISBN 978 1 4724 0909 6

The Architecture Chronicle
Diary of an Architectural Practice
Jan Kattein
ISBN 978 1 4094 5186 0

Expanding Disciplinarity in Architectural Practice
Designing from the Room to the City
Tom Holbrook
ISBN 978 1 4724 8173 3

Architecture of Resistance
Cultivating Moments of Possibility within the Palestinian/Israeli Conflict
Yara Sharif
ISBN 9781472447883

A Musicology for
Landscape

David Nicholas Buck

Routledge
Taylor & Francis Group

LONDON AND NEW YORK

First published 2017
by Routledge
2 Park Square, Milton Park, Abingdon, Oxon OX14 4RN

and by Routledge
711 Third Avenue, New York, NY 10017

Routledge is an imprint of the Taylor & Francis Group, an informa business

British Library Cataloguing-in-Publication Data
A catalogue record for this book is available from the British Library

Library of Congress Cataloging-in-Publication Data
Names: Buck, David N. Title: A musicology for landscape / David Nicholas Buck.
Description: Abingdon, Oxon ; New York, NY : Routledge, 2017. | Includes bibliographical references and index.
Identifiers: LCCN 2016049110| ISBN 9781138694422 (hb : alk. paper) | ISBN 9781472479389 (pb : alk. paper) | ISBN 9781315208879 (ebook)
Subjects: LCSH: Music--20th century--Philosophy and aesthetics. | Landscape architecture.
Classification: LCC ML3877 B83 2017 | DDC 781.5/3--dc23
LC record available at https://lccn.loc.gov/2016049110

ISBN: 978-1-138-69442-2 (hbk)
ISBN: 978-1-4724-7938-9 (pbk)
ISBN: 978-1-315-20887-9 (ebk)

Typeset in Avenir and Baskerville
by Servis Filmsetting Ltd, Stockport, Cheshire

Printed in the United Kingdom
by Henry Ling Limited

To Y.

Contents

CONTENTS

Figures

Notations

All notations are created by David Buck.

N23 *923 Above*. Qualities of landscape sounds defined. 2013.

N24 *923 Above*. Detailed development of sound qualities. 2013.

N25 *923 Above*. Further development of notation. 2013.

N26 *923 Above*. Layers of sound and landscape qualities. 2013.

LIST OF FILMS

All films were created by David Buck, 2011–2014.

Lines Burnt in Light. 2012. www.db-land.com/films/LinesBurntInLight

Pink Elephants. 2013. www.db-land.com/films/PinkElephants

655. 2013. www.db-land.com/films/655

923 Above. 2013. www.db-land.com/films/923Above

Land of Flowers. 2013. www.db-land.com/films/LandOfFlowers

Acknowledgements

This musicology for landscape would not have been 'realised' without drawing on the generous support of numerous individuals over many years.

This book grew directly out of my PhD at The Bartlett School of Architecture, UCL, and I would like to thank my dedicated supervisors: Dr Penelope Haralambidou (Coordinator MPhil/PhD Architectural Design, UCL) for nurturing the thesis, for her crucial advice on the process of developing research through design, and for her considered comments on the text in its various iterations; Professor Jonathan Hill (Professor of Architecture and Visual Theory and Director of the MPhil/PhD Architectural Design, UCL) for his enthusiastic support, insightful comments throughout the research, and for his patience while waiting for landscape to appear; Professor Neil Heyde (Royal Academy of Music) for generously supporting the research and for his critical advice in the selection of the music notations. I would also like to thank Professor Iain Borden (Professor of Architecture and Urban Culture, UCL) and Professor Katja Grillner (Dean of Faculty KTH Royal Institute of Technology, Stockholm) for their generous support at the critical final stage.

I would like to thank Peter Zinovieff for generously loaning me his original and fascinating notation for *December Hollow*, which was an early inspiration for this investigation of music and landscape. I would like to acknowledge the fantastic support over more than a decade from Howard Riley, one of jazz's most innovative pianists, for my own musical studies. To Michael Finnissy I offer thanks for his generous discussions of time, landscape and music at his home in Steyning, while to Paul Griffiths my appreciation for introducing the book with an epigraph from his own extensive writings on music.

I would like to thank the Bartlett Architectural Research Fund for supporting my visit to the Paul Sacher Foundation, and for the following staff in Basel for their generous support in the access of the archive materials that form critical aspects of this book: Dr Felix Meyer (Director), Dr Heidy Zimmermann, Ms Sabine Hänggi-Stampfli.

I would like to thank Valerie Rose for initially commissioning this book, also the wonderful editor and team at Routledge, Fran Ford, Grace Harrison, Trudy Varcianna, Ting Baker and Lucy Loveluck for their care and nurturing the book during its development and delivery. And to the editors of *Design Research in Architecture* I offer particular thanks for generously including me in their fascinating series: Murray Fraser, Jonathan Hill, Jane Rendell, Teddy Cruz.

Special mention must be given to the wonderful friends who have contributed through their open discussions on landscape and music over many years: Alexandra Blum, David Chapman, Steve Douglas, Stephen Hryncewicz, Toru Mitani, Makoto Noborisaka, Sofie Pelsmaker, David Rathbun, and Yoji Sasaki.

I would like to offer particular thanks to my wonderful mother for nurturing my creative talents since childhood, for her tireless encouragement and enthusiasm, and for a lifetime of ceaseless support.

Lastly, this book is dedicated to my father, Derek Thomas Buck (1926–2002), for inspiring a lifetime of learning and for showing me that anything is possible.

Fide et fortitudine.

IN AN OPEN FIELD

REFLECTIVE WINDOW

One might like to believe that musical notation is a glass window, through which those of us on the outside see into the study of the composer's intentions, experience the sounds exactly as they were imagined. The twentieth century, however, taught us that notation is not a neutral code, that the process of writing affects what is written. Moreover, if the light outside were to dim and the crowd go away, then the window might begin to reflect back the composer's own image, and the incursion of notation into the process of composition become inescapable.[1]

This book addresses a silent aporia in landscape architecture discourse, the paucity of design tools to adequately address landscape's inherent temporality and seeks to investigate new notations for landscape architecture through a synthesis with music notation. It accepts the assertion of English composer Cornelius Cardew (1936–1981) that 'notation and composition determine each other',[2] and in investigating music notation provides a reflective window through which to consider new ways of conceiving, understanding, and constructing landscape. The Hungarian composer György Ligeti (1923–2006) presciently noted that 'one often arrives at something qualitatively new by uniting two already known but separate domains',[3] the approach taken in this book, which draws directly and conceptually from music, the discipline with the longest and broadest history of notating time. Casting light onto both landscape architecture and music, as though we are standing between two mirrors, allows us to reflect on both. In a form of infinite recursion we see each field reflected in the other, a reciprocal study examined through the shared prism of notation. This reciprocal relationship can curiously be traced back

to the earliest history of the development of Western Art music notation. Called in Latin *in campo aperto*, 'in an open field', it referred to the non-diasematic method of providing mnemonic prompts to singers of ecclesiastical music, drawing the first connotation between the temporality of music and landscape.

MADE BY WALKING

The long history of this book was inspired by two encounters, separated by 23 years. Firstly, my interest in landscape lies in the experience of a seminal year spent in Canada when I was 12 years

1.1 Extract from the Cantatorium of St Gall, an example of *in campo aperto* notation, and the oldest surviving complete music manuscript of neume notation. This form of non-diasematic notation was without horizontal stave lines and, consequently, a means of accurately representing relative pitch. 922–925. Courtesy of St Gallen, Stiftsbibliothek, Cod. Sang. 359: Cantatorium, f. 4v (http://www.e-codices.unifr.ch/en/list/one/csg/0359).

old. Considered by my father to be still too young for drinking and driving, he instead bought me a gun. I wandered hours and days, passing weeks and months through the forests of northern Ontario near our lake shore cottage, a vastness undefinable by a sense of dimensional space. It was actually the duration of the walks that gave a sense of scale to the landscape, and the thousands of trees that provided its visual and auditory experience. As English landscape architect James Corner recognises, we perceive landscape through 'the accumulation of often distracted events and every day encounters'.[4] This was certainly the case for me and this walking experience gave me the confidence to get lost, to enjoy the unexpected, and to understand that time is the builder. As the Spanish poet Antonio Machado (1875–1939) reminds us, 'there are no paths, paths are made by walking',[5] and like those old walks I took in Canada, this book grew out of an exploratory journey, examining aspects of music and landscape architecture along the way.

Secondly, I was inspired by the discovery of American musicologist Thomas S. Reed's *Directory of Music Notation Proposals*[6] in 1997, a compendium of over 500 new music notations developed in the latter twentieth century. Subject to some inevitable repetition, this study showed the rich possibilities of reinvestigating an existing notational language, which instinctively one might presume to have become fully developed, and rigidly fixed. The implication of Reed's publication on landscape architecture seemed profound. If such variety of new forms of notation could be created through a detailed study of alternative modes of representation in music, then surely similar possibilities must also exist for landscape architecture, which like music,

is conceived and constructed through drawing, and which like music, is centrally located around time.

EVERYTHING UNDER THE SKY

The word landscape, having both practical and philosophical dimensions, has never easily been defined by a single etymological strand. Derived from the Dutch word *landschap* referring to units of agrarian or enclosed land, a more widely understood connotation has come from its extensive use in art, such as the Venetian painter Giovanni Bellini's (1459–1516) *Saint Jerome Reading in a Landscape* from 1485. This painting shows a landscape progression from Saint Jerome in his wilderness sanctuary reading from the Bible with the mythical lion at his feet, towering rock formations, to a distant walled city. This landscape is not a natural construct, but synthesised from stylised and allegorical references.

The interconnectedness between different aspects of landscape's meaning has a long history but by the early eighteenth century notions of landscape encompassed three ideas that were to have long-standing resonance. Reference to each of these can be found in a single series of articles on the pleasures of imagination written in the summer of 1712 by the founder of *The Spectator*, Englishman Joseph Addison (1672–1719). Firstly, that landscape was constructed through vision. Building upon English philosopher John Locke's (1632–1704) notion of a sensory hierarchy, Addison noted that 'our sight is the most perfect and most delightful of all our senses. [. . .] It is this sense which furnishes the imagination with its ideas; so that by the pleasures of the imagination [. . .] I hear mean such as arise from visual objects'.[7] Secondly, that landscape is a mental construct as much as a physical realm. Addison noted that the sensory delight he spoke of arose 'either when we actually have them in our view, or when we call up their ideas into our minds by painting, statues, descriptions, or any the like occasion'.[8] He went on to state that the ability to picture in our imagination is so strong that 'a man in a dungeon is capable of entertaining himself with scenes and landscapes more beautiful than any that can be found in the whole compass of nature'.[9] Thirdly, that landscape was not nature but was constructed and this could be achieved through the active manipulation of the world around us. He wrote that:

> fields of corn make a pleasant Prospect and if the Walks were a little taken care of that lie between them, if the natural embroidery of the Meadows were helpt and improved by some small Additions of Art, and the Several Rows of Hedges set off by Trees and Flowers that the soil was capable of receiving, a Man might make a pretty Landskip of his own possessions.[10]

Later, the English novelist and politician Horace Walpole (1717–1797), writing in 1752, wonderfully described the designer of Rousham Gardens in Oxfordshire, Englishman William Kent (1685–1748), as 'the inventor of an art that realises painting, and improves nature'.[11] More recently, in 2012, architects Davide Deriu and Krystallia Kamvasinou noted that:

> whether we look at professional fields such as landscape architecture [. . .] or, more generally, at the place of landscape in the wider realm of architectural and urban cultures, [. . .] the ways of seeing and representing the landscape are inextricably bound up with design practices.[12]

This book refers to three aspects of landscape, which are respectively termed: landscape space, both natural and manmade external spaces, defined by American landscape architect Kathryn Gustafson as 'everything under the sky';[13] landscape art, the representation of external space in painting and other artistic media; and landscape architecture,[14] a term first used by English designer J.C. Loudon in 1840 in reference to the works of English landscape architect Humphry Repton (1752–1818), albeit in connection with buildings, and which is now the recognised professional term for the design of external spaces. While focusing on landscape architecture this book necessarily also draws upon aspects of landscape art, and upon landscape space.

Music in this research uses the definition of English musicologist John Blacking (1928–1990) from 1973 as 'humanly organised sound', the title of the first chapter of his book *How Musical is Man*.[15] Blacking's definition, broader than the Oxford English Dictionary's of music as 'the art or science of combining vocal or instrumental sounds to produce beauty of form, harmony, melody, rhythm, expressive content',[16] creates more open possibilities to examine parallel aspects of music and landscape architecture than a narrower definition might provide. Also, except where otherwise noted, in Chapter 5 titled *Meadows*, the term music in this research explicitly refers to Western Art music. This is the musical culture where the writing of sounds has the longest and richest history with records dating back to 830 A.D., and where the notation of musical sound has been instrumental in its changing conception and development. I do not include the study of folk music as its history is often un-notated. Nor do I include jazz improvisations where the notation indicates the structural framework of chord progressions, although American landscape architect Walter J. Hood has referred to this in his writings[17] and urban design projects.[18] Also excluded is tablature notation, which is used not in the description of sounds, but to describe the manner of their production.

THE DECEPTION OF THE EYE

Writing in 1992, Corner identifies three difficulties in landscape architecture representation, the designer's indirect and 'remote access to the landscape medium; [. . .] its abstractness with respect to the actual landscape experience; and the anterior, prevenient function of the drawing, its generative role'.[19] As part of the challenges of landscape architecture representations, their failure to capture the encompassing scale of landscape space within the inherent flatness of a drawing means that representations' two-dimensional nature creates a conflict between the space of representation, and the space represented. If architectural space can ultimately be connected back to anthropometric scale, the vastness of landscape space often requires landscape architects to draw it at one five-hundredths, one thousandths, even one five-thousandths of its actual size, further distancing the drawings from the qualities of landscape space. This distancing is not just spatial but material as well. Landscape architecture lacks the edaphic and climatic qualities inherent in landscape spaces creating a disjunction between the relative materiality of drawn and drawing. As French landscape architect Christophe Girot noted, 'the finest discourse in plans, whether layered or simple, cannot hide this inherent absence of site'.[20] The representations of landscape architecture are also inevitably experienced visually, which limits the way in which our senses can operate in its apprehension. American cultural geographer Yi-fi Tuan reminds us of the varying operation of the senses, that 'the eyes explore the visual field and abstract from it certain objects, points of focus, perspectives. But the taste of lemon, the texture of warm skin, and the sound of rustling leaves reach us as just these sensations'.[21] Through the nature of their production, landscape architecture representations are not just visual constructs, but constructed and then viewed statically. If landscape is an alchemy between place and time and as Corner notes 'there is a duration of experience',[22] then attempting to freeze these experiences into static instances in time in order to draw them, will inevitably exclude the temporal qualities of the experience.

This book builds upon this broad critique and directly addresses two critical omissions in conventional landscape discourse: the development of design tools to specifically address the rich temporality of landscape space within landscape architecture, and sound as a vital constituent of it. Conventionally, landscape architecture drawings have shared with architecture the rendering of three-dimensional space in two dimensions through the use of linear perspective. The Irish cultural geographer John Wylie noted the parallel development of the geometric rules that supported cartography, astronomy and surveying, with perspectival techniques of landscape depiction, 'allowed artistic representation to approximate the realities of perceptual experience, by offering on the canvas a "realistic" and plausible portrayal of the visible world'.[23] But this visual 'reality' came with consequences. Landscape space as represented by orthographic or perspectival techniques separated the observer from the subject, an isolation that is temporal as much as visual, freezing landscape experience and materiality into a single moment of visual time. Linear perspective not just represented space, but also 'enabled a commanding, objective and controlled grasp of space and spatial relations'.[24] Corner's own summary of the implications of linear perspective for landscape architecture are that 'they are based upon the illusionary logic of the picture plane rather than the sensual arrangement of [. . .] spatial, temporal and material qualities'.[25] The French art historian Hubert Damisch in *A Theory of / Cloud/* summarises it this way:

> perspective only needs to "know" things that it can reduce to its own order, things that occupy a place and the contour of which can be defined by lines. But the sky does not occupy a place, and cannot be measured; and as for clouds, nor can their outlines be fixed or their shapes analysed in terms of surfaces, [. . .] it reveals perspective as a structure of exclusion.[26]

Damisch's concerns that perspective excludes elements that cannot be reduced to clearly delineated outlines, so any constituents of landscape without surfaces, codifies the limitations perspective imposes on representing the temporal aspects of landscape architecture. Perspective's limitations were, of course, known to those credited with its development. Italian Filippo Brunelleschi (1377–1446) in his experiments in Florence, unable to capture the temporal qualities of the sky through drawing, 'covered the corresponding part of the panel with a surface of dark silver in which the real air and heavens were reflected'.[27] Brunelleschi brought the ephemeral sky into the field of drawing indirectly through reflection. Italian Leon

Battista Alberti (1404–1472) whose *On Painting*[28] first appeared in 1435–36, noted regarding outlines that 'the painter, in describing this space, will say this, his guiding an outline with a line, is circumscription',[29] while affirming that vision was the focus, stating that 'painting strives to represent things seen'.[30]

Linear perspective in landscape architecture therefore creates a double deception. Firstly, from the very nature of its mode of representing landscape space, it necessarily excludes both time and sound. Secondly, as Finnish architect Juhani Pallasmaa suggests, perspectival representation, 'not only describes but also conditions perception',[31] narrowing our perception of landscape architecture. This book actively addresses these historic concerns by examining the potential for notation to provide alternative representational models for landscape architecture, and as American philosopher Nelson Goodman (1906–1998) critically noted, 'the allographic art has won its emancipation not by proclamation but by notation.'[32]

TIME REVEALED, TIME CONCEALED

The challenges facing the landscape architect in the representation of landscape time can be found in a number of works from the eighteenth century. Typifying many is French artist Jacques Rigaud's (1680–1754) ink and wash of Stowe Gardens titled *View of the Queen's Theatre from the Rotunda* from 1734. We see the Rotunda, Stowe House, King Georges Column and Queen Caroline's Monument as we scan from left to right. Focus is brought to the enjoyable activities taking place in the foreground, the sky is muted with no clouds reflected in the water's surface. With the Rotunda to our left and King Georges Column in the centre of the scene,

View of the Queen's Theatre *from the* Rotunda . Veüe du Theatre *de la* Reine *prise a coté de la* Rotonde .

we are looking due north-east. The sun is low in the sky to the west and our attention is brought to time most strongly through Rigaud's care with shadows. Also, from the 1730s we see a different attempt in Kent's *Woodland Scene by Moonlight*, part of a series of drawings of Chatsworth House, currently in their Devonshire collection. Here, two people walk through the woods past a pond, and yet the water's surface is central to bringing our focus to time. The long reflection piercing through the darkening tree canopy immediately captures a moment in early evening repose. Time of day, the windless reflection on the water, both bring a temporal landscape sense quite different from Rigaud's. Yet, these and other drawings from this period still typically crystallise

frozen moments in landscape space. The first notable English attempt to explicitly reconcile time in landscape architecture drawing can be found in the *Red Books* of Humphry Repton (1752–1818), the originator of the term landscape gardener. Unlike Lancelot 'Capability' Brown (1716–1783) whose design business included construction and consequently whose designs were largely realised, the majority of Repton's landscape work is to be found in over 400 books produced for clients including the Duke of Bedford. Repton's work likely grew out of the late eighteenth-century drawings of places that have been termed 'topography' where artists recorded the geography of places and captured them in watercolour views. Their direct observations

of landscape may have been useful to Repton in developing his own drawings, which like those of the topographical draughtsman, focused on the real, rather than the idealised, landscape. Each bound in red leather, Repton's books were a compendium of sketches, explanations and drawings that helped his clients envisage his proposals. Best known within each book are the 'before' and 'after' representations of his designs, an overlay flap opened by the reader to reveal the completed scheme at a future location in time.[33] In the case of *Purley in Berkshire*, as suggested by Repton in 1793, the existing landscape is shown as symmetrically divided. A meander of the river occupies the middle distance on the left of the drawing, rolling hills to the right. Evenly aged mature trees on either side imply a landscape extending beyond the picture frame in both directions. The cultivated fields on the crest of the hill with furrows sharply drawn suggest a post-harvest autumn scene, but otherwise there are few hints to reveal the time of the landscape. The activities depicted in the landing of a boat, the leading of animals, or figures on horseback, are specific to neither time nor locale. In Repton's proposal the cultivated landscape is replaced by the pastoral and arboreal, while creating in the mind of the observer a time period spanning at least several decades. The proposed landscape was drawn fully mature: the trees that surround the folly on the distant hilltop are over ten metres in height, and again, uniformly so. In the creation of a future landscape, Repton has structured it through the architectural intervention of the folly, and one that

1.4 Humphry Repton. 'Status quo' and 'ideal view' watercolours from Repton's *Red Book* titled *Purley in Berkshire – A Seat of Anthony Morris Storer Esq.* Sketch 11: View from the suggested new house. Top: status quo, with two overlays. Bottom: Ideal view, as improved by Repton. 1793. Private Collection, England. Picture credit André Rogger, Basel.

references the iconography of the past. Perhaps this misrepresentation of time was a result of Repton's brief encounter with the site and the time spent on production of this book. As Swiss landscape historian Andre Rogger has noted, 'Repton and Storer spent three days investigating the landscape potential of the site [. . .] three weeks after his visit, on 22 November 1793, Repton sent Storer his Red Book.'[34] Rogger argues that the didactic nature of Repton's representations often made the 'viewers feel as if they are standing within a landscape, rather than merely looking at it'.[35] He continues with the suggestion that

the *Red Books* created the 'potential to generate "real-time" experiences [. . .] to render the experience of someone moving through a real landscape'.[36] Perhaps the first attempt to explicitly 'realise' time in the representation of designed landscapes, Repton's *Red Books* contain a paradox in their approach to drawing temporality. While proposing to reveal the client's land in change and improvement, they fail to include seasonality, diurnal variation, an indication of growth and decay in landscape space. Even a sense of occupation or the activities of the agrarian poor that might have indicated the connection between time and these landscape spaces, is absent. The time of Repton's representations is neither emblematic nor specific, but generic and abstract. He captures two separate times but at the expense of the detail and ambiance of each. Perhaps Repton had inadvertently discovered that the representation of landscape time, and through it, landscape space and materiality, contained significant challenges.

UNCERTAIN PRECEDENTS

The American landscape architect Stephen Krog writing in 1983 stated that 'landscape architecture cannot afford to overlook or neglect the very necessary, though admittedly unsettling, confrontation with the interactive, non-mappable, non-quantifiable and difficult-to-predict components'.[37] The possibilities of drawing the invisible aspects of landscape space, using notation's specific ability to operate beyond the limits of representation, were set out by Goodman in 1976 in an explanation of the critical difference between autographic and allographic arts. He noted 'where the works are transitory, as in singing and reciting, or require many persons for their production, as in architecture and symphonic music, a notation may be devised in order to transcend the limitations of time and the individual'.[38] In fact, the standard text on the criteria for a notational system, Goodman's own *Languages of Art*,[39] specifies five syntactic and semantic requirements, which forbid ambiguity, overlap and indeterminacy in and among characters, including under the category *unique determination* that 'ambiguity of inscriptions is forbidden'.[40] He further noted that 'amenability to notation depends upon a precedent practice that develops only if the works of art in question are commonly either ephemeral or not productible by one person. [. . .] symphonic and choral music, qualifies on both scores, while painting qualifies on neither',[41] criteria that also apply to landscape architecture. The field of notating landscape temporality is surprisingly both under-researched and under-theorised. Corner has written that 'apart from Halprin, however, notational developments specific to landscape architecture have been few and far between, and yet the analogous qualities of landscape to narrative, dance, theatre, or film, suggest that notations would be a promising area of research'.[42] Notation in a range of other temporal practices that provide possible analogies with landscape architecture are reviewed below, each of them drawing directly or tangentially on music notation in their development. These notations provide precedents of past efforts to link music and landscape architecture, and also reveal the varied approaches adopted by others.

LABANOTATION

This was developed in the 1920s by Austrian dancer and choreographer Rudolf Laban (1879–1958) to describe a motive experience through time and space in dance, which is analogous with the movement through landscape space and has been drawn upon by other design notation as mentioned below. Unlike Benesh Movement Notation (of English ballet), which uses a five-line stave with time running horizontally (the lines correlating to head, shoulders, waist, knees, floor), Labanotation priorities space over time. Currently considered to be solely a dance notation, originally 'Laban conceived his system as a notation not merely for dance but for human movement in general'[43] and it is this that has led to its influence on landscape architecture notations with a concern for movement. Time is shown by bar-lines like music notation, with double bar lines at the beginnings and endings, but time now runs vertically up the page, a device adopted by some twentieth-century notations including Klavarskribo devised by Cornelis Pot in 1931. In Labanotation there are symbols for 27 human movements, with abstract symbols defining four interconnected parameters: the direction of movement, the part of body, the level of movement, and the length of time the movement lasts. Labanotation, however, has two embedded weaknesses in its potential application for landscape architecture notations: it is a descriptive notation to record movement but not a prescriptive one that could be used for composition, and significantly it offers considerably reduced temporal precision than music. The smallest temporal interval indicated by the symbols in Labanotation[44] is one sixteenth of a beat, while in music notation it is 1/128th, with five flags to a note head.[45]

THE VIEW IN MOTION

First published in 1965, *The View from the Road* by American urbanists Donald Appleyard (1928–1982), Kevin Lynch (1918–1984), and John Myer (1927–2009) specifically aimed to 'deepen the observer's grasp of the meaning of his environment: to give him an understanding of the use, history, nature or symbolism of the highway and its surrounding landscape'.[46] Their notation analyses three aspects of motion and space: apparent self motion, apparent motion of the visual field, and the characteristics of the space including enclosure, light quality, proportions, objects and surfaces. Their abstract notation also drew reference from music, as the authors noted it doesn't 'present a sequence of time and space as in a movie but rather symbolises it by placing elements along a continuous line or staff as in musical notation'.[47] This is reviewed in more detail later in Chapter 4 *Clouds*.

SPACE-SEQUENCES

The notation described above drew upon earlier investigations by the American architect Philip Thiel (1920–2014), who proposed a system for a graphic notation to represent the experiences of space sequences, emphasising their temporal qualities. He noted that:

> the perception of our visual world is a dynamic process involving the consumption of time. The spaces, surfaces, objects, events and their meanings which [. . .] constitute both our natural and man-made landscapes cannot be seen simultaneously, but must be experienced in some temporal sequence.[48]

His research, the beginnings of which he dates to 1951,[49] grew from the observation that:

> movement in time is of course a constant preoccupation of the musician, the dancer, the film editor. Today it is also beginning to preoccupy the architect, the urban designer, the city planner and the landscape architect as it never has before.[50]

Thiel's own critique was while 'the musician has a score: the dancer has Labanotation and the film editor a "storyboard" [. . .] the architect and designer for their part have either only a series of perspective sketches, or orthographic projections'.[51] Thiel's space notation assumed the space experienced at any moment would be 180 degrees vertically and horizontally, which included an allowance for the movement of one's head. Thiel's 'space-form' notation was developed through the use of symbols in order to denote vertical and horizontal elements, the cross appearing in the right of each box marks the location of a viewer's eyes, mimicking the vanishing point of linear perspective, as does his use of planes in orthographic projection as an understanding of the experience of landscape space. He noted that 'in a given experience of space, however, there is one constant element: time; and one variable constant, or parameter: that of movement. Movement in space is characterised by rate and direction'.[52] He borrowed from Labanotation the use of a vertical time line running up the page, with equal time intervals on one side of the line, but amended it by adding distance travelled on the other. In doing so he fixed time and space as being directly correlated, both being scaled in a metronomic and regular way. These two notational strategies, a spatial notation for time and a symbolic notation for aspects of space creating elements, he then combined into a 'duration line and space-form notation'. The space zones along the horizontal axis show the relative distance from the viewer of the spatial extent, while the words 'ends', 'ports', and 'merges' show the spatial connections. Thiel freely acknowledges the influence of music notation on his work, noting that 'if a "rest" occurs in a given space, then the duration line would be dotted for the length of time of the rest',[53] while in conclusion stating that 'the space score described above has certain analogies with the musical score, and indeed borrows some terms from musical notation'.[54] Thiel's adaptation, however, is an uncertain precedent, borrowing aspects from music, but focusing on the rhythmic certainty of pre-twentieth century music, overlooking contemporary music notation that pre-dates his own investigations.

1.5 Philip Thiel. An extract from Thiel's duration line and space-form notation. Movement is read vertically up the page, and space zones on the horizontal axis. 1961. Courtesy the Town Planning Review.

MOTATION

The noted American landscape architect Lawrence Halprin (1916–2009), writing in *RSVP Cycles: Creative Processes in the Human Environment*[55] and referring in part to Labanotation, writes that:

> on the one hand we have been able to score motion itself, and on the other hand score for the environment. We have never really been able to correlate the two [...] scores where motion and environments are mutually interrelated and affect each other [...] the need for new notation arises out of the inability of the traditional approach to express new concepts.[56]

Halprin's response to that question, his *motation* developed for his landscape architectural projects

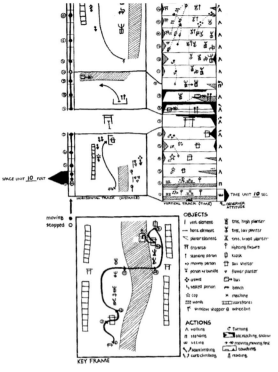

1.6 Lawrence Halprin. His space and time notation for his design for The Nicolett Mall, where time is delineated in inches along the vertical axis. 1969. Used by kind permission of the publisher, Georges Braziller, Inc.

including the Nicolett Mall, Minneapolis, included a scalable axis with space measured in units of ten feet and time in units of ten seconds, mapping movement through the space and the effect of objects on the actions within it. His notation charts human actions, both motive (such as walking, moving fast) with static (such as standing, reading, sitting), and the objects in the urban landscape that are implicated in these movements. These also include objects' relative motility, such as the movement of individual people or crowds, and the static (vertical and horizontal surfaces, benches, lighting and trees). Like Thiel, he proposes a vertical time axis with rigid increments, but then extends the development of a symbolic notation for landscape architecture through the addition of a more comprehensive set of symbols to embellish and

record the experience of urban landscape spaces. It is intriguing that this notation has not enjoyed more widespread adoption.

PATH-NOTES

A more contemporary attempt to notate time in landscape architecture is the work of Israeli musicologist and designer Galia Hanoch-Roe. Her notation for the scoring of paths, published in 2011, draws on the shared properties of linear sequences in music and in space. She states that 'the idea of perceiving space as a stream of voices each representing a different aspect of the experiential quality of a linear sequence, could broaden the visual approach to design into a means for a richer experience'.[57] This notion of multi-dimensional experience allows her to incorporate other senses including smell and sound along a line in time and space, which the vehicle-based movement of *The View from the Road* excluded. To these, she further added seasonality, sense of enclosure, rhythm, pace and odour and auditory stimuli, which together formed 'a simultaneous score representing the polyphony of concurrent experiences'.[58] Her notation borrows heavily from the language of music: 'path notes' representing 10 imperial feet are combined into 'measures' of 40 feet; the path experience has 'rhythm'; and at the beginning of the score descriptive words such as 'mysterious' and 'energetic' evoke the expressive language of music notation, such as in the imperative *allegro vivace* (fast and full of life) at the start of the notation of Russian composer Pyotr Tchaikovsky's 1864 work for string quartet titled *Allegro vivace in B flat major*. Referring to decisions about rhythm, she suggests we ask 'what are the indicators of resting point and the elements of visual rhythm;

should they be constant or changing; should they relay a strict or a flowing rhythm [. . .]?'[59] While drawing upon her musical background, she seems to treat time as a monovalent entity and rhythm as a function of the sense of sight, suggesting a rigid interpretation of how music might influence the development of notation for landscape architecture.

MAP-DRAWINGS

Corner, in the preface to *Taking Measures across the American Landscape* in 2000, wrote that, 'how a particular people view, value, and act upon the land is in large part structured through their codes, conventions, and schemata of representation'.[60] His landscape architecture notations contained within his book also make reference to music notation. He explains his use of the term measure, for example, by noting the 'various representational, reconciliatory, and poetic capacities of measure (as in the rhythms and harmonies of music, art, and cosmography)'.[61] His publication contains aerial photographs by American photographer Alex MacLean together with Corner's representations, which he refers to as 'a series of map-drawings',[62] rather than using 'notation', a term he instead uses for preparatory drawings rather than the published representations. Describing their development, he explains a two-stage process, starting with scribbles on old maps that draw out structural relationships, then noting that 'these notations prompted me to make a series of map-drawings, which became composites of maps with photographic and satellite images, often overlaid with dimensional and logistical equations and other invisible lines of measure'.[63] Noting that 'the map-drawings play on certain planning abstractions, such as making visible strategic organizations of elements across a ground plane or revealing certain scale and interrelational structures',[64] for the *Longhouse Cave* at Mesa Verde in California, Corner combined photographic images, with shadow diagrams, a scaled plan, and two sections showing the light penetration into the space in summer and winter. The work contained in this book explores and captures the temporality of landscape through layers of visual images and cartographic techniques.

EVENT, MOVEMENT AND SPACE

There have also been notations by others, seeking to address time and landscape space. The Swiss architect Bernard Tschumi stated in 2004 that design notation's explicit purpose 'is to transcribe things that are normally removed from conventional (architectural) representation', and his design notations in *Manhattan Transcripts* from 1977, which spanned from landscape, through architectural, to urban spaces, 'were a first attempt to test concepts and to reformulate some of the traditional means of architectural representation through the inclusion of the dynamic component',[65] addressing a primary concern of this research. The *Manhattan Transcripts* are divided into four parts: MT1, 'the park' (units of open space); MT2, 'the street' (units of urban organisation); MT3, 'the tower' (units of architecture); MT4, 'the block' (units of the city). His notation investigated three intersecting fields: E denoting events, M denoting the movement of bodies through space, and S denoting the fabrication of physical spaces. Tschumi's notations are addressed in more detail in Chapter 3 *Horizons*.

THE TIME OF MUSIC

The notations reviewed above seem to contain three critical weaknesses in a comprehensive critique of

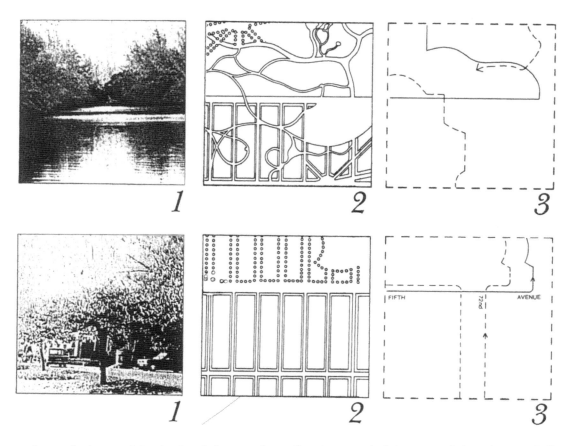

music notation's potential to lead to design notation for landscape architecture.

Firstly, while they acknowledge potential similarities between the time of landscape architecture and the time of music, they draw specifically and exclusively on historic notions of musical time. It seems remarkable that the notation of time from the Baroque, Classical and Romantic periods of musical history are so persistent in design notations. The works reviewed above persist in seeing the time of music as regular, linear and metric, overlooking more contemporary notions of musical time including the writings of American musicologist Jonathan Kramer for whom musical time extends into the a-periodic and for whom 'one of the central tenets [. . .] is that musical time is both linear and nonlinear'.[66]

Secondly, following on from this they have perhaps inevitably focused on restricted notational precedents and on drawing only from symbolic music notation. Not just in the examples reviewed above but even as recently as 2011, the Japanese architect Sou Fujimoto in a lecture at Harvard GSD titled *Primitive Futures* refers to bar lines defining the flow of time, illustrated through reference to the music by German composer Johann Sebastian Bach (1685–1750) titled *Aria mit verschiedenen Veränderungen BWV 988* from 1741, more commonly known as the Goldberg Variations. Within design notations that draw on historic music notations, there is an overwhelming predominance of symbolic notation, ignoring the precedents from the twentieth century including other notational methods developed in music since 1950.[67] I believe that by deliberately drawing on these wider source materials, and by contributing to an understanding of musical time and notational strategies that reflects current knowledge in the field of music, this will allow us to make this broader knowledge available for landscape architectural research. It is no coincidence that the flowering of musical innovation in the last 100 years has been directly accompanied by an equal blossoming of notational strategies and methods.

Thirdly, with the exception of Hanoch-Roe in the examples above, notations for landscape architecture persist in deferring to vision as the primary quality of landscape space to the detriment of the other senses. In bringing aspects of music notation into landscape architectural notations, incredibly, and most curiously of all, they leave sound behind.

The notion that music notation has no spatial concerns and so is subsequently unsuited as a precedent for landscape architecture that might also need to address not just time but space is addressed by English art critic Simon Shaw-Miller who argues that one function of notation is to allow the composer to see the music during the process of composition. He states that 'this visual and temporal interplay with past and future confounds the definition of music as an art that exists purely in time: it exists in many different times and spaces'.[68] As Lynch also reminds us 'the precise, abstract time of science and efficiency is certainly far removed from that of inner experience'.[69] And yet the time of temporal design

notations has been dominated by absolute time, by chronology. Halprin's '*motation*' used time intervals of ten seconds, for example, and even as recently 2010, Kamvasinou asserted that 'timelines are crucial for exploring issues to do with duration, speed and perception during the analysis stage, and for showing how design unfolds in time during the design stage'.[70] Yet, although the extended duration of experience of landscape space means that information is encoded in sequential steps, does this mean that time in landscape is limited to absolute time? Even Lynch himself writing in 1972 in *What Time is this Place?* admits that landscape time is not the absolute time of science, saying:

> we have two kinds of evidence of the passage of time. One is rhythmic repetition – the heartbeat, breathing, sleeping and waking, hunger, the cycles of sun and moon, the seasons, waves, tides, clocks. The other is progressive and irreversible change – growth and decay, not recurrence but alteration.[71]

In music certainly time is not presumed to be only regular, linear and unidirectional. Kramer identifies qualities of time in music that co-exist together with the quantities of absolute time, terming them gestural time, linear time, multiple directed linear time, and vertical time.[72] By expanding the range of music notations into contemporary examples, allows us to better incorporate what Swedish musicologist Ingmar Bengtsson refers to as the 'essential qualities of the material',[73] which in this case includes aspects of landscape temporality and sound.

CREATIVE TRANSCRIPTION

English music critic Hugo Cole (1917–1995) offers a broad definition of notation as 'ways in which directives may be issued'.[74] According to Cole, notation serves four main purposes in the Western cultural tradition of music:

1 To allow the writer to invent new music, and to calculate effects in advance and at leisure.

2 To provide an exact timetable, so that independent parts may be closely co-ordinated.

3 To provide the performer with an artificial memory.

4 To describe the sounds of performed music for purposes of analysis or study.[75]

The extraordinary spread and popularity of music has undoubtedly been derived from these critical aspects contained within its notation. Through the act of writing down sounds, as either performed or as conceived, music notation has both fixed specific moments of music at a particular time, while also allowing for its long-term preservation for the future. Through fixing a fluid practice, it has created a permanent record of temporal practices within music, allowing for the promotion of authorship, the communication of ideas, and the composition of sounds. This nature of fluid practice, not just within individual works but over longer durations of time, has also created a fluid relationship between music and notation. A more open reading of music notation suggests that the precision of symbols used in it need not be solely organised on the strict monomial basis of one sign equalling one meaning. All notations, in fact, contain degrees of ambiguity, and as Cole argues:

symbols with a broad, ill-defined content of meaning have their place in all organic languages and notation systems, their special advantage being that they allow for subtle shades of meaning that can never be suggested if connotations are rigidly fixed.[76]

So, precision of description need not be a prerequisite of notation. In studying the development of new landscape architecture notations such precision and clarity can surely be temporarily sacrificed in order to allow for new methods to be explored. After all, landscape architectural notation does not to be read at speed like music notation; there is time for the eyes to regress and revisit places in the notation. We can scan backwards as well as forwards: the limitation is not visual capacity but, rather, comprehension. Being a deliberate innovation, these into new landscape architectural notations are inevitably unable to provide output clarity at their beginnings. They are tools first for personal investigation rather than for public dissemination. Tschumi acknowledged similar references in his work, noting that his own transcripts 'are literally a work in progress, in so far as the method of work becomes increasingly precise in the later stages, as if the search for new tools always passes through uncertainties, intuitions'.[77]

Rather than a rigid definition of notation, my research draws on an alternative idea by the Italian composer Ferruccio Busoni (1866–1924) who stated that 'every notation is, in itself, the transcription of an abstract idea'.[78] Busoni, a critical figure in twentieth-century music,[79] asserted that notation's value was not only as the written document, a record of the composer's intention, but was also the act of writing down sounds. From his own transcriptions of Hungarian composer Franz Lizst's (1811–1886) *Spanish Rhapsody* Busoni noted that 'out of his "tenets" I constructed my "technique"'.[80] He also proposed including the performance of the notation as a transcription, stating that:

> the musical idea becomes a sonata or a concerto [. . .] that is an Arrangement of the original. From this first transcription to a second the step is comparatively short and unimportant. [. . .] Again, the performance of a work is also a transcription.[81]

This critically challenged the notion that the purpose of notation was to ensure fidelity between each performance of a work, the essence of Goodman's definition. As a composer as well as pianist, he asserted that transcription was also a form of composition, and the music he created often contained material from other composers' work. These key Busoni transcription works include *Fantasia nach J. S. Bach, for piano* catalog number BV 253 (*Fantasia after J.S. Bach, for piano*) from 1909.[82] According to the Canadian musicologist Marc-Andre Roberge, these show 'the importance of creative transcription, which is much closer to composition than to arrangement'.[83] The American musicologist Jeremy Grimshaw notes that in composing this piece, which was dedicated to his recently deceased father, Busoni drew on three Bach compositions, *Christ, du bist der helle Tag* (BWV 766), *Gottes Sohn is kommen* (BWV 708), and *Lob se idem allmächtigen Gott* (BWV 602), and that 'the Fantasia contains new and borrowed material in roughly equal measure'.[84] This reworking of others notations was not only confined to the deceased but also his living contemporaries. The Austrian composer Arnold Schoenberg (1874–1951), for example, sent Busoni a composition for comment titled *Klavierstuck, op.11, No.2*, only to have it returned, Busoni replying that 'let me tell you that I have (with total lack of modesty) "rescored" your piece'.[85] Busoni wrote to

Schoenberg on 26 July 1909 informing him that what he noticed was that 'your music "*as a piano piece*" is the limited range of textures in time and space'.[86] The American musicologist Erinn Kynt has noted that for Busoni each composition:

> began with an *Idee* (idea) in the composer's mind. He considered such *Ideen* abstract, idealistic and "non-musical" entities taken from human experience. These ideas need not be entirely new, personal, or even musical; they can be drawn from other realms such as literature, architecture, or even from everyday events. Originally unrelated to music these abstract thoughts become musical conceptions [. . .] that are then *transcribed* into musical realizations and *arranged* into larger structures.[87]

This compared with Schoenberg, for example, who saw composing as beginning 'with the novel conception of a personal, concrete, and new musical idea [. . .] either a composer's overall musical conception for an entire piece, or the reasoning behind the musical unfolding of the composition'.[88] Busoni, writing a letter to his wife on 22 July 1913, noted that, 'transcription has become an independent art; no matter whether the starting-point is original or unoriginal. Bach, Beethoven, Liszt, and Brahms were evidently all of the opinion that there is artistic value concealed in a pure transcription'.[89]

Busoni's ideas resonate with the search for new landscape architecture notations in three ways. First, that examining the notation of others can be used to create new notations, that transcription can be of tremendous value in the development of new notations and compositions. Second, that abstract ideas including non-musical ones can be the basis for temporal compositions. Whereas Busoni proposed that ideas from outside music could be utilised in musical compositions, I invert this through the detailed study of music notation in order to investigate new temporal notations for landscape architecture. Thirdly, that notation is an act as well as an object, a temporal process of drawing out ideas, and that this is an equally valid use of notation as the production of a finish composition. These three aspects of Busoni's work together inform this book's research methodology, which investigates aspects of three musical notations in order to investigate the temporality of landscape architecture, and in doing so record the temporal research processes involved.

This notion of creative transcription is developed further in the chapter *Horizons* through examining the process of 'realising' notation undertaken by American pianist David Tudor (1926–1996). Tudor, in interpreting the notation of other composers in order to undertake a detailed study of them, literally drew out aspects from the notations he studied as a precursor to their performance. This musical process in which ideas are drawn out through the act of drawing is echoed in the word design, which the English architect Jonathan Hill has argued in its original meaning in Italian, *disegno*, suggested 'both the drawing of a line on paper and the drawing forth of an idea'.[90] This shared connotation of the drawing out of ideas, is part of the reciprocal relationship between landscape architecture and music created in this research, and we can also say that in this regard, that music composition is a corollary with design.

A MUSICOLOGY FOR LANDSCAPE ARCHITECTURE

In this study of a musicology for landscape architecture, three music notations and their specific approaches to time are examined. In investigating whether the temporality of the music notated is similar to aspects of landscape time, I examine what notational tools for landscape architecture might be derived from the strategies contained within each of these music notations. Each of the three music precedents selected for these chapters are non-vocal music notations, following Kramer's suggestion that compared with vocal music, 'non-texted music really is about time'.[91] This book is structured into six components: this introduction, a parallel history of time in music and landscape, three research investigating a particular theme developed from an aspect of the investigation of notating time, and a conclusion. The three central chapters – titled *Horizons*, *Clouds*, and *Meadows* – are italicised as each explores a distinct facet of the notation of time in music and landscape architecture. Each of these chapters is both analysis and synthesis.

In order to investigate this reciprocal relationship between music and landscape architecture, I examine the notational strategies of three contemporary music notations in fine detail. These special works, spanning a period of particular musical innovation, are American composer Morton Feldman's (1926–1987) *Projection I* from 1950, Hungarian composer György Ligeti's (1923–2006) *Lontano* from 1967, and English composer Michael Finnissy's *Green Meadows* from 1977. These are juxtaposed against the designed landscapes of New York city, the cinematic landscape in *Onibaba*, the natural landscape at Girraween National Park in Australia, and the historic landscape at Rousham garden. Each of these landscape spaces is examined through the prism and possibilities of the respective music notation. A common method has been applied to this diverse range of music and landscape architecture sources. Firstly, each music notation is transcribed in order to investigate its notational strategies. This includes whether aspects of the notation or the sounds created from it are analogous to aspects of landscape architecture. Selecting a notational precedent from music allows the detailed examination of how components of the work interact over time and how these temporal relationships are notated. Starting with the time of music, rather than the time of landscape, allows the extended temporality of the former to immediately inform the investigation of landscape architecture temporality. Starting with the notation of a musical work, rather than its performance, leads directly to the primary research tool, notation itself. Secondly, I study a landscape architecture notation that explores similar themes to those of the specific music notation, supporting this translation from music to landscape. Thirdly, I create through a process of transcription new notations that allow for detailed of the shared aspects of music and landscape architecture.

The notations described in this book, analytical, descriptive, prescriptive, are a form of creative transcription that draws out aspects of the precedents examined. The inscriptions developed in them in pen, chalk, pencil and charcoal, form a static notation in the first chapter *Horizons* but in the following chapters *Clouds* and *Meadows* are filmed to form notations. In these latter two the new landscape architectural notations are framed temporally by the determined durations of the music created by the primary source notations: 11'37" from *Lontano* in *Clouds*, and 10'55" from *Green Meadows* in *Meadows*.

In addition to the creative transcription process described above, music also imbues this book in other ways. The three chapters *Horizons*, *Clouds*, and *Meadows* reference the tripartite and ubiquitous nature of the sonata form in music where three sections of a musical work are perceived both individually and through their correspondences with the adjacent ones. Here, the three chapters can be read as self-contained investigations of music and landscape architecture, and yet also through their juxtaposition, encourage the reader to see their interconnections. *Horizons*, *Clouds*, and *Meadows* each draws upon a range of histories of music notation and landscape architecture, bringing them into one work so that they can be reviewed together now. There is a duality within each. I study three aspects of music, sounds in space in *Horizons*, unfolding temporality in *Clouds*, the materiality of sound in *Meadows*, but simultaneously three aspects of landscape architecture – space, time and material – addressing Corner's concern that 'there are three phenomena unique to the medium of landscape [. . .] that evade reproduction in other art forms and pose the greatest difficulty for landscape architectural drawing [. . .] landscape spatiality, landscape temporality, and landscape materiality'.[92] The creation of three themed investigations also draws analogies with the dominant structural unit of music, the triad. In a musical triad three materials (tones) are brought together to give an identifiable quality to a particular place, not just within the material of the composition, but also temporally, as the Welsh musicologist Paul Griffiths has noted 'what may matter as much, or more, is how the triad works as a signpost [. . .] in time'.[93]

Chapter 3 *Horizons* investigates the notation of landscape architectural space, exploring the relationship between the space of the notation and the space notated. Music notation in *Horizons* provides dual historic and contemporary precedents for the study of the musical relationship between time and space and for understanding the development of a drawn spatial language with a central concern for time. I start by studying the notation of space and time in Feldman's composition *Projection I*. This is followed by a diachronic review of the role of space in music notation from our earliest surviving records, examining how the syntax of music notation has developed. Next, I investigate the notation of space from Swiss architect Bernard Tschumi's *Manhattan Transcripts MT1* from 1994 and how his notation frames space. This is followed by a study addressing the landscape architectural sounds of New York from a seminal description by the Italian film director Michelangelo Antonioni.

Chapter 4 *Clouds* investigates the notation of landscape architectural time, exploring the notation of unfolding time. Music notation in *Clouds* provides the opportunity to explore how symbolic notation can notate unfolding, ephemeral temporality. I investigate qualities of time in the notation of Ligeti's *Lontano*, termed 'vertical time' by musicologist Kramer.[94] While in *Projection I* I investigated the terminations of sounds in space, *Lontano* looks at the implications of their relative beginnings through the notion of Interonset Intervals. Next I investigate the notation of real and perceived motion by Appleyard *et al.*[95] from *A View from the Road*, before applying these two to an investigation of a cinematic landscape in the Japanese film *Onibaba* by Kaneto Shindo, examining landscape temporality through the prism of music, notation, and a particular place.

Chapter 5 *Meadows* investigates the notation of landscape architectural materiality, exploring sound as a material. Music notation in *Meadows* functions in three ways: a notation creating sounds of an imagined English landscape; a study from ethnomusicology of the development of a notational language that addresses parameters of sound in landscape architecture that fall outside of those found in music; and a model for the development of a composition notation for the creation of a landscape through sound. I initially focus on a composition titled *Green Meadows* by Finnissy, examining the notational strategies used in the evocation of the Sussex Downs. Next, the chapter moves to the Australian hinterland, adopting a tripartite approach to the notation of landscape sounds. Firstly, I investigate the limitations of Western music notation, secondly, I apply an ethnomusicological approach to the transcription of a-periodic time and non-diatonic tonality, before developing new notational strategies and tools to address the components of landscape sound that fall outside of both precedents. Lastly, the research then applies these notational tools to the composition of a new auditory landscape. Chapter 5 *Meadows* then looks at how sound investigates and creates landscape space through its introduction into an English landscape, Rousham garden in Oxfordshire, before concluding by proposing that sound can now be included in the picturesque.

This book is not just about notation but is seen as being constructed from two forms of it, one drawn, one written. The written text[96] itself is a notation, a symbolic representation of sounds, of thoughts, on space, time, and materials, and their intersection in music and landscape architecture. The text functions as an ekphonetic notation in this design research, as signs to assist in the apprehension of the landscape architectural notations. The text – a written notation – and the films – from drawn notation – are brought together so that the established written language and the developing notational one, both draw and draw out, sounds and ideas. The tangible and conceptual are contained within each.

The landscape architecture notations in Chapters 4 and 5, *Clouds* and *Meadows*, can be accessed in two ways: the full notations are available at their respective web links which appear in the book and are listed as films. They should be viewed when they first appear in the text. Critical aspects of them are also contained within the book where they are listed as notations in both the contents and the text. The full notations should be watched together with the sound from which they are derived. Ligeti's music from Chapter 4 *Clouds* is contained within the film *Lines Burnt In Light*, while Finnissy's from Chapter 5 *Meadows* is contained within the film *Pink Elephants*, each available from the Apple iTunes Store.

NOTES

1 Griffiths, 'Sound-Code-Image' (1986), 5.

2 Cardew, 'Notation: Interpretation, etc.' (1961), 21.

3 Ligeti, 'Etudes for Piano' (1988), 4.

4 Corner, 'Representation and Landscape' (2002), 148.

5 Machado, *Selected Poems* (1982), xxix.

6 Reed, *Music Notation Proposals* (1997).

7 Addison, 'Pleasures of Imagination', (21, June 1712).

8 Addison, 'Pleasures of Imagination', (21, June 1712).

9 Addison, 'Pleasures of Imagination', (21 June 1712).

10 Addison, 'Pleasures of Imagination' (25 June 1712).

11 Walpole, *Anecdotes of Painting* (1849), 57.

12 Deriu and Kamvasinou, 'Critical Perspectives on Landscape' (2012), 1.

13 Kathryn Gustafson in conversation with the author in London, 2000.

14 The term landscape architecture is used in preference to the term landscape design, which has recently fallen out of common usage.

15 Blacking, *How Musical is Man?* (1973).

16 http://www.oed.com.libproxy.ucl.ac.uk/view/Entry/124108?rskey =pevggP&result=1&isAdvanced=false#eid.

17 Hood, *Blues & Jazz Landscape Improvisations* (1993).

18 Hood, *Dooryard Blues and Green Jazz* (1994).

19 Corner, 'Representation and Landscape' (2002), 146.

20 Girot, 'Vision in Motion' (2006), 95.

21 Tuan, *Topophilia* (1974), 10.

22 Corner, 'Representation and Landscape' (1992), 147.

23 Wylie, *Landscape* (2007), 144.

24 Wylie, *Landscape* (2007), 58.

25 Corner, 'Representation and Landscape' (2002), 155.

26 Damisch, *A Theory of /Cloud/* (2002), 124.

27 Damisch, *A Theory of /Cloud/* (2002), 124.

28 Alberti's book was published in both Italian and Latin and is known as both *Da pictura* (in old Italian), and *Della pittura* (in modern Italian).

29 Alberti, *On Painting* (1970), 22.

30 Alberti, *On Painting* (1970), 22.

31 Pallasmaa, *The Eyes of the Skin* (2005), 16.

32 Goodman, *Languages of Art* (1976), 122.

33 Rogger, *Landscapes of Taste* (2007), 54.

34 Rogger, *Landscapes of Taste* (2007), 50–51.

35 Rogger, *Landscapes of Taste* (2007), 79.

36 Rogger, *Landscapes of Taste* (2007), 83.

37 Krog, 'Creative Risk Taking' (2002), 62.

38 Goodman, *Languages of Art* (1976), 120.

39 Goodman, *Languages of Art* (1976), 186–7.

40 Goodman, *Languages of Art* (1976), 148.

41 Goodman, *Languages of Art* (1976), 121–122.

42 Corner, 'Representation and Landscape' (2002), 153.

43 Goodman, *Languages of Art* (1976), 217.

44 Hutchinson, *Labanotation* (1961), 52.

45 Goodman, *Languages of Art* (1976), 183.

46 Appleyard, Lynch and Myer, *View from the Road* (1965), 21.

47 Appleyard, Lynch and Myer, *View from the Road* (1965), 21.

48 Thiel, 'Sequence-Experience Notation' (1961), 33.

49 This is noted by Thiel as a reference that his clearly precede those of Appleyard *et al.*, which ultimately received broader recognition than his own.

50 Thiel, 'Sequence-Experience Notation' (1961), 34.

51 Thiel, 'Sequence-Experience Notation' (1961), 34.

52 Thiel, 'Sequence-Experience Notation' (1961), 50.

53 Thiel, 'Sequence-Experience Notation' (1961), 51.

54 Thiel, 'Sequence-Experience Notation' (1961), 52.

55 Halprin, *RSVP Cycles* (1969).

56 Halprin, *RSVP Cycles* (1969), 71.

57 Hanoch-Roe, 'Linear Sequences' (2007), 134.

58 Hanoch-Roe, 'Linear Sequences' (2007), 111.

59 Hanoch-Roe, 'Linear Sequences' (2007), 123.

60 Corner, *Taking Measures* (1996), xi.

61 Corner, *Taking Measures* (1996), xvii.

62 Corner, *Taking Measures* (1996), xii.

63 Corner, *Taking Measures* (1996), xvii.

64 Corner, *Taking Measures* (1996), xvii.

65 Walker, 'Avant-propos' (2004), 121.

66 Kramer, *The Time of Music* (1988), 2.

67 Spatial notation uses horizontal spacing of sounds and silences. So, time is scalable, and any duration can be notated, bringing far greater precision than symbolic notation particularly for a-periodic compositions where there are constantly changing durations of sounds and silences. Space-time notation was pioneered by the American composer Earle Brown in 1953 with his composition *Twenty Five Pages*. Conceptual notation was developed by music theorist Heinrich Schenker whose analytical notation uses stem-less note heads with beams to show structure rather than rhythm, analysing existing scores by removing all ornamentation and dividing the music into background, middle distance and foreground. Implicit graphic notation, such as Earle Brown's *December 1952*, created a form of notational ambiguity to change the relationship between composer and performer to allow the later greater involvement in the 'composition' of the music. In indeterminate or aleatoric notation the composer allows for choices to be selected during the performance. In the case of the French composer Pierre Boulez's *Piano Sonata No.3*, the parts of the score in parenthesis can be omitted or played, and if selected for performance can be repeated at will.

68 Shaw-Miller, 'Thinking Through Construction' (2006) 41.

69 Lynch, *What Time is this Place?* (1972), 65.

70 Kamvasinou, 'Notation Timelines' (2010), 416.

71 Lynch, *What Time is this Place?* (1972), 65.

72 Kramer, *The Time of Music* (1988), 452–4.

73 Cole, *Sounds and Signs* (1974), 111.

74 Cole, *Sounds and Signs* (1974), 42.

75 Cole, *Sounds and Signs* (1974), 9.

76 Cole, *Sounds and Signs* (1974), 14.

77 Tschumi, *Manhattan Transcripts* (1994), 9.

78 Busoni, *Sketch of a New Esthetic* (1911), 17.

79 Busoni in 1910 published *An Attempt at an Organic Piano Notation* with the aim of simplifying sight-reading. Busoni, *Selected Letters* (1987), 106.

80 Busoni, *Essence of Music and Other Papers* (1957), 86.

81 Busoni, *Sketch of a New Esthetic* (1911), 18.

82 This composition was inspired by the death of Busoni's father. Kynt, 'How I compose' (Spring 2010), 234.

83 Roberge, 'The Busoni Network' (1991), (82).

84 http://www.allmusic.com/composition/fantasia-nach-j-s-bach-for-piano-kiv-253-mc0002358702.

85 Busoni, *Selected Letters* (1987), 386.

86 Busoni, *Selected Letters* (1987), 384.

87 Kynt, 'How I compose' (2010), (230–231).

88 Kynt, 'How I compose' (2010), (231).

89 Busoni, *Essence of Music and Other Papers* (1957), 95.

90 Hill, *Weather Architecture* (2012), 82.

91 Kramer, *Time of Music* (1988), 167.

92 Corner, 'Representation and Landscape' (2002), 146.

93 Griffiths, *A Concise History of Western Music* (2006), 45.

94 Kramer, *Time of Music* (1988), 55.

95 Appleyard, Lynch and Myer, *View from the Road* (1965).

96 Nelson Goodman noted that 'the text [. . .] is a character in a notational system. As a phonetic character, with utterances as complaints, it belongs to an approximately notational system' (Goodman, *Languages of Art* (1976), 207).

A PARALLEL HISTORY OF TIME IN MUSIC AND LANDSCAPE

In order to locate this research within a broader context, this chapter briefly charts a parallel history of time in music and landscape. This shared history reflects not just the centrality of time to both fields but also their long inter-relationship. As Canadian musicologist R. Murray Schafer notes, music is both our source of 'the best permanent record of past sounds'[1] and also the manner in which 'throughout the history of Western music, the sounds of nature (particularly those of wind and water) have been frequently and adequately rendered'.[2] Welsh musicologist Paul Griffiths structures the changing temporality of music as 'time whole, time measured 1100–1400, time sensed 1400–1630, time known 1630–1770, time embraced 1770–1815, time escaping 1815–1907, time tangled 1908–1975, and time lost 1975–',[3] the eight epochs he delineates form the divisions that are examined in more detail below, before a comparable study of landscape.

MUSIC

TIME WHOLE

When Tudor sat down at the piano on 29 August 1952 in Woodstock and played for the first time the three movements (30 seconds, 143 seconds, 100 seconds) of American composer John Cage's *4'33"* it followed Cage's assertion that a determined duration could now create music, with pitch, timbre and volume secondary. It is perhaps ironic that it is often assumed that this marked the beginning of an idea of music in which time was its essential materiality, and yet Griffiths, however, dates the first record of music to hollow bone fragments of simple wind instruments found in Slovenia over 40,000 years ago, noting that 'being sound and shaped time, music begins'.[4] This long early history of shaping time culminated with

the appearance in 'the middle of the ninth century, [. . .] Latin neumes – so called from the Greek *neuma*, a sign or nod'.[5] This was followed by the publication of the treatise *De Institutione Harmonica* by French music scholar Hucbald (*c*.840–930), 'a monk of St. Amand in the diocese Tournai'.[6] This is our earliest written record of the simultaneous sounding of notes, polyphony, which required a means to coordinate voices over time. Slightly later in his *Prologue to His Antiphoner*, dated around 1025, Guido of Arezzo (dates of birth and death not recorded) importantly noted that by standardising the staff, with lines in yellow for C and red for F, 'in every melody those lines or space which have one and the same colour [. . .] sound alike throughout, as though they were all on one line'.[7] Pitch, and therefore time, could flow from one notation to another, anchored to a datum that connected across music to its homes in many different landscapes.

TIME MEASURED – 1100–1400

Further development during this period was marked by two critical publications. Firstly, *Ars cantus mensurabilis* (*The Art of Measured Song*) by German music theorist Franco of Cologne (dates of birth and death not recorded) in around 1260. His treatise not only marked the systemisation of music notation from many simultaneously occurring disparate methods including wide variations in the number of lines in a stave but critically, in noting that music is 'song measured by long and short units of time',[8] changed the notation of time 'to individual, sign-specific durational values'.[9]

By removing the relative subjectivity of earlier music notation, which depended upon the context to define the values of each note, he codified the use

2.1 Extract from a 91-page collection of melodies and plays. An early example of neumes set into four scribed lines with one in red ink denoting the pitch F. Eleventh to twelfth century. Courtesy Einsiedeln, Stiftsbibliothek, Codex 366(472): Fragmenta Sequentiarum, 40v. (http://www.e-codices.unifr.ch/en/list/one/sbe/0366).

2.2 Extract from a fourteenth-century transcription of an original by Guido of Arezzo, showing diastematic neumes with different symbols denoting different temporal values. The music starts with the words, *Ecce dies uenient* (Behold, the days come). Fourteenth century before 1314. Einsiedeln, Stiftsbibliothek, Codex 611(89): Antiphonarium pro Ecclesia Einsidlensi. 001r (http://www.e-codices.unifr.ch/en/list/one/sbe/0611).

2.3 Giovanni Gabrieli. Extract from *Sonata Pian'e Forte*. 1597.

of symbolic notation for time, which was to continue over the following centuries.

The second critical development in music notation during this period came from the publication in around 1320 of *Ars nova* (*The New Art*) by French composer and theorist Philippe de Vitry[10] (1291–1361). His treatise allowed for greater temporal complexity, including the idea of a time signature, which created the means in which sub-divisions of time could be measured, as well as recognising that rhythmic values divisible by two and three were of equal validity. American musicologist Carl Parrish (1904–1965) has noted that a significant innovation of this period was the use of notes drawn in red ink, 'marking as it does the emergence in written music of the *hemiola* ("one and one-half"), that is, the use of time values in the relationship of three to two'.[11] This ability to link the main rhythmic groups and their subdivisions allowed for the growing complexity of polyphonic music, multiple instruments or voices coalescing through time.

TIME SENSED – 1400–1630

As Griffiths notes, changes to music now were the result of 'a wish to mirror reality as perceived by the senses: the reality of time (newly experienced as smoothly continuous and orderly in the fifteenth century, when the first accurate clocks were made) and the reality of hearing'.[12] This period included the music of Flemish composer Guillaume Dufay (1397–1474), whose composition *Nuper rosarium flores* is noted through its harmonic proportions echoing those of Brunelleschi's design for the dome of Florence's Basillica, to be an early connection between architectural and musical space. Additionally and importantly this period included the works of Italian composer Giovanni Gabrieli (*c.*1554–1612) whose *Sonata Pian' e Forte* brought the first sense of spatial depth to music. Composed for a cornet and three sackbuts (early trombones), this composition, the first with direct instructions for volume, used alternating soft and loud dynamics to create an acoustic space of varying scale. Space, like time, could also be scaled. The

2

DIE KUNST DER FUGE

Contrapunctus 1

BWV 1080, 1

2.4 Johann Sebastian Bach. The beginning of Bach's *Contrapunctus 1* where the four notes of the first two bars, D-A-F-D, are reintroduced as the opening four notes of the left hand in bars nine and ten, and raised up a fifth in bars five and six. 1742. Breitkopf & Hartel.

Belgium composer Johannes Tinctoris (1435–1511) writing in 1477 noted that in counterpoint where the pitches are related but the rhythms independent that this could be created 'by means of the various quantities represented by the shapes of the longs, breves, and semibreves'.[13] Slightly later in 1510 in Belgium composer Josquin des Prez's (1450–1521) chanson for four voices, *Mille regretz*, a sense of this temporal perspective is created from the four-part vocal counterpoint, where the same words are sung by different voices in varying locations within the composition. Time flows through these one thousand regrets.

TIME KNOWN –1630–1770

Griffiths states that 'time was now as absolute and knowable as space. And it was to this absolute, knowable time – this clockwork time – that the music of the next century and more fixed itself'.[14] Although this period includes the music of Englishman Henry Purcell (1659–1695), German composer George Frideric Handel (1685–1759) and Italian Antonio Vivialdi (1678–1741) as the newly consistent notation spread across Europe, it is the music of Bach, born in Eisenach, Germany, that most exemplifies this Baroque music and clocks are 'often pictorially represented in Bach's cantatas'.[15]

2.5 Franz Joseph Haydn. The opening five bars for strings from *Symphony No. 99*. 1793. CCARH.

In his 1742 *Die Kunst der Fuge* (*The Art of the Fugue*) BWV 1080, the 19 movements for one or two harpsichords developed organically as melodic ideas repeatedly reappear, enriching the emotions they evoke, as the music develops over time. For example, the motif starting the first movement, *Contrapunctus 1*, is modified in the second movement, inverted in the third, note values augmented or diminished in the seventh iteration, and become triplet note values in *Contrapunctus XVI*. Time flowed metronomically through his music and yet the very repetition seemed to play 'on our expectations and render us somehow changed through the experience of any particular piece'.[16]

TIME EMBRACED – 1770–1815

This brief 45-year span, known as the Classical period in music, was 'to seize time into itself, to embody not only our observation but also our experience of time'.[17] As the German musicologist Johann Philipp Kirnberger (1721–1783) noted 'the composer must never forget that every melody is supposed to be a natural and faithful illustration or portrayal of a mood or sentiment, insofar as it can be represented by a succession of notes',[18] and that time was central to this experience. He argued that the 'tempo must be correctly captured by the composer to conform with the sentiment he has to express'.[19]

This period included the music of Austrian composers Wolfgang Amadeus Mozart (1756–1791) and Franz Joseph Haydn (1732–1809), and the early works of German Ludwig van Beethoven (1770–1827). Haydn's *Symphony No.99 in E-flat major*, composed in 1793 and consisting of four movements, embraced time expressly in its evocation of mood, as the composition moves from an *adagio* in 4/4, to one in 3/4, a *menuetto: allegretto* in 3/4, before ending in a *vivace* finale in 2/4 time. One of a series of 'London' symphonies, Haydn brought great attention to time through the use of slurs and accented beats so that the framing of the time signature was recast in further detail, echoing both the Enlightenment notion of reflecting man's emotions in the creative arts and the urge to measure and classify.

TIME ESCAPING – 1815–1907

This, the Romantic period of music, grew out of recognition that:

> the universe was becoming ever more complicated as nineteenth-century science began uncovering its age and its extent. But a symphony could [. . .] grant an experience of wholeness, continuity and comprehensibility, or at least a deeper knowledge of how these things were escaping.[20]

The Classical precedents of order and balance were now replaced with greater dissonance and the use of previously distant keys, less ordered musical structures than the rondo[21] or sonata form, longer works to accommodate this greater variation and personal expression, and the use of dramatic contrasts of volume. Regarded practitioners from this period include Austrians Anton Bruckner (1824–1896) and Franz Schubert (1797–1828), Czech Gustav Mahler (1860–1911), and Hungarian Franz Liszt (1811–1889). It was Liszt, writing in 1855, who noted that, 'the artist may pursue the beautiful outside the rules of the school without fear that, as a result of this, it will elude him'.[22] Within the single movements of his symphonic poems Liszt clarified time and mood through adding instructions to the score, including 'beat divisions directly under each note in an effort to indicate its duration more precisely',[23] as well as the extensive use of words to describe the mood to be evoked.

TIME TANGLED – 1908–1975

Griffiths notes that the year 1908 was a critical year,

> the completion by Schoenberg of the first compositions to dispense with the harmonic system based on major and minor keys [. . .] also, there was no force impelling the music towards resolution in the home key, for there were no keys now and no homes.[24]

Music moved away from tonality, was now often atonal and without reference to a key. This was accompanied by music of increasing temporal complexity, supported by the discovery 'by Einstein in 1905, that time is not a universal constant but can vary with the position and movement of the point of view – that time is not one but many'.[25] In the same year as Schoenberg but in America, Charles Ives composed *The Unanswered Question*, which as American musicologist Jan Swafford noted, contained 'most of the devices associated with musical Modernism: polytonality, polyrhythm, free dissonance, chance and collage effects, spatial music',[26] decades before they found their way into the work of other composers.

In 1913, French composer Claude Debussy (1862–1918) called for greater attention from composers of the beauty of nature noting that fine art 'can capture only one of its aspects, preserve only one moment. It is the musicians alone who have the privilege of being able to convey all the poetry of night and day, of earth and sky',[27] arguing that the new media of film and the techniques of cinematography would 'show us out of this disquieting labyrinth'.[28] The route ahead lay in new notations, to allow music to break free of its past. As American composer Earle Brown (1926–2002) noted in regard to his work and that of

others, notation was central to the development of new ideas, which 'could not be notated traditionally and that the sound of the work is of an essentially different character because of the new notation'.[29] Referring to his own experiments with notation, which led to his 49 stave notation, American composer Harry Partch (1901–1974) noted that 'a musical system does not evolve as it does because it lends itself to being translated into notation. It evolves, basically, from the capacity of the ear, and is formulated and articulated by scientific insight and creative speculation'.[30] American composer John Cage (1912–1992) constantly asserted the imperative of the new when, referring to his own experiments, he stated 'that nothing was lost when everything was given away'.[31]

TIME LOST – 1975–

After the flowering of new musical and notational possibilities in the preceding period, Griffiths notes

Hawthorne 30 *Played by using a strip of board 14¾ ins, long and heavy enough to press the keys down without striking.

2.7 Charles Ives. Extract from *Piano Sonata No.2 'Concord, Mass., 1840–60'.* (1921?).

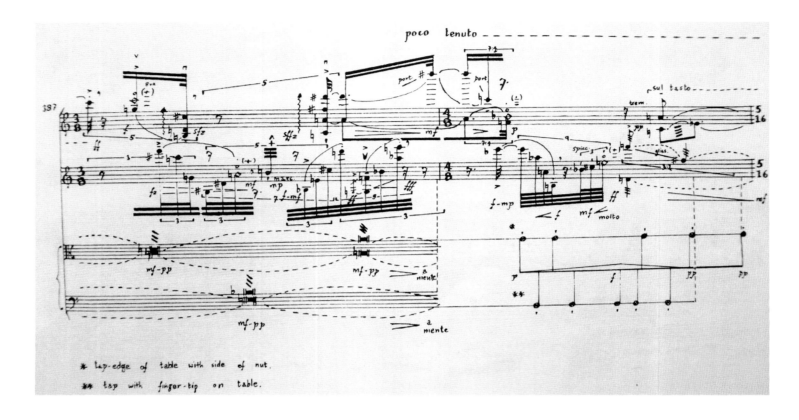

* tap-edge of table with side of nut.
** tap with finger-tip on table.

2.8 Brian Ferneyhough. Extract from *Sonatas for String Quartet*. 1967. Edition Peters

that from 1975 onwards, that although this is a rich time for music innovation, it is tinged with melancholy, that 'lost in the labyrinth, music seems unable now to call out to the unknown future – as Beethoven did [. . .] as Chopin and Du Fay did. Those times are gone – or they are here, and we cannot shake them off'.[32] Notions of musical time expanded in binary explorative tracks, towards greater freedom from the limitations of notation, in which much of the music was determined in the performance itself, or conversely towards a restless search for greater precision, notational practices epitomised in the work of English composer Brian Ferneyhough where in essence the complexity of

the notation could not be fully rendered in any performance. Both approaches sought to understand the complexity and indeterminacy of musical time.

LANDSCAPE

TIME OVERLOOKED

The *Doomsday Book* started in 1066 by William the Conqueror (1028–1087), but 20 years in its production, was a national survey not of the English landscape, but of the land itself. The units of measure were agricultural productivity and human settlements, not the possibilities that passing time might produce for the enhancement of either. Land was, above all, quantitative.

TIME PERCEIVED – 1605–1725

In England, the Dutch *landschap* was now termed *landskip*, where it came to have the meaning of a scene – a rural one – from a single viewpoint, with the connotation that it referred to the intrinsic physical qualities of a place. The first *Oxford English Dictionary* definition of landscape appeared in 1605, defining it as 'a picture representing natural inland scenery as distinct from a sea picture, a portrait etc'.[33] In English author Thomas Blount's (1618–1697) *Glossographia* published in 1656, his extended definition was 'Landskip [...] an expression of the Land, by Hills, Woods, Castles, Valleys, Rivers, Cities, &c. as far as may be shewed in our Horizon. All that is not of the body or argument thereof is Landskip.'[34] Landscape could now also include not just the natural, but also the manmade, an extent of visual space. In Jan Siberechts's *View of a House and its Estate in Belsize, Middlesex* from 1696, the elevated perspectival viewpoint captures a house and enclosed formal gardens with an extensive kitchen garden beyond. If time in Baroque music was regular and precise, in landscape a similar visibility was also given to time. Even more than in the English landscape, the garden of Vaux-le-Vicomte in France encouraged the steady ambulation of visitors, the sculpted topiary and spaced statues marking out measures of the journey with the regularity of music by J. S. Bach.

TIME FROZEN – 1725–1803

The OED definition of landscape was now 'a view or prospect of natural inland scenery, such as can be taken in at glance from one point of view; a piece of country scenery'.[35] In an engraving from 1739 of the landscape at Chiswick, a plan is surrounded by thirteen views. Time was frozen as each episode in the journey around the garden was to be apprehended from a single viewpoint. These were constructed vistas, sequentially arranged. In the title page from a guide to Stowe Gardens published in 1746 by Englishman Thomas Bowles, the key lists one plan and fifteen views. The scenes are either titled 'view of', 'view at', or 'view from', emphasising the static imperative in the experience of each. We are placed in the eyes of a visitor, instructed in a direction of gaze. We may be looking out, or looking in, but we are not presumed to be apprehending landscape space in motion or focused on its temporality. Commonly references from ancient civilisations were incorporated in the creation of these new landscapes. Time may have been frozen but it could also be conflated, aspects of historic iconography superimposed on their contemporary present. The English landscape critic Richard Payne Knight (1750–1824) writing in *The Landscape, A Didactic Poem* from 1794, noted that landscape was constructed in the viewer's mind, but with the thoughts of a painter to guide them:

> For though in nature oft the wand'ring eye
>
> Roams to the distant fields, and skirts the sky,
>
> Where curiosity its loo invites,
>
> And space, not beauty, spreads out its delights;
>
> Yet in the picture all delusions fly,
>
> And nature's genuine charms we there descry;
>
> The composition rang'd in order true,
>
> Brings every object fairly to the view;
>
> and, as the field of vision is confin'd,
>
> Shews all its parts collected to the mind.[36]

Outliving fashions for formal then picturesque landscapes, in English artist Alexander Cozens's

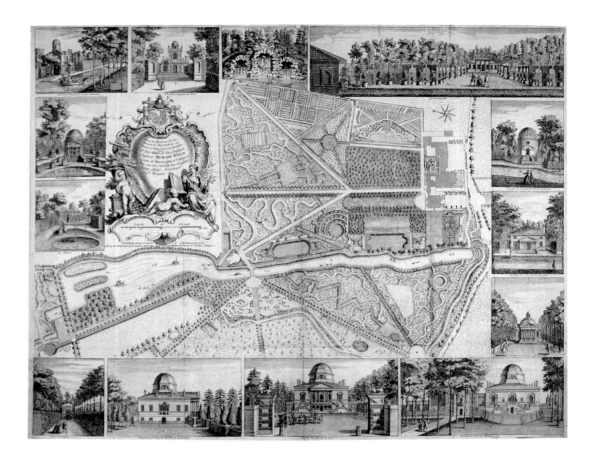

2.9 John Rocque. Extract of engraving of Chiswick showing the plan and associated views. 1739. From *Vitruvius Britannicus IV*. Heritage Image Partnership Ltd / Alamy

(1717–1786) ink and watercolour from 1763 titled *Landscape*, a companion work to *A Lake* from the same year, direct observation of nature is used. This notion of a static scene is perhaps the most persistent one in landscape. It not just survives, but flourishes. English cultural geographers Stephen Daniels and Denis E. Cosgrove (1948–2008), writing in 1988, in an introduction to *The Iconography of Landscape*, give the definition 'a landscape is [. . .] a pictorial way of representing or symbolising surroundings'.[37] This understanding of landscape as an area of space to be seen, something Wylie describes as 'a unit of visual space',[38] continues to retain dominance in understandings of landscape. Landscape, in effect, a way of seeing the world, is summarised by Cosgrove writing in 1985:

> Landscape is thus a way of seeing, a composition and structuring of the world so that it may be appropriated by a detached individual spectator to whom an illusion of order and control is offered through the composition of space according to the certainties of geometry.[39]

These are advantages not to be despised, when observations are to be noted once or oftener in the day. It is only necessary that they be inserted in a column headed *Clouds*; that the Modifications which appear together be placed side by side, and those which succeed to each other in the order of the column, but separated by a line or space from the preceding and succeeding day's notations.

\ Cirrus: ⌒ Cumulus: — Stratus: \⌒ Cirro-cumulus: _ Cirro-stratus: ⌒_ Cumulo-stratus: \⌒_ Cirro-cumulo-stratus, or Nimbus.

TIME NATURALISED – 1803–1928

In his 1803 *Essay on the Modification of Clouds*, English amateur meteorologist Luke Howard (1772–1864) allowed for changing phenomena to be captured through their morphology, using a Linnaean classification system developed as part of a wider interest in using scientific knowledge to understand the world around us. Howard's classification included symbols he created for the three main cloud groups of Cirrus, Cumulus, and Stratus and three compound symbols for their combinations, noting that 'the modifications which appear together be placed side by side, and those which succeed to each other in order of the column, but separated by a line or space from the preceding and succeeding day's notations'.[40] With the publication of English naturalist Charles Darwin's (1809–1883) thesis *On the Origin of Species* in November 1859, time became visible, 'we see nothing of these slow changes in progress, until the hand of time has marked the long lapses of ages'.[41] In America, five years before Darwin, American author Henry David Thoreau (1817–1862) writing in *Walden: Or, Life in the Woods* had eulogised landscape and the inherent persistence of its temporal qualities,[42] re-evoked by Cage's re-reading of it in 1968 as 'music is continuous, only listening is intermittent'.[43]

2.10 Luke Howard. Extract from *Essay on the Modification of Clouds* with Howard's cloud notation. 1803.

TIME STILLED – 1928–1969

With Czech architect Sigfried Giedion's (1888–1968) foundation of CIAM (Congrès Internationaux d'Architecture Moderne) in 1928, modern ideas of landscape were born. Modernity could re-imagine time in progressing towards the future, while including past notions of landscape time, but perhaps in unanticipated ways. In German architect Mies van der Rohe's (1886–1969) *Resor House Project* in Jackson Hole, north-west Wyoming, from 1937–41, in an interior perspective view of the living room looking out through a glass wall to the Grand Teton Mountains, we see the distant mountain scenery through the frame of the north facing window. The landscape is ground to the architectural figure, and vision again dominates the experience of landscape. The exterior is no more in motion or dynamic than the materials of the interior, which is frozen into the collaged view. Time is, once again, stilled.

TIME NOTICED – 1969–1984

The publication in 1969 of American landscape architect Ian McHarg's (1920–2001) *Design with Nature* started a wide-reaching dialogue regarding our interaction with the world. As the author himself noted in September 1991, its ripples included fields as diverse as 'religious studies and environmental psychology [. . .] conservation, environmental science, landscape architecture, architecture and regional planning'.[44] The book's central premise was 'that nature is process, that it is interacting, that it responds to laws, representing values and opportunities for human use with certain limitations and even prohibitions to certain of these'.[45] He measured and mapped a range of natural processes, investigating and recording them on same scale plans.

These were then conflated into composites where, in the case of his study for the Washington and the Potomac River Basin, their collective values indicted factors such as their unsuitability for urbanisation, their value as agricultural land, even the soils' load-bearing capacity for septic tanks. McHarg's proposition was that in order to understand landscape time what was needed was to isolate each edaphic and climatic parameter so that they could be better understood, creating understanding of individual parameters in static contemplation. What we gained was an understanding of the components of landscape processes. What we curiously didn't, was an understanding of their individual and collective operation and change over time. Yet, this notion of a landscape created by processes was reinforced in the following year with the designation of the first *UN Year of Conservation*. Based on the ideas that the causes of change in landscape spaces were as much the result of human processes as natural ones, the United Nations proposed that they could therefore be reversed over time, that time could effect repair as well as decay.

TIME HUMANISED – 1984–1994

In 1984 the American cultural geographer J. B. Jackson (1909–1996) proposed an alternative notion of landscape, one that emphasised our human connections. Classifying this as *Landscape Three*, the time of landscape is no longer that of the natural processes underpinning physical spaces, but a human one, he proclaimed that:

> my search for a definition has led me back to that old Anglo-Saxon meaning: landscape is not scenery, it is not a political unit; it is really no more than a collection, a system of man-made spaces on the surface of the earth.[46]

He further explained his belief in a new landscape that was never simply natural, and stated that, 'it is *always* artificial, always synthetic, always subject to sudden or unpredictable change. [. . .] We create them and need them because every landscape is the place where we establish our own human organization of space and time'.[47] This readjustment of humanity's role in shaping landscapes was recognised in 1992 with UNESCO's formation of the World Heritage Cultural Landscapes, acknowledging that landscape was the combined works of nature and man, and 'paving the way for a new thinking in human beings and their environment, linking culture and nature, with a vision of sustainable development'.[48] Jackson argues that *Landscape Three*, in fact, means we have returned to operating with landscape temporality in the same way of the medieval peasant, that we are no longer tied or attached to a physical landscape, but rather we make connections with others at a particular place and time, 'an unending patient adjustment to circumstances'.[49] The time of landscape no longer needs to be captured in ways of viewing or frozen in formal designs to express our knowing supremacy over nature.

TIME IMPLICATED – 1994–

English anthropologist Christopher Tilley, in *A Phenomenology of Landscape*, states that 'space does not and cannot exist apart from the events and activities within which it is implicated'[50] and that time forms part of these processes, suggesting that 'the landscape is both medium for and outcome of action and precious histories of action'.[51] This view of landscape is close to Wylie's definition of landscape phenomenology where 'landscape is defined primarily in terms of embodied practices of dwelling – practices of being-in-the-world in which self and landscape are entwined'.[52] The English anthropologist Tim Ingold has likewise argued against the separation that earlier definitions of landscape implied, stating that 'I reject the division between inner and outer worlds – respectively of mind and matter, meaning and substance – upon which such distinction rests'.[53] He continues by noting that 'the landscape is the world as it is known to those who dwell therein, who inhabit its places and journey along the paths connecting them'.[54] For others, nature continues to provide an opposing aspect to humanity, with French landscape architect Gilles Clement calling for the Third Landscape, a space left over from human habitation, 'the genetic reservoir of the planet, the space of the future'.[55]

This rich interconnected history of time in music and landscape, which has both charted and informed their respective developments, forms the background to the following chapters, which examine contemporary music by three key practitioners of the twentieth century. Within the history of landscape time outlined above, many of the distinctions that define these categories are widely recognised and accepted, while to me 1803 stands out as a critical moment. While Howard and his influence upon artists of the day are known through his contribution to the representation of time in landscape art, in landscape architecture his name appears less frequently. Darwin is more often thought of as a seminal figure, establishing a scientific basis for a new understanding of landscape space. Yet, Howard's publication, which predates Darwin's by 56 years, is critical in two ways. In using the word notation for his cloud classification system,

he presciently opens the door to investigating the temporality of landscape through notation, while his system of notational pictograms that are amended in meaning through their formation into compound structures is analogous to the beginnings of music notation and implies a little-noticed early connection between the representation of time in music and landscape.

NOTES

1 Schafer, *The Soundscape* (1993), 103.

2 Schafer, *The Soundscape* (1993), 105.

3 Griffiths, *A Concise History of Western Music* (2006), vii–viii.

4 Griffiths, *A Concise History of Western Music* (2006), 1.

5 Abraham, *Concise Oxford History of Music* (1979), 62.

6 Abraham, *Concise Oxford History of Music* (1979), 75.

7 Strunk, *Source Readings in Music History* (1998), 212.

8 Strunk, *Source Readings in Music History* (1998), 227.

9 www.cengage.com Franco of Cologne, *Art of Measured Song*.

10 Abraham, *Concise Oxford History of Music* (1979), 72.

11 Parrish, *Notation of Medieval Music* (1978), 146.

12 Griffiths, *A Concise History of Western Music* (2006), 44.

13 Strunk, *Source Readings in Music History* (1998), 402.

14 Griffiths, *A Concise History of Western Music* (2006), 97.

15 Butt, *Century of Bach and Mozart* (2008), 112.

16 Butt, *Century of Bach and Mozart* (2008), 120.

17 Griffiths, *A Concise History of Western Music* (2006), 136.

18 Strunk, *Source Readings in Music History* (1998), 763.

19 Strunk, *Source Readings in Music History* (1998), 763.

20 Griffiths, *A Concise History of Western Music* (2006), 165.

21 The rondo is a musical form in which the main thematic idea (A) is interposed with contrasting material before being returned to, such as a form of A-B-A-C-A.

22 Strunk, *Source Readings in Music History* (1998), 1159.

23 Kregor, *Liszt as Transcriber* (2010), 64.

24 Griffiths, *A Concise History of Western Music* (2006), 227.

25 Griffiths, *A Concise History of Western Music* (2006), 229.

26 Swafford, *A Question is Better than an Answer*, http://www.charlesives.org/ives_essay/.

27 Strunk, *Source Readings in Music History* (1998), 1432.

28 Strunk, *Source Readings in Music History* (1998), 1434.

29 Brown, *Notation and Performance of New Music* (1986), 181.

30 Partch, 'Experiments in Notation' (1998), 219.

31 Cage, *Silence* (1961), 8.

32 Griffiths, *A Concise History of Western Music* (2006), 302.

33 http://www.oed.com/view/Entry/105515?p=emailAacUGlP2BE XFI&d=105515.

34 http://www.oed.com/view/Entry/105515?p=emailAacUGlP2BE XFI&d=105515.

35 http://www.oed.com/view/Entry/105515?p=emailAacUGlP2BE XFI&d=105515.

36 Knight, 'The Landscape' (1975), 344.

37 Cosgrove and Daniels, *The Iconography of Landscape* (1988), 1.

38 Wylie, *Landscape* (2007), 91.

39 Cosgrove, 'Prospect, perspective' (1985), 55.

40 Howard, *Modifications of Clouds* (1865), 14.

41 Darwin, *Origin of Species* (1859), 84.

42 'Time is but the stream I go a-fishing in. I drink at it; but while I drink I see the sandy bottom and detect how shallow it is. Its thin current slides away, but eternity remains.' Thoreau, *Walden, Or, Life in the Woods* (1882), 155.

43 John Cage interview with Robin White at Crown Point Press, Oakland California, 1978. http://writings.heatherodonnell.info/Messiaen_and_Thoreau.html#_ftn7.

44 McHarg, *Design with Nature* (1992), iii.

45 McHarg, *Design with Nature* (1992), 7.

46 Jackson, 'Concluding with Landscapes' (1984), 156.

47 Jackson, 'Concluding with Landscapes' (1984), 156.

48 http://whc.unesco.org/documents/publi_wh_papers_26_en.pdf.

49 Jackson, 'Concluding with Landscapes' (1984), 151.

50 Tilley, *Phenomenology of Landscape* (1994), 10.

51 Tilley, *Phenomenology of Landscape* (1994), 23.

52 Wylie, *Landscape* (2007), 14.

53 Ingold, 'The Temporality of the Landscape' (1993), 155.

54 Ingold, 'The Temporality of the Landscape' (1993), 156.

55 Clement, *The Third Landscape*. http://www.gillesclement.com/cat-tierspaysage-tit-le-Tiers-Paysage.

HORIZONS

This chapter investigates the notation of space in music and landscape architecture, informed by a detailed examination of *Projection I* by the American composer Morton Feldman from 1950, and the innovative representation of time and space in this notation. By introducing the background to Feldman's history of composition we are also able to look back to the role of space in the early developments of music notation, drawing connections between the language of Feldman's notation and those from European mediaeval music. This connection has been noted by Griffiths, who together with Italian critic Umberto Eco (1932–2016) sees parallels between the late middle ages and the present, noting, 'what was new in the early fifteenth century, and curiously anticipatory of the twentieth, was the composition of works which could not have been imagined without notation, works whose notational form is an integral part of their existence'.[1] This binary musical history is then followed by a study of Tschumi's *MT1 'The Park'* from 1977. By juxtaposing his design notation, one that 'frames' space, the space of New York within a grid of fictitious incidents, we see corollaries with Feldman's notation. These studies from music and landscape architecture are then used to investigate the notation of the sounds of spaces from New York, from a landscape close to the location of *MT1* on the eastern edge of Central Park. Taken from a written account of the city over 40 years ago, they vividly describe the genesis and qualities of a now departed landscape space, a space captured in new landscape notations.

MORTON FELDMAN

Feldman was a New York composer whose work spanned a range from compositions for solo instruments including piano (*Preludio* from 1944, *Three Dances* from 1950, *Last Pieces* from 1959, *Triadic Memories* from 1981), small groups including piano and violin (*Spring of Chosroes* from 1977, *For John Cage* from 1982), string quartets (*String Quartet* from 1979, *String Quartet II* from 1983), and orchestra (*In Search of an Orchestration* from 1967, *On Time and the Instrumental Factor* from 1969, *Coptic Light* from 1985).[2] His work drew upon a range of source materials, including influential figures from Philip Guston (1913–1980) to Bunita Marcus, Christian Wolff to Aaron Copeland (1900–1990), John Cage (1912–1992) to Franz Kline (1910–1962), although landscape hardly featured. His only known composition to directly refer to landscape was a tone poem for four instruments titled *That Landscape*, from which we have only three bars from 88 to 90 from an undated sketchbook in the collection of the Paul Sacher Foundation in Basel. But his music is most regarded for two periods of works, firstly for his early series titled *Projections* and *Intersections* written between 1950 and 1953, and secondly for his extended compositions from the late 1970s, where performances of his *String Quartet II*, for example, could last up to six hours.

He developed an early interest in graphic notations and new ways of representing sounds from friendships with leading painters from the New York School of American artists, including Willem De Kooning (1904–1997), Mark Rothko (1903–1970) (later, in 1971, to inspire a Feldman composition titled *Rothko's Chapel*), Robert Rauschenberg (1925–2008) (Feldman owned a large black painting of his),[3] and Jackson Pollock (1912–1956). The influence of these painters on his work was profound. As he noted, 'the new painting made

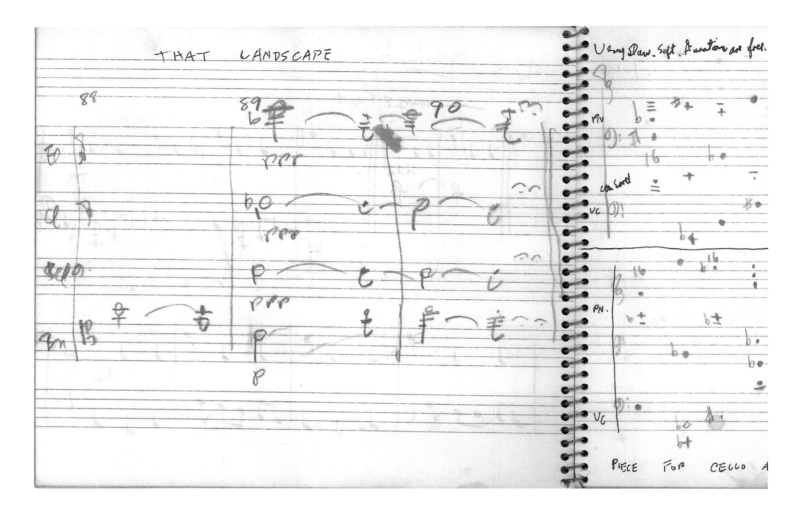

3.1 Morton Feldman. *That Landscape*. Undated.
©Morton Feldman Collection, Paul Sacher
Foundation, Basel.

me desirous of a sound world more direct, more immediate, more physical than anything that had existed heretofore'.[4] In order to achieve this intimacy between sound and the audience he developed a form of graph notation, noting that 'the degree to which music's notation is responsible for much of the composition itself is one of history's best-kept secrets'.[5] Drawing upon the approach in his friends' Abstract Expressionism paintings, which removed the figure–ground relationship of earlier art and replaced it with a new focus on the paint itself, Feldman's graphic notations achieved a similar effect, focusing attention now on the material of sound. He was open in acknowledging the influence of painting on his work, writing, 'I prefer to think of my work as: *between categories*. Between Time and Space. Between painting and music. Between the music's construction, and its surface.'[6] There were also musical necessities in place in the decision to explore alternatives to the symbolic representation of sounds in conventional music notation. Writing in a series of essays published in 1985 he stated that:

> between 1950 and 1951 four composers – John Cage, Earle Brown, Christian Wolff and myself – became friends [. . .] Joined by the pianist David Tudor, each of us in his own way contributed to a concept of music in which various elements (rhythm, pitch, dynamics, etc.) were de-controlled. Because this music was not 'fixed', it could not be notated in the old way. Each new thought, each new idea within this thought, suggested its own notation.[7]

Feldman sought new possibilities for sounds and music, noting that, 'the history of music has always been involved in controls, rarely with any new sensitivity to sound. Whatever breakthroughs have occurred, took place only when new systems were devised.'[8] Feldman writes explicitly of the limitations all notations contain for both performer and the sound materials. He noted that:

> most notation merely limits the range of choices open to the performer (a passing chromatic G# on the violin must lie somewhere between a presumably established G and A, and probably not closer to G than A). From this point of view, 'indeterminate notation,' which exaggerates the performer's freedom of choice, is a useful reminder of the relativity of all notation.[9]

It is within these contexts of sound as materials in space, of pushing on the limits of notation, that his notation for *Projection I* forms the basis for these landscape studies.

SPACE IN THE DEVELOPMENT OF MUSIC NOTATION

The space of music notation, defined here as the surface of the manuscript or score, has been the location for the development of music notation since our earliest surviving records of this written language. These historic records reveal how symbolic music notation developed from centuries of experiments into ways in which aspects of musical material, space and time could be notated. The oldest recorded written melody known to us dates from the ninth century and the original is currently held in the National Library in Paris. On page 16 of this parchment document are four columns of text written in the spaces created by lines incised into the page. The third column is in Greek, with the adjacent one titled *Idem Latine* (the same in Latin), containing the familiar words to the hymn *Gloria in Excelsis*. The first 12 lines of the Greek version contain an additional symbolic script of marks above the words, sometimes dots, sometimes tiers of dashes or marks evocative of accents. These mnemonic signs indicate the upward and downward movement of melody and this notation marks the beginning of a 350-year history of *neumes*, derived from their meaning in Greek of 'nod' or 'sign'. The American musicologist Carl Parrish (1904–65) notes that the origins of neumes, although indistinct, 'lay in accentuation signs of Greek and Roman literature, ascribed to Aristophanes of Byzantium (ca. 180 B.C.), which were used to indicate important points of declamation by marking the rise and fall of the voice'.[10] Two vocal markings, a rising tone of the voice, termed *acutus*, and an opposing lowering tone, termed the *gravis*, gave rise to the earliest neumatic symbols.

The earliest of these neumes were chironomic from the Greek word 'hand', and referring to the gestures used by the choir leader to indicate the relative location of the sound, marked out their indicative location in the space of their performance. They occupied, through association, a spatial relationship to the words being sung. Each of the neumes were like polarised atoms, held within the proximity of their associated word, but without a means of particular reference that might allow them to operate independently. These early neumes were termed in Italian, *in campo aperto*, literally 'in an open field' and functioned as *aide memoires* to the singers

of Gregorian chant, who knew the words by heart.[11] An example of this from the earliest complete musical manuscript in the world, the Cantatorium of St Gall, was found in the Abbey of St Gallen, Switzerland, dating from about 922–925, which in an extraordinary coincidence was the location that the Italian humanist Poggio Bracciolini discovered Vitruvius's *De architectura* in 1414.[12]

Subsequently, a stronger spatial connection between the text and the neumes was developed. Now termed diastematic neumes, they were located

3.3 An extract from the Cantorium of St Gall, illustrating non-diastematic neumes. Circa 922–925. Courtesy St Gallen, Stiftsbibliothek, Cod. Sang. 359 St Gall, f. 55r.

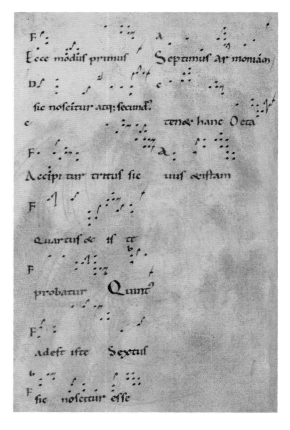

when the guidelines, previously implied, were now made explicit. Lines were no longer just scored into the surface, but drawn directly on it. In the fluid experimentation of the period, alternative systems also concurrently developed. In some notations, letters from A to G were used to denote pitch, but the letters were also placed diastematically, rising and falling as the melodic contour traversed the page as they traced each successive tonal interval. This method advantageously gave a shorthand way to read the notation, as no new symbolic language was necessary, although it also contained a redundancy: as the letters indicated the pitch, there was no reason for them to be spatially located: the rises and falls a double indication of the same information.

A further development was the use of coloured lines to show the location of the pitches F and C, lines that later became the clef signs of modern music notation.[13] The development of these guidelines, coloured red for F and yellow for C, is credited to Guido of Arezzo.[14] Guido also noted an important secondary aspect of these guidelines concerning their ability to connect works across time and space, in that sounds on one notation could be identified as identical to the same on another. Writing in his *Prologus antiphonarii sui* (*Prologue to His Antiphoner*), thought to have been published around 1025, he stated that:

> it is then most certainly true that all neumes or sounds similarly positioned on lines of the same colour or letter sound alike throughout, and they do so even if differently shaped so long as the line has the same colour or letter; while on different lines and in different spaces even similarly formed neumes sound not at all alike.[15]

above the relevant text and positioned according to an imaginary datum line that gave them a relative position not just to the words, but to the pitch of adjacent tones. In this extract from a *Tonarium*, or vocal exercise, lines can be faintly seen scored into the surface of the manuscript. These guidelines for the scribe allowed for the first attempts to give a spatial scale to the notation of pitch, while the remaining parameters of timbre, volume, and rhythm followed later. It is noteworthy that the earliest notation was concerned with drawing the materiality of pitch, rather than the temporality of rhythm. Diastematic neumes were further developed

3.4 An extract from *Ecce modus primus*. Late eleventh century. Courtesy Bibliothèque Nationale de France. Latin 7211, fol. 127v.

The sounds in the space of a single manuscript could now, through the coloured datum lines, be related to those in the space of others.[16]

The development of notation described above covers the period of unmeasured Gregorian chant, termed *musica plana*. Notation was now able to locate pitch with adequate precision but another musical parameter, time, subsequently developed solely as a symbolic language. *Musica mensurata* as it came to be known, regular measured polyphonic music, developed in a period starting around the middle of the thirteenth century. One of the most significant advances during this period was the development of symbols for silence as well as sound, in other words symbols for time without composed sounds. Time could now flow continuously through the notation and music. American musicologist Willi Apel (1893–1988) noted that in the period from 1225–1260, a key innovation was the notation of rests, 'this sign is no longer a stroke of indefinite length, drawn carelessly through the staff, but is written very accurately and appears in four different lengths'.[17] Each increasing length of rest was shown by extending the vertical line by one more line of the stave. Franco of Cologne then developed a system in which the note shapes had distinct durations and this was codified in his treatise *Ars cantus mensurabilis* (*The Art of Measured Song*), *c.*1260. In this treatise, he wrote about time without sounds, explaining that:

> time is the measure of a sound's duration as well as of the opposite, the omission of a sound, commonly called a rest. I say 'rest is measured by time', because if this were not the case two different melodies—one with rests, one without—could not be proportionally accommodated to one another.[18]

The notation of time now changed from subdivisions of rhythmic patterns to individual signs, each with specific durational values. This led to the systemisation of notation in Europe after the earlier history of disparate investigations spread among a range of countries and musical cultures, creating a template for music notation that was to last until the twentieth century, and providing a model for the innovative notation of Feldman's 1950s compositions.

TIME REPRESENTED BY SPACE

Feldman says in reference to the *Projections* series of five consecutively numbered compositions that:

> my desire here was not to 'compose', but to project sounds into time, free from a compositional rhetoric that had no place here. In order not to involve the performer (i.e., myself) in memory (relationships), and because the sounds no longer had an inherent symbolic shape, I allowed for indeterminacies in regard to pitch.[19]

Unlike Cage's aleatoric compositions, Feldman's intention was on freeing the sounds, not the performer. *Projection I* was remarkably only his third published musical composition. The first had been three years earlier with *Only* in 1947 for solo voice published by Universal Edition, No.16519.[20] *Projection I*, a composition for solo cello, was one of the first by Feldman to use graph paper as the base for its notation. Similar to the early scored lines in manuscripts of medieval music, this grid helped locate sounds in the space of the notation. The composition indicates three timbres or sound qualities (harmonic, pizzicato, arco – all three modes of sound production on the cello), three relative pitches (high, middle, low), while duration was 'indicated by the

PROJECTION 1

FOR SOLO CELLO

TIMBRE IS INDICATED: ◇ = HARMONIC; P=PIZZICATO; A=ARCO

RELATIVE PITCH (HIGH, MIDDLE, LOW) IS INDICATED: ⊓ = HIGH; ⊡ = MIDDLE;

⊔ = LOW. ANY TONE WITHIN THE RANGES INDICATED MAY BE SOUNDED.

THE LIMITS OF THESE RANGES MAY BE FREELY CHOSEN BY THE PLAYER.

DURATION IS INDICATED BY THE AMOUNT OF SPACE TAKEN UP BY THE

SQUARE OR RECTANGLE, EACH BOX (: :) BEING POTENTIALLY 4 ICTI.

THE SINGLE ICTUS OR PULSE IS AT THE TEMPO 72 OR THEREABOUTS.

amount of space taken up by the square or rectangle, each box [. . .] being potentially 4 icti. The single *ictus* or pulse is at the tempo 72 or thereabouts.'[21] *Projection I* consists of 204 units of time, *icti*, spread over approximately 170 seconds, depending upon the performers interpretation of the tempo in each performance. There are no changes between Feldman's initial handwritten notation, and the one published in 1962 by C. F. Peters of New York to the pitches or their spatial arrangement, only to the extent of guidelines used. The score starts and ends with silence, three *icti* of silence at each end, leaving space for the ambient sounds of the performance space to be heard. Before the first sounded note, a mid-range tone produced from plucking a string (pizzicato), are durations of ambient sounds and the composition

ends in similar manner as the final produced sound is also pizzicato. Incredibly, silence accounts for 58 per cent of the composition's duration: so 42 per cent are sounds *in* space, the remainder sounds *of* space. The silences vary in length from one *icti* to eleven *icti* in duration, and are located throughout the whole score, but slightly more prevalent towards the end. The sounds are located in the notation via means of discontinuous guidelines, running in both X and Y directions at 90 degrees to each other. Vertically, they are dotted lines that help to align the 'measures' of each four beat unit, calibrating the location of the composed sounds in time to support the performers interpretation of tempo; horizontally they are solid lines defining the edges of the four *icti* boxes and so aiding the positioning of the range of the pitch within

3.5 Morton Feldman. Page one of the notation of *Projection I*. 1950. Edition Peters.

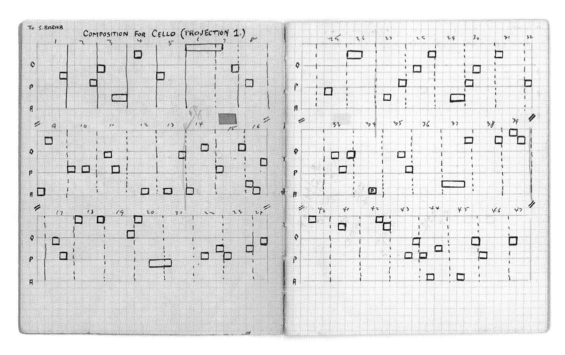

PROJECTION 1

Morton Feldman

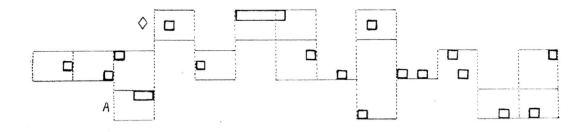

1.

COPYRIGHT © 1962 BY C.F. PETERS CORPORATION, 373 PARK AVE. SO., NEW YORK 16, N.Y.

3.6 Morton Feldman. His autographic notation on the left and the published version on the right. The composer's original sketch for *Projection I*, titled *To S. Barab Composition for Cello*. This composition was dedicated by Feldman to the American cellist and composer Seymour Barab. 1950. ©Morton Feldman Collection, Paul Sacher Foundation, Basel.

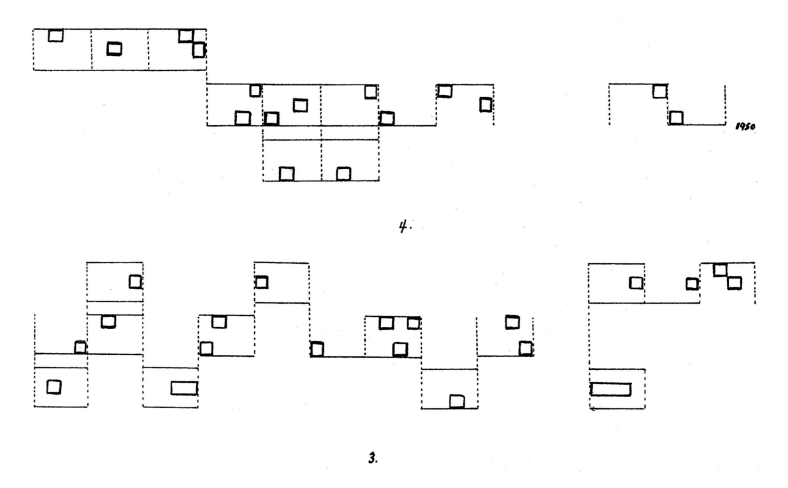

1950

4.

3.

3.7 Morton Feldman. The notation of silence in the final page of *Projection I*. 1950. Edition Peters.

3.8 Morton Feldman. Guidelines locating sounds in space in *Projection I*. 1950. Edition Peters.

each mode of production, and between adjacent sounds. These horizontal lines are discontinuous in only two locations, from beats 140 to 144, and from beats 188 to 196, both in the final third of the composition. Perhaps this reveals Feldman's intent that the composed sounds are not in themselves diminished as the piece ends, but rather are gradually surrounded by an increasing proportion of space.

The mode of sound production is unevenly divided between the pizzicato, arco and harmonics, in the corresponding proportions 47 per cent, 24 per

cent, and 29 per cent. On the cello the harmonic notes require faster bowing in order to produce the sound and also ring on the other strings as well as on the one being directly played.[22]

These harmonics are by the nature of their production through overtones, of higher pitch and less full sound. A consequence of harmonically produced higher pitches is that they are easier for the ear to determine the direction of, and so give a varied spatial sense to the listener. This is also true of higher pitches notated by Feldman from his high, medium,

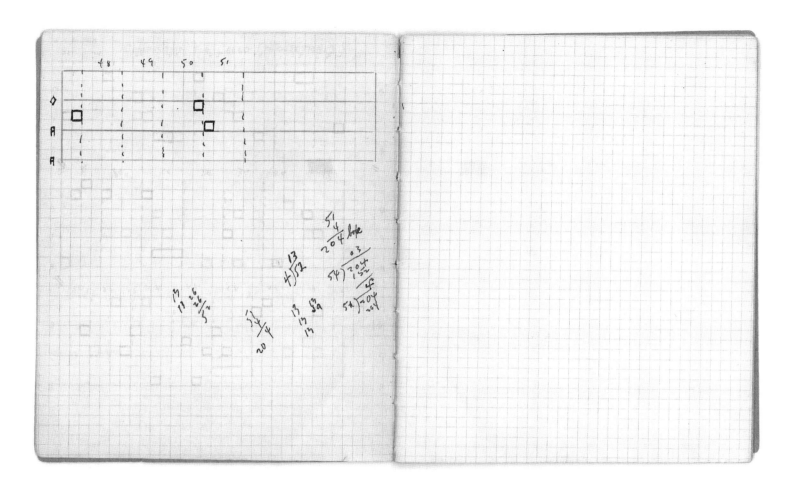

3.9 Morton Feldman. Composer's original sketch for *Projection I*, titled *To S. Barab Composition for Cello*. This sketch notation shows the possibility that time continues beyond the formal extent of the composition. 1950. ©Morton Feldman Collection, Paul Sacher Foundation, Basel.

and low categories. In the analysis of *Projection I*, 32 per cent are higher pitches, 25 per cent medium, and 29 per cent lower. The majority of the tones produced by the cellist in the performance of this piece are towards the extremes of the instruments range. This tendency for the pitches to be widely spaced is counterbalanced by the consistency of the volume of the sounds, which, although not explicitly notated by Feldman, reveals a consistent dynamic spread.

He subsequently gradually abandoned the graphic form of notation that had supported the development of *Projections*, moving away from this over a five-year period between 1953 and 1958. He explained this as a realisation of a flaw in his notation, stating, 'I was not only allowing the sounds to be free – I was also liberating the performer. I never thought of the graph as an art of improvisation, but more as a totally abstract sonic adventure.'[23] Feldman himself was conscious

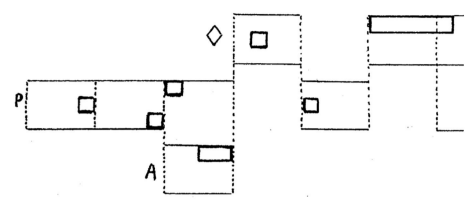

PROJECTION 1

of the space of his compositions, writing that, 'the scale of what is actually being represented [. . .] is a phenomenon unto itself'.[24] His work from 1979 onwards changed to an expansive scale of time. *Violin and Orchestra* from that year lasts over one hour, *String Quartet* from the same year over ninety minutes, while by 1983 his *String Quartet II* lasted close to six hours, and four hours for his 1984 piece *For Philip Guston*. He explained this development saying:

> My whole generation was hung up on the 20 to 25 minute piece. It was our clock. [. . .] As soon as you leave the 20–25 minute piece behind, in a one-movement work, different problems arise. Up to one hour you think about form, but after an hour and a half it's scale. Form is easy – just the division of things into parts. But scale is another matter.[25]

The scale Feldman created in these large pieces was one of both time and space. The forward progression of the music creates a transient space, one large enough to allow us to be both simultaneously in it, and yet passing through.

THIS DEPARTING LANDSCAPE

Dutch cellist Taco Kooistra's performance of *Projection I* at Hilversum Conservatorium, the Netherlands, recorded in 2005, starts with the note G, followed by A flat, F, C, D, D flat, G, and G again. Each of these sounds, and the subsequent ones, resonate in the space of the hall. The constant reverberation time created by the hall's acoustics and the consistent volume of the sounds produced draw immediate attention to the pitches selected by the performer, but subsequently, and more compellingly, to their qualities. The different modes of sound production in operation by the cellist as they interpret the notation create a vivid contrast and each sound is suspended in the space created by the non-performed sounds (silences) notated in the score. As Feldman noted, 'only by "unfixing" the elements traditionally used to construct a piece of music could the sounds exist in themselves – not as symbols, or memories which were memories of other music to begin with'.[26] In connection with the production of the sounds, Feldman sought to bring attention, not to their commencement, but to their conclusion. He wrote that:

> though tonality has long been abandoned, and atonality, I understand, has also seen its day, the same gesture of the instrument attack remains. The result is an aural plane that has hardly changed since Beethoven, and in many ways is primitive – as Cezanne makes us see Renaissance space as primitive.[27]

Although his notational system of sounds delineated by boxes, that show their relative spatial distribution as well as their level of pitch and mode of production, denotes the beginning and end of each sound equally, Feldman's concern for sounds was for the spatiality created by their ending. Writing in 1985, he said that:

> Since music is increasingly obsessed with this one idea – variation – one must always be looking back at one's material for implications to go on. Change is the only solution to an unchanging aural plane created by the constant element of projection, of attack. This is perhaps why in my own music I am so involved with the decay of each sound, and try to make its attack sourceless. The attack of a sound is not its character. Actually what we hear is the attack and not the sound. Decay, however, this departing landscape, *this* expresses where the sound exists in our hearing – leaving us rather than coming towards us.[28]

This is at odds with the conventional understanding as noted by Cole, that 'musical meaning is invested in the beginning, not the end, of a note'.[29] The idea of a spatial extent created through sound has a long history in music. As Schafer mentions:

> such is the music of the classical concert and its high points are the chamber music of Bach and Mozart. In such music distance is important, and the real space of the concert hall is extended in the virtual space of dynamics—by which effects may be brought into the foreground (*forte*) or allowed to drift back toward the acoustic horizon (*piano*).[30]

This relationship between dynamics and space for Schafer also connects music to the visual construct of perspective. As he states:

> When Giovanni Gabrieli composed his *Sonata Pian'e Forte* (literally, to be sounded soft and loud), he introduced perspective thinking into Western music. Before this date we have no record of dynamic contrast in music, by which we must not infer that it did not exist, but may deduce that it had not become an articulated desideratum of performance. Gabrieli's *piano* and *forte* were the first steps towards the quantification of sound level, just as the foot and furlong had earlier quantified space: Just as objects are rank-ordered in perspective painting, depending on their distance from the viewer, so musical sounds are rank-ordered by means of their dynamic emphasis in the virtual space of the soundscape.[31]

In conventional music the interconnections between successive tones, its harmonic structure, pushes the music forward. Tudor referring to the music of French composer Pierre Boulez (1925–2016) noted that 'the space seems to be in front of one, in one's line of aural vision, as it were'.[32] In *Projection I*, however, each sound exists in its own space by nature of its independent location. As Belgium music critic Herman Sabbe has noted, 'the full and the void, the transparent and the opaque, the ephemeral and the enduring are no alternating categories in Feldman's music, they are simultaneous and interdependent features of it'.[33] If Feldman's notation locates sounds within the space of the score, the sounds of the performance space are not directly and similarly located. His notation is not a direct representation of the sound, a direct sonorous image, as it fails to include the effect of the performance space on the sounds it creates. Feldman saw space as defined through the combination of timbral and temporal structures together rather than simply time alone. He noted in his sketchbook 'time structure then makes it possible to create music as on a canvas or better yet not unlike the architect's four walls'.[34]

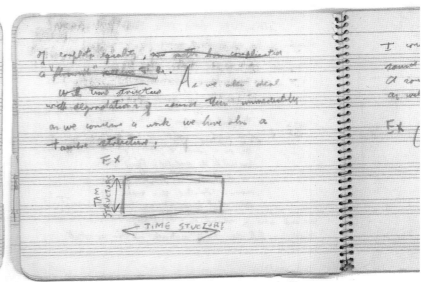

3.11 Morton Feldman. Structure and the Structural Cell from his undated sketchbook. ©Morton Feldman Collection, Paul Sacher Foundation, Basel.

'REALISING' FELDMAN

In order to further investigate *Projection I*, I return to Busoni's notion of creative transcription, transcribing Feldman's *Projection I* to develop the tools to allow for an in-depth study. Developing a new notation from *Projection I* allows us to separate out aspects of Feldman's work, creating a new reading of it that opens up potential un-noticed correlations with landscape architecture. This transcription method shares analogies with those of Tudor who is most closely connected with the performance of the music of Cage during the years 1951 to the late 1960s, the period that included many of his aleatoric scores including *Winter Music* (1957) and *4'33"* (1952). Tudor transcribed composers' scores in a process termed 'realisations', defined by musicologist John Holzaepfel as translating 'the composer's notation into a single instance of an infinity of possibilities, [. . .] the abstract concrete'.[35] Tudor created these

'rigorous preparatory steps, including measurements, computations, conversion tables [. . .] translated into a more or less conventional notation for his own use in performance'[36] in order to reduce the increasing freedom that Cage's notations created. Intriguingly, given the broad recognition given to his realisations of Cage's music, Tudor actually first wrote them for a composition by Feldman, his *Intersection 3* in 1954.[37] One example of Tudor's use of realisations was the way in which they allowed him to draw time precisely. In the case of *Winter Music*, for example, Tudor used a scale of 'one inch equals one-sixteenth of sixty seconds, or 3.75 seconds'.[38] For *4'33"* he adopted the scale of 'one half-inch to M.M. = 60, or one second',[39] creating the following spatial scale for the three movements of the piece, 30" becomes fifteen inches, 2'23" becomes 71½ inches, and the final movement of 1'40" becomes 50 inches of the score. In this sense they are analogous to the early music

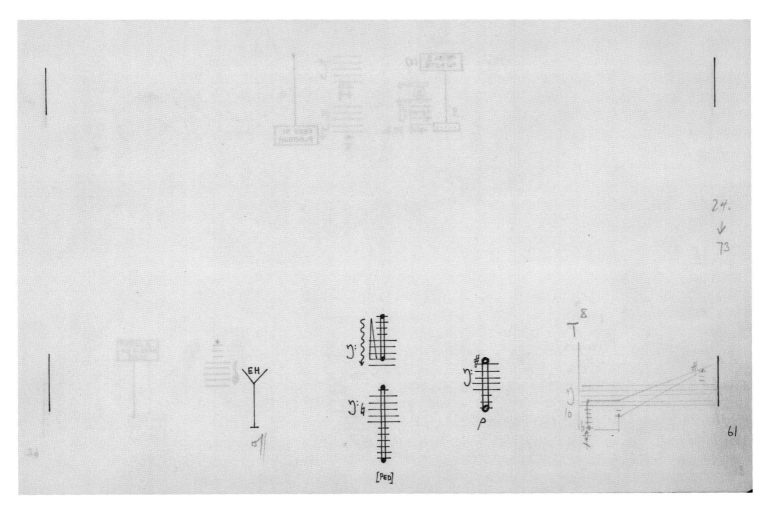

3.12 David Tudor. Tudor's realisation of John Cage's Concert for Piano and Orchestra – Solo for Piano (p. 61), Getty Research Institute, Los Angeles (980039). Unknown date. ©J. Paul Getty Trust.

notations where having known pitches to perform, the notational challenge then becomes one of visualising time. The process of developing these realisations was, predictably given the open nature of Cage's original notation, not a single transcriptive process. Tudor's second realisation of *Concert for Piano and Orchestra / Solo for Piano* clearly shows fainter marks, referred to by Isaac Schankler as 'read through from the next two pages'[40] together with Tudor's

own pencil additions that supplement his inked transcriptions. Tudor's realisations were a kind of expulsion of ideas, an aspiration of thoughts in order to synthesise and construct a performance of the music located within the notation, a music obscured by the aleatoric nature of Cage's compositions. My realisations are also an unpacking, but they are less concerned by the music encoded within Feldman's original and are more a deconstruction

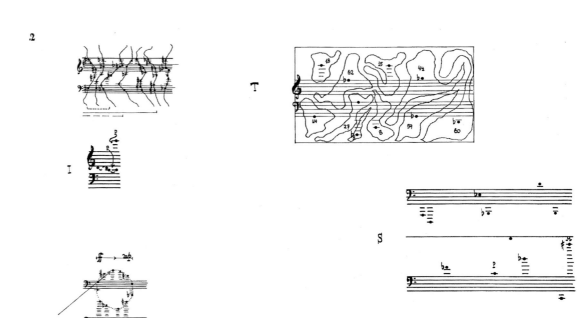

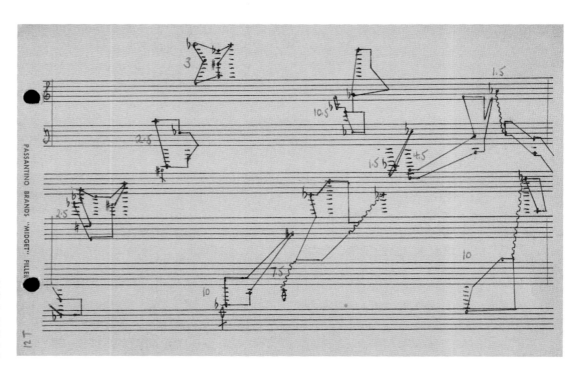

3.13 John Cage. Notation from page twelve of *Concert for Piano and Orchestra* with T in the upper right hand corner. 1958. Edition Peters.

3.14 David Tudor. David Tudor's realisation of John Cage's Concert for Piano. Getty Research Institute, Los Angeles (980039). 1957–1958. ©J. Paul Getty Trust.

of one notation in order to understand its strategies through the construction of a new notation. The 'performance' of Tudor's realisations was a single, discrete temporal event, a duration determined by the notation. The performance of these landscape realisations is neither singular nor discrete but an extended process of developing new notations for landscape, one that includes thoughts as well as actions, readings as well as writings.

SOUND AND SHAPED TIME

As Griffiths has noted, 'being sound and shaped time, music begins'.[41] In the simple gestural language at work in Feldman's score, there are echoes in interconnected ways with the beginnings of music notation described earlier. Firstly, in this composition Feldman develops symbols that simply draw, almost pictorially, sound's spatial qualities. By echoing their relative rise and fall, tones are broadly located within their relative position on the notation, evocative of earlier chironomic neumes. Simple guidelines, aids to help locate the pitches, occur in the developing notation of both diastematic neumes and *Projection I*. While the development of rhythmic complexity in these neumes led to the development of a complex symbolic system to allow different durations to be scaled to the score, Feldman simply and directly draws them to scale. Sounds and silences are equally scaled and from this we can assume are awarded equal significance in his work. This is similar to the early notation of silence in music except that in Feldman' work a proportional notation rather than a symbolic one is employed. Feldman's guidelines in *Projection I*, 'measure' temporal units and material qualities. Spatial depth is created by the quantity of space which is itself created by the measures of

silence. Feldman's notation draws the boundaries of immateriality, of silence. It inverts the conventional figure – ground relationship (performed sounds – background sounds) and what is actually created is a spatial depth from the ambient sounds of spaces, working together with the composed sounds. In *Projection I* the depth to this representation of sound is less through the volume the performer selects, which was consistent in Feldman's music of this period, and more through a combination of mode of sound production and relative pitch. Although, overall, the volume from this notation, like many others of Feldman's throughout his career, is quiet, the mode of sound production from arco, to pizzicato, to harmonics, as well the volume produced by the performer, creates subtle differences in sonic depth. The effect of these is to create spatial depth – we are not slicing through space as in Eckbo's elevation but both temporal and spatial scales are created in Feldman's notation for *Projection I*.

Feldman's notation allows for the simultaneous representation of time and space as an alternative to orthogonal or perspective drawing. His notation shares the ambiguity of the early notation of music, and in doing so opens a model for multivalent representation in landscape architecture. Alberti's *On Painting*, published in 1435, used guidelines to locate materials in space, which post-dated similar developments in music. As English architectural critic Robin Evans (1944–1993) notes, 'Alberti's method gives a perspective of a squared pavement behind the picture plane. The tiles are aligned with the picture plane, and aligned therefore with the prince of rays',[42] in reference to the term given to the line travelling from the observer's eye, and parallel to the ground, and which the picture plane is perpendicular to. It is curious that landscape architecture has been drawn closely to the Albertian perspective when other models, not just in music, but also in landscape art have long been available. In Giovanni di Paolo's *Saint John the Baptist Retiring to the Desert* from 1454 we see different spaces compressed within the painting. First, the moment Saint John leaves the city, his toe just across the threshold at the precise moment his journey commences, and second, in seemingly mountain terrain as he progresses towards his desert destination. There are layers within the painting that could correspond to fore, middle, and background, but no sequential relationship between them, and no vanishing point. The temporal implications of the painting come from Saint John's journey, while the spatial aspects from the ambiguous duality of the elements of the landscape where sculpted pale green forms seem to signify both tree canopies and rugged mountain peaks in the same moment. In addition to perspective's exclusion of time from landscape through the necessity of a static viewpoint, Australian architect Nicholas Temple has noted that perspective created a new understanding of depth:

> the notion of distance before Alberti's survey was less about length and more about time or effort. The time taken to traverse the city by foot for example constituted an acceptable measures of distance, which was expressed not so much in numerical terms as by certain vernacular expressions, such as 'a hike'.[43]

So, Feldman's notation, in providing a representation of time and space, synthesises aspects of music and landscape art, connecting us back to the era of non-perspectival drawing, when time was closely correlated with space and when space could be a dimension in time.

TRANSCRIBING MANHATTAN

Bernard Tschumi's *MT1 'The Park'* was the first of four studies from his seminal 1977 investigations in *Manhattan Transcripts*, which drew upon notational precedents in music and dance in its development. Tschumi saw the *Manhattan Transcripts* as part of a larger study of notations, noting in the foreword that 'although other forms of notation were devised in various stages of the total project (words, sounds, installations), the *Transcripts* are composed mainly of drawings, for drawings are both key means and limitations of architectural inquiries'.[44] Like my own earlier transcriptions of *Projection I*, Tschumi also saw his notations as transcriptions, aiming to 'propose to transcribe an architectural interpretation of reality'.[45] Although the sequences are fictitious, as Tschumi noted the origin of each *Transcript* was real and could be found within the city, stating, 'Manhattan is a *real* place; the actions described are *real* actions [...] they isolate, frame, "take" elements from the city'.[46] *MT1* consists of twenty-four sequences of events, spaces, and movements that shadow the story of an anonymous murder. Each consists of three elements, 'a special mode of notation – the three-square principle – underlines the deadly game of hide and seek between the suspect and the ever-changing architectural events'.[47] The first square in each line of three is composed of a photograph, a single event within both the notation and the wider story of life in New York. These photos witness the unfolding murder, providing twenty-four moments in the reveal from the victim being stalked to the murderer's capture. The second square is derived from 'the world

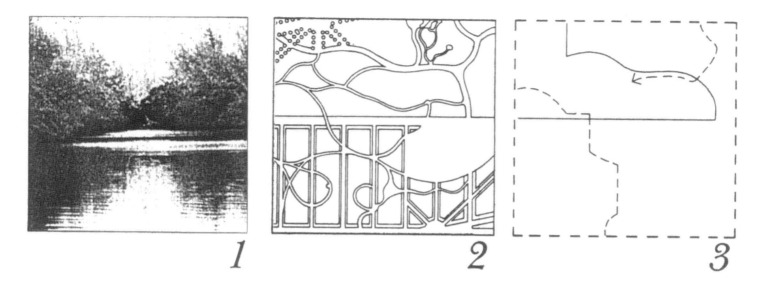

of objects, composed of buildings abstracted from maps, plans',[48] while the third denotes movements abstracted from choreography, or other movement diagrams concentrating on their spatial effects. Tschumi asserted that the 'original purpose of the tripartite mode of notation [. . .] was to introduce the order of experience, the order of time – moments, intervals, sequences',[49] questioning the conventional ways in which the city is represented in architectural drawing. Central to *Manhattan Transcripts* is the temporal organisation of events taking place in the city; their sequential nature represents 'both time and consequence, temporality and logic'.[50] Similar to Russian film director Sergei Eisenstein's (1898–1948) notion of 'montage' explained in *Film Form*,[51] Tschumi saw each element of the notation as like a cinematic frame. He believed that we understood each image first through its immediate adjacent juxtapositions, and then secondly through its cumulative sequence. Tschumi noted that the notation is constructed from 'two conflicting fields: first, the framing device

– square, conformist, normal and predictable, regular and comforting, correct. Second, the framed material, a place that only questions, distorts, compresses, displaces.'[52] The frames that contain the events, spaces and movements are not equally delineated. The frames of the two former are continuous lines, while the latter are discontinuous, shown in dashed lines. Tschumi does not explain this in the text, other than noting that each sequence of three frames is to be read in chronological succession, and we are to understand them not in isolation but through their cumulative meaning. Is he suggesting that movement, actions over time, is the component most open to unexpected cross-pollination? Or perhaps we are being invited to see the boundaries of movement as the most temporal of the three components that constitute the landscape architectural spaces represented through his new notation.

In transcribing Tschumi's notation I created a composite notation, titled *New York Interstices*, that was a synthesis of the real and imagined, the fictitious and

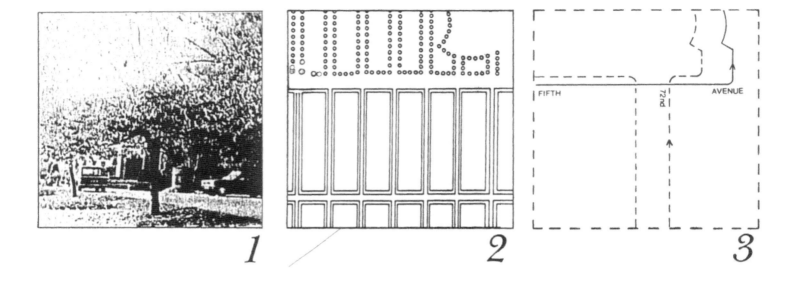

the recorded. It was also a synthesis between music and landscape architecture, focusing on resonances between a music notation, a design notation, and a detailed record of sound and space. I continued working on the same paper as the earlier analysis of *Projection I* so that potential similarities between the two works might appear. I started with rotating *MT1* counter-clockwise by 90 degrees so that time is running horizontally from left to right. This aligns the sequential unfolding with that of *Projection I*, drawing parallels between the space-time relationships of Feldman's notation with that of Tschumi. Both of these notations, by isolating the materials of their compositions in framed boxes – timbral and tonal in *Projection I*, pictorial and planimetric in *MT1* – emphasise their spatial qualities over time. I focus on four specific sequences, numbers, 1, 11, 12, and 13, selected as they either locate the notation within identifiable landscape spaces within the city, or incorporate elements of music notation. The first

sequence locates the story around the area of Fifth Avenue and East 72nd Street, at the eastern edge of Central Park, the space spanning six blocks from 68th Street to 74th Street. With each block 80 × 274 metres, the 'movement' square denotes a space of 313,600 m^2. Here, I add the scaled plan of Central Park, locating Tschumi's fiction within the real space of New York. Sequence 11 finds us back in Central Park itself, seeing the legs of detectives in close-up on the site. The movement and space frames in this sequence include Bethesda Fountain, and the path leading to it from the south called The Mall, a formal feature from American landscape architects Frederick Law Olmsted (1822–1903) and Calvert Vaux's (1824–1895) design. The following real locations from Central Park are noted in Tschumi's notation: Cherry Hill, The Esplanade at the north end of the Mall, the Lake, Cleopatra's Needle, and The Ramble. Unlike in sequence 1 where we are firmly located in a precisely notated landscape

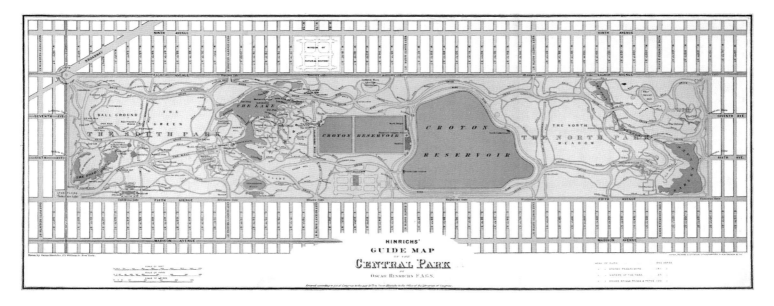

3.17 Frederick Law Olmsted and Calvert Vaux. Extract from the Map of the Central Park showing the progress of the work up to 1860, showing the location of The Mall, Ramble, and Lake. 1860.

space, these spaces are no longer accurately spatially arranged, but are rather relocated within the frame of the notation's sequence. In sequence 11 I re-draw the locations to scale, using dashed lines to position the notated and the notation in scaled landscape space. In the following sequence, number 12, we now witness these events in the city from the air. The movement frame is closely related to the previous one but the central focus now moves west, implying movement not just within the story as we progress from the previous sequence, but across the space of Central Park. This space frame is one of only two that directly draws upon music notation. We see a stave marked with a bass clef and three continuous waving lines. These are then redrawn at enlarged scale, revealing that the pitches Tschumi selected, although stacked like a conventional chord, are, in fact, in intervals of fourths. This brings the introduction of sounds into the *Transcripts* closer to music of the twentieth century, which adopted the more dissonant

fourth over the long history of chords composed of intervals of a third. In sequence 13, the three lines are supplemented as single note below the fourth lower ledger line. In sequence 13, Tschumi's notation also includes two defined pitches that are separated by an interval of exactly three octaves, the typical range of pitch of the human voice, delineating the range of human sounds within the city of New York. These two sequences, numbers 12 and 13, introduce sound as a component of space. Perhaps this is the sound of movement created by the characters of this part of the narrative and the layering of these different sounds denoted by the meandering lines implying varying pitch over time.

Echoing ideas from Feldman's *Projection I*, Tschumi noted that:

> ultimately, the *Transcripts* try to offer a different reading [. . .] in which space, movement and events are independent, yet stand in a new relationship to one another, so that the

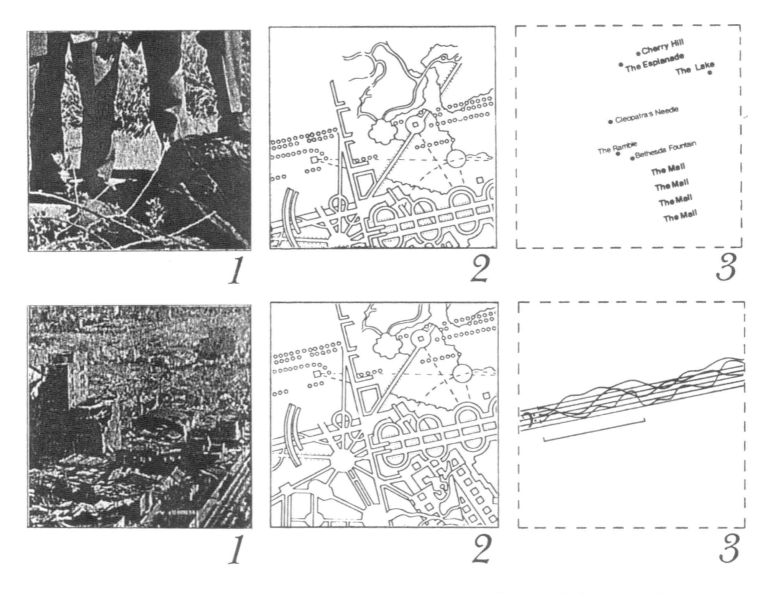

3.18 Bernard Tschumi. Sequence eleven from the Manhattan Transcripts, Part 1: The Park. 1977. ©Bernard Tschumi.

3.19 Bernard Tschumi. The musical stave from sequence twelve from the Manhattan Transcripts, Part 1: The Park. 1977. ©Bernard Tschumi.

conventional components of architecture are broken down and rebuilt along different axes.[53]

For Feldman, the three modes of sound production specified in the notation also create three modes of space production, as space is created through the material of sound. If, as Corner suggests, that materiality is one of the special qualities of landscape space that landscape architecture representation must seek to address – in addition to its special spatial and temporal properties – then the *Transcripts* strangely omit this. Tschumi himself acknowledged this omission in 2004: 'so I would now say that each of the concepts that I developed at the time of the *Manhattan Transcripts* is still valid for the work, but there was a missing component: materiality',[54] the focus for the following transcription.

SOUNDS OF THE CITY

As the *Transcripts* combine both the fictitious and factual, *New York Interstices* now introduces sound as an aspect of landscape architectural space and notation. The selected sounds are connected with the location of Feldman's and Tschumi's notations, being based within the space of New York. The Italian film director Michelangelo Antonioni (1912–2007) is recorded making a diary of three hours of sound from 6 a.m. to 9 a.m. during a visit to the city around 1970[55] from his room on the 34th floor of the Sherry-Netherland Hotel. In this text he describes both the sounds' production, such as 'a huge truck passes. It seems so close that I feel I am on the second floor' and their qualities, for example, 'then a hollow boom, barely audible, but lingering in the air. A faint hum suddenly stops.'[56] His description, which in its English translation runs to only 1129 words, both locates sounds within known locations of the city, such as the lines of cars snaking through the roads at the southern end of Central Park along the East and West Drive, as well as the difficulties of identifying sound source locations and directions from his room. For example, at quarter past six he notes 'a terribly noisy truck seems just outside the window. But it is an aircraft. All the sounds increase [. . .] and then they recede, gradually. But no, another rumble, another siren. Irritating, persistent, right across the horizon'.[57]

His vivid description brings to life the spatial qualities of this area of New York, the impact of the city's architecture on its landscape spaces as it amplifies and distorts sounds, both amplifying and distorting the sense of distance and proximity they create.

Each sound described by him I notate as a spatial envelope. I indicate pitch via vertical location within the notation, duration via relative length of symbol, and where known geographic location within this part of New York via dashed lines to the location in New York. Intriguingly, given that the hotel is located adjacent to the park, in his diary he does not describe natural sounds except the wind, or their direction, which is interrupted by the surrounding buildings. What he instead describes, in a way eerily reminiscent of Feldman, is a sound quality and a sense of duration including the nature of the sound's decay. Where Tschumi brought together events, movements and spaces, my notations bring together the time-space relationships in the notation of *Projection I*, the events-movements-spaces of *MT1*, and the sounds of New York so vividly described by Antonioni. These are set together in the space of one notation. They can be read individually or as a composite of the time-space of music and landscape architecture.

In this chapter 204 beats of Feldman's composition together with the 180 minutes of Antonioni's description are conflated into one notational space (see notation N1). What is lost is accuracy of temporal scale, but what appears in its place are striking similarities between Antonioni's observations and Feldman's composition. Was *Projection I* his musical response to the experience of a life in the sounds of New York? *New York Interstices* includes dashed lines that link sounds described by Antonioni with similar sounds in *Projection I*,

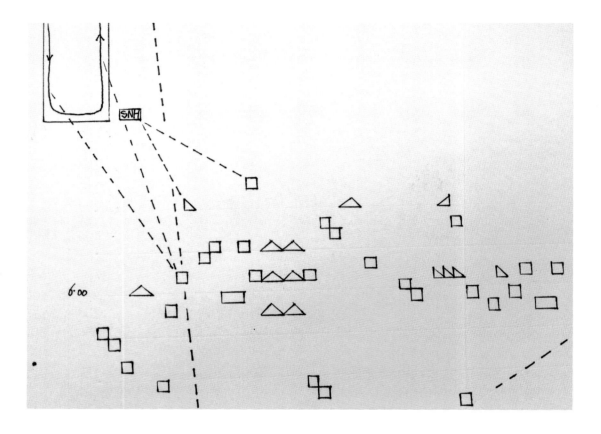

3.20 David Buck. Extract of *New York Interstices* showing correlations between sounds in *Projection I* and Antonioni's description. 2011.

such as sounds repeated, or low pitched sounds separated by space. The sounds in *Projection I* and the sounds of New York city seem to reverberate in our minds. Feldman composed this music while sharing an apartment with Cage on Broad Street and this is appears in the notation as CFH, Cage-Feldman House, located 3.8 miles from the Sherry-Netherland Hotel, drawn to scale south-east of the corner of Central Park. Intriguingly, at the same time Antonioni wrote his vivid description of New York's sounds, Feldman's was composing *The Viola in My Life I*, the first of a four-part composition for viola, flute, piano, percussion, violin and cello.

This composition echoes aspects of *Projection I*, but now each tone rings extendedly and the multi-instrumentation provides a greater timbral range. Although Feldman had by 1970 abandoned graphic notations for over a decade, it is as though *Projection I* continues to be reflected in this later work, and also resonates in my own.

NOTATION OF SPACE

As Evans noted, 'projection operates in the intervals between things'.[58] As we have seen in this chapter *Horizons*, the notation developed in *New York Interstices* is also a form of projection, an externalisation of

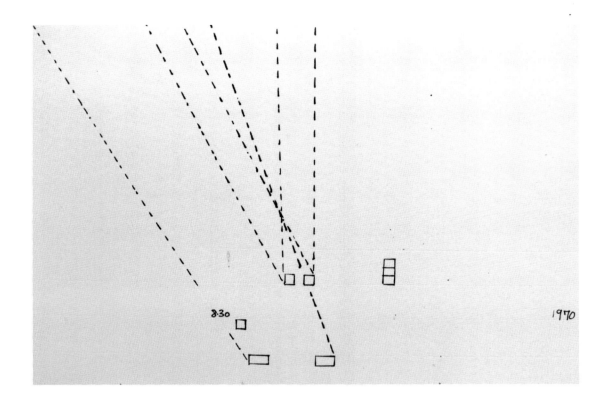

3.21 David Buck. Extract of *New York Interstices* showing correlations between sounds in *Projection I* and Antonioni's description. 2011.

personal thoughts on the space between music and landscape architecture. The selection of Feldman's notation of *Projection 1*, which through its open nature in musical terms invites the performer to be actively involved in its realisation, became an invitation into my own landscape architecture investigations, as though I was the performer of Feldman's notation. The openness of *Projection I* allowed me to be creatively involved in its interpretation. In *Horizons*, we see that there are correspondences between Feldman's notation and the history of music notation's development, revealing similarities between space in early music notation and Feldman's work, which itself contributed to the development of open notations in the music of the mid twentieth century.

We can also see that the notation of space in *Projection I* allows us to fill in a void in *MT1*, addressing the deficiency of sound in urban landscape space which is conventionally overlooked. The works of Feldman, Tschumi, and Antonioni share a common location in New York, creating a common space to investigate aspects of landscape architecture notation. The corollaries in the framing of space in *Projection I* and *MT1* led to the development of *New York Interstices*, which draws out similarities between the notation of space in music and landscape architecture. This notation, through the transcription of earlier notations created by Feldman and Tschumi, provides a means of 'realising' intersections between these two fields of music and urban landscape.

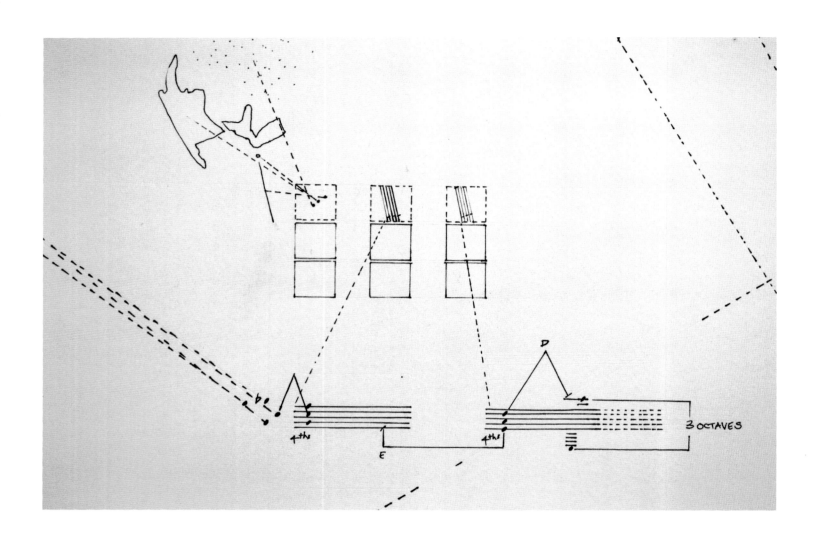

3 OCTAVES

3.22 David Buck. Extract of *New York Interstices*
showing the location of sound sources, pitch
range, and geographic location in New York.
2011.

3.23 David Buck. Extract of *New York Interstices*
showing the location of the Cage-Feldman house
on Grand Street, New York. 2011.

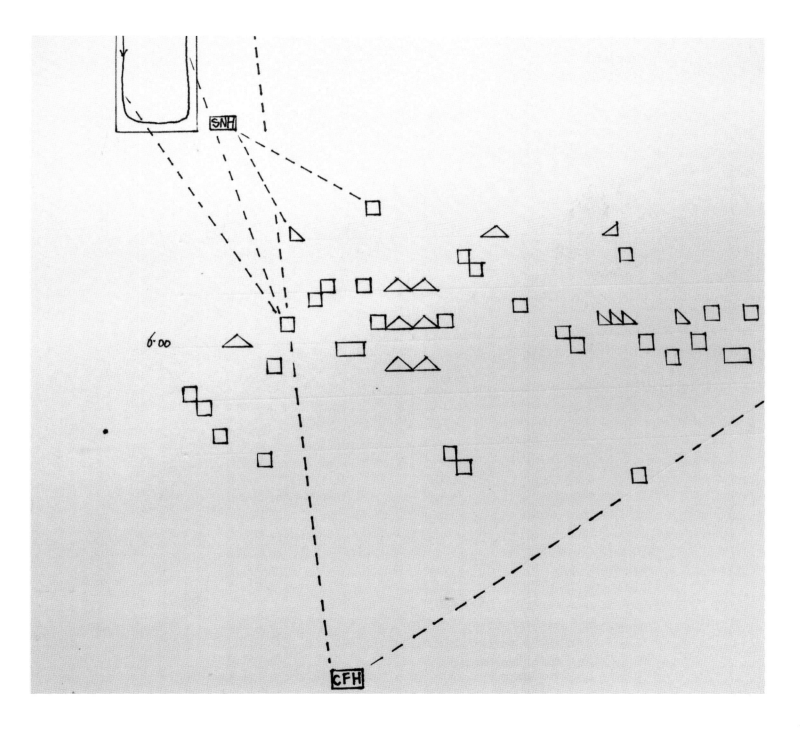

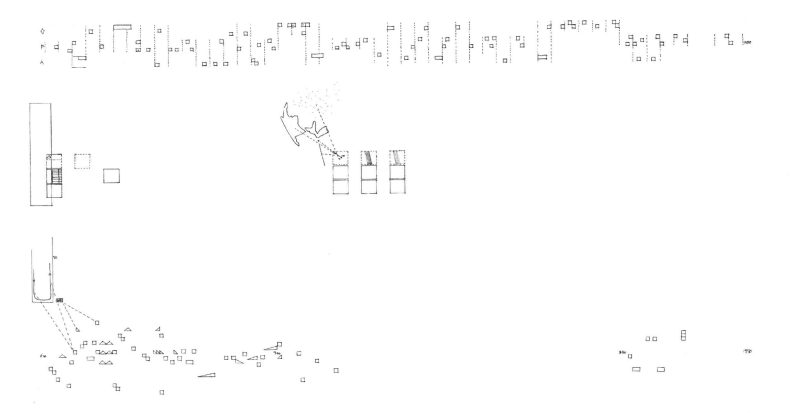

N1 *New York Interstices.* Initial analytical notations of Feldman, Tschumi and Antonioni. 2011.

NOTES

1 Griffiths, 'Sound-Code-Image' (1986), 5–6.

2 http://www.cnvill.net/mfworks.pdf.

3 Bernard, 'Feldman's Painters' (2002), 179.

4 Feldman, *Morton Feldman – Earle Brown* (1970), 1.

5 Feldman, *Essays* (1985), 132.

6 Feldman, 'Between Categories' (1988), 5.

7 Feldman, *Essays* (1985), 48.

8 Feldman, *Essays* (1985), 91.

9 Boretz and Cone, *Perspectives on Notation* (1976), viii.

10 Parrish, *Notation of Medieval Music* (1978), 4.

11 As Parrish has noted 'these pieces would obviously be impossible to interpret accurately today if they did not exist in later versions in which the notation is definite in pitch.' Parrish, *Notation of Medieval Music* (1978), 9.

12 I am indebted to Professor Jonathan Hill, UCL, for bringing this to my attention.

13 The choice of F and C may have been due to the fact that within the scale of C (the white notes on the modern piano), that they are the only two tones whose lower adjacent tones are a semitone (half-step) away, all others are a whole tone. These might have functioned as a warning to the singers that a less frequent interval was located.

14 Rastall, *Notation of Western Music* (1983), 32.

15 Strunk, *Source Readings* (1965), 119.

16 Parrish, *Notation of Medieval Music* (1978), 66.

17 Apel, *Notation of Polyphonic Music* (1942), 302.

18 Strunk, *Source Readings* (1965), 140.

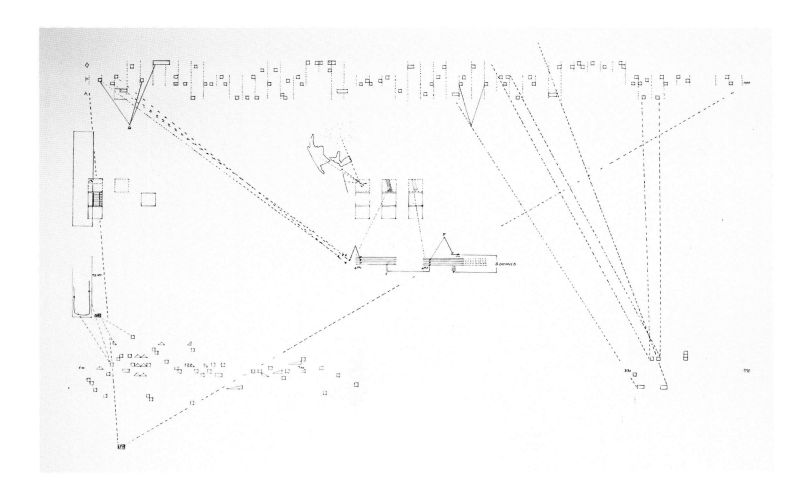

19 Feldman, *Essays* (1985), 38.

20 http://www.cnvill.net/mfworks.pdf.

21 Feldman, *Projection 1 for Solo Cello* (1962), 1.

22 I am indebted to Professor Neil Heyde, RAM, for bringing this to my attention.

23 Feldman, *Essays* (1985), 38.

24 Feldman, *Give My Regards* (2000), 137.

25 Griffiths, *Modern Music* (2010), 280.

26 Feldman, *Essays* (1985), 49.

27 Feldman, *Essays* (1985), 88.

28 Feldman, *Essays* (1985), 89.

29 Cole, *Sounds and Signs* (1974), 82.

30 Schafer, *The Soundscape* (1993), 117.

31 Schafer, *The Soundscape* (1993), 156.

32 Holzaepfel, 'Cage and Tudor' (2002), 174.

33 Sabbe, *Music of Morton Feldman* (1996), 13.

34 Feldman, *Structure and the Structural Cell* from his undated *Sketchbook*. Copyright Morton Feldman Collection, Paul Sacher Foundation, Basel.

35 Holzaepfel, 'Painting by Numbers' (2002), 163.

36 Holzaepfel, 'Cage and Tudor' (2002), 176.

N2 *New York Interstices*. Three initial analytical notations of Feldman, Tschumi and Antonioni. 2011.

37 Holzaepfel, 'Cage and Tudor' (2002), 176.

38 Holzaepfel, 'Cage and Tudor' (2002), 180.

39 Holzaepfel, 'Cage and Tudor' (2002), 175.

40 http://www.newmusicbox.org/articles/cage-tudor-concert-for-piano-and-orchestra/.

41 Griffiths, *Concise History* (2006), 1.

42 Evans, *The Projective Cast* (1995), 110–111.

43 Temple, *Disclosing Horizons* (2007), 133.

44 Tschumi, *Manhattan Transcripts* (1994), 6.

45 Tschumi, *Manhattan Transcripts* (1994), 7.

46 Tschumi, *Manhattan Transcripts* (1994), 8.

47 Tschumi, *Manhattan Transcripts* (1994), 8.

48 Tschumi, *Manhattan Transcripts* (1994), 8–9.

49 Tschumi, *Manhattan Transcripts* (1994), 9.

50 Tschumi, *Manhattan Transcripts* (1994), 10.

51 Eisenstein, *Film Form* (1949).

52 Tschumi, *Manhattan Transcripts* (1994), 11.

53 Tschumi, *Manhattan Transcripts* (1994), 7.

54 Walker, 'Avant-propos' (2004), 122.

55 The date is disputed in a recent book by Antonella Sisto who notes that the diary excerpts first appeared with a different date of April 1966. Sisto, *Film Sound in Italy* (2014), 198.

56 http://bldgblog.blogspot.co.uk/2007/07/new-york-city-in-sound.html.

57 http://bldgblog.blogspot.co.uk/2007/07/new-york-city-in-sound.html.

58 Evans, *The Projective Cast* (1995), 366.

CLOUDS

This chapter investigates the notation of aperiodic time in music and landscape architecture, commencing with a detailed study of the notation of the Hungarian composer György Ligeti's composition from 1967, *Lontano*, examining the strategies used within its symbolic notation to address complex notions of time. This is followed by an analysis of a landscape architectural notation from 1965, contained in a publication titled *The View from the Road*, exploring whether its approach to drawing motive experience in landscape might resonate with Ligeti's notation and his notions of unfolding time. These studies from music and landscape architectural notations are then used to investigate the cinematic landscape contained within the film *Onibaba*, by Japanese director Kaneto Shindo (1912–2012). Ligeti's music is strongly connected with film, most noticeably through director Stanley Kubrick's extensive use of it in his 1968 film *2001: A Space Odyssey*, and later when *Lontano* appeared three times in Kubrick's 1980 film *The Shining*.[1] Perhaps Kubrick selected Ligeti's music for these films due to the absence of a conventional rhythmic pulse, and instead we are drawn into listening to what seems like slow, transient, awakenings, in which time floats expansively around us.

GYÖRGY LIGETI

Ligeti's compositions spanned from operatic (*Aventures* in 1961), to orchestral (most notably *Apparitions* from 1958–59, *Atmospheres* in 1961, and *San Francisco Polyphony* from 1973–1974) to concerto, choral and chamber music as well as three influential books of piano etudes between 1985 and 2001. However, it was *Lontano*, together with *Apparitions* and *Atmospheres*, that explored a multi-layered,

dense sound that became strongly associated with Ligeti's work. Termed 'micropolyphony', Ligeti first used this approach in *Apparitions*, which has been described by English musicologist Richard Steinitz as 'microscopic counterpoint, an internally animated yet dense structure in which large numbers of instruments play slightly different versions of the same line'.[2] Ligeti himself described the effect of micropolyphony in *Lontano* as, 'you hear a kind of impenetrable texture, something like a very densely woven cobweb [. . .] The polyphonic structure does not actually come through, you cannot hear it; it remains hidden in a microscopic, underwater world, to us inaudible'.[3] Ligeti's ability to map out each contributing instrument's movement with immense care, while retaining the integrity of the whole composition, became the hallmark of his orchestral scores. From 1966 onwards these polyphonic networks become less dense and Ligeti noted that, 'typical of this thinned-out micropolyphony – now resembling the transparency of a drawing rather than the opaqueness of a painting – are the *Second String Quartet* (composed 1968) and the *Chamber Concerto* for thirteen players (composed 1969–70)'.[4] There are a number of references to the changing phenomena found in landscape in his work, including his *Chamber Concerto, Clocks and Clouds*,[5] and *San Francisco Polyphony*. In reference to the first movement of the *Chamber Concerto* from 1969–70, for example, Ligeti noted that his overall idea was the image of 'the surface of a stretch of water, where everything takes place below the surface. The musical events you hear are blurred; suddenly a tune emerges and then sinks back again.'[6] A similar interest is referenced in his later work from 1974–77, *San Francisco Polyphony*, where Ligeti noted:

this piece starts with a cluster full of various tunes [. . .] as they are intertwined like creepers. Then slowly a very clear melodic pattern emerges from this dense structure, it is discernible for a while before it sinks back into the billowing mass.[7]

Lontano was composed in the same year as the Beatles' *Lucy in the Sky with Diamonds*, and only seven years after Ligeti launched his international career when his composition *Apparitions* was performed at the International Society for Contemporary Music festival.

SOUND ON PAPER

The American musicologist Jonathan Bernard has noted that Ligeti's approach to notation was rather traditional, 'essentially a direct and accurate representation of a specifically envisioned sonic realization'.[8] The only notable exception to Ligeti's use of conventional notation is in the graphic notation employed in his 1961–62 composition for solo organ titled *Volumina*. But the notation of some of Ligeti's earlier compositions can be seen to have influenced the notation of *Lontano*. For example, in his compositions *Apparitions* from almost a decade earlier, on page five for each of the eight brass and cellos, Ligeti notated the precise volume changes of each, before amending in red pencil the volume of notes starting in bar 47 to *ppp*. The notation for *Lontano*, for a full orchestra but without percussion, starts with an individual flute, playing a single note that increases in volume from *pppp* to *p*, before decreasing and dying away seven beats later. A second flute enters slightly less than two and a half beats (five-twelfths, in fact) after the initial tone is first sounded, playing the same pitch, to the same peak

4.1 György Ligeti. Extract from *Apparitions* with Br. denoting brass instruments and Vc cellos. Composer's handwritten annotations on the published score of *Apparitions*. Undated. ©György Ligeti Collection, Paul Sacher Foundation, Basel.

of volume before dying away on the second beat of the third bar. Other flutes enter, before clarinets, winds, and then strings, until in bar 68 (Section O) 57 different instruments are simultaneously sounding notes of differing durations, and volumes. The piece ends on bar 165 with two clarinets and one bass clarinet, the notes fading away with their length dependent upon the clarinetists' breath capacity, but

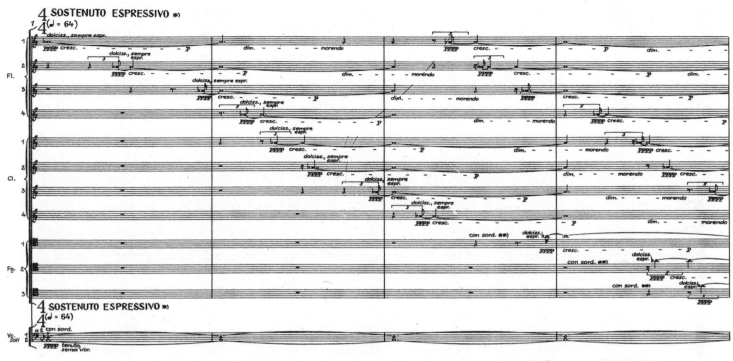

4.2 György Ligeti. Extract from the notation of
Lontano. 1967. Schott, Mainz.

stopping simultaneously. The score of *Lontano* utilises the conventional symbols of music in the notation of pitch, duration, volume and timbre: time order is read left to right, there is one symbol for each sound, there is one level on the stave for each pitch, and time relationships of notes are shown through note heads, stems and flags. The musical term *sostenuto espressivo* (sustained expressive) is written at the beginning of the score, together with the conventional time markings of 4/4. The beginnings of the notes are marked *Dolciss. sempre esp* (for *dolcissimo* – as sweet as possible, and *sempre espressivo* – always expressive), while the endings are marked *morendo*, dying away. There are small variations in the treatment of different instruments as the music progresses. In bar five, for example, the pitches of the four clarinets no longer die away, but, rather, end with the marking *ppp*, pianissimo, which is slightly louder than their beginnings, which are notated *pppp*. There are not only singular increases followed by decreases in volume for particular notes, but the volume also fluctuates within the sounding of some notes. The

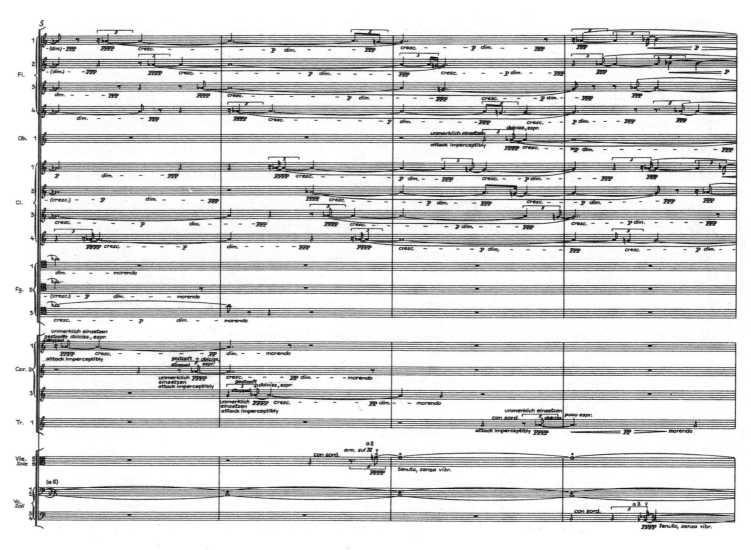

4.3 György Ligeti. Extract from the notation of
Lontano. 1967. Schott, Mainz.

second clarinet, for example, in bar 6 starts with an
A flat *pppp*. This note then increases in volume to *p*
before decreasing to *ppp*, then increasing to *p* before
becoming quieter and ending *ppp*. The tone also
changes to a G at *ppp* so each tonal particle of the
phrase, both the A flat and the G, are, in fact, dealt
with similarly. The volume of both rises and falls

away again, but this time these two adjacent notes
are joined together, rather than being separated by a
period of silence. This continuity of sound brings
this sonic landscape closer to the listener as it is now
unbroken, the previously distant space of silence
now replaced by a perceptibly closer one of sound.
Griffiths notes that the instrumentation also affects

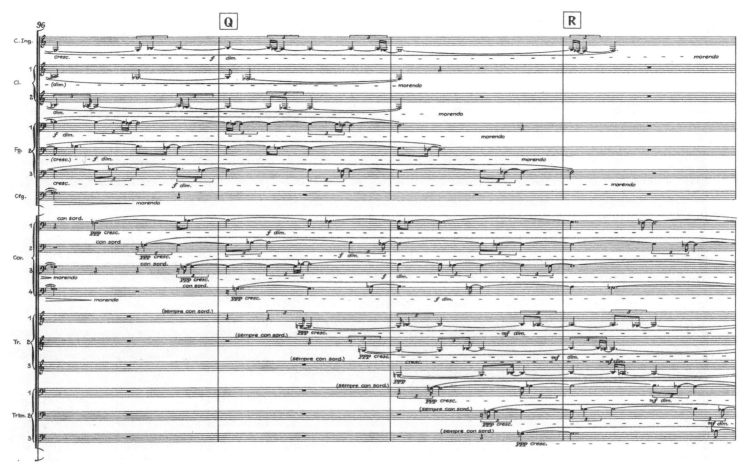

4.4 György Ligeti. Extract from the notation of *Lontano*. 1967. Schott, Mainz.

the auditory experience, that 'a chime of octaves, for instance, sounds closer than a more complex chord, [. . .] the register (high and low notes tend to sound far away) and the orchestration (the brass, for instance, have more presence than the strings).[9] What is most distinctive about the notation is the precision with which the durations of each note and their volumes are notated, as well as the durations of silences that separate these almost inaudible beginnings and endings. Ligeti explained that he felt it necessary to move away from bar lines with their rigid delineation of duration into equal units, and that he used them 'only for practical purposes, so that the works can be conducted. The bars are not bars in the traditional sense, but merely a means of synchronizing the parts.'[10] This idea that bar lines were for practical realisation of the music, lines to coordinate the performance in time rather than as a temporal grid for the conception of time, meant that for Ligeti, his 'music is a continuous flow, unbroken by bars, like a Gregorian melody',[11] and so creating music that has 'something artificial about it: it is an illusion'.[12] The

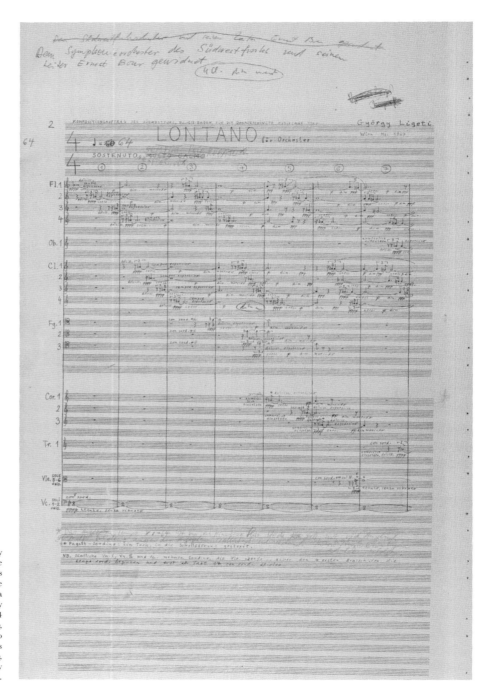

4.5 György Ligeti. Blueprint of the fine copy of *Lontano* with handwritten notes by the composer. In blue pen at the top of the score is the dedication 'This piece is in honour of the Southwest German Radio Symphony Orchestra and their conductor Ernest Bour'. On this copy Ligeti had changed the tempo from 60 to 64 beats per minute, and underneath from *sostenuto, molto calmo* (sustained, very calm) first, then to *sostenuto, sempre poco rubato* (sustained, always with a little freedom of time), then to *sostenuto, expressivo* (sustained, expressively). 1967. ©György Ligeti Collection, Paul Sacher Foundation, Basel.

detailed composition of the relationship between the 687 sound endings and beginnings, was both complex and time consuming. Ligeti, however, saw that *Lontano* could only be created by the attention created through the detailed notation that he used:

> If I were to notate that in an undifferentiated way, the result would not be the same. As an example I should like to make this comparison: only a very small part of an iceberg is visible, the largest part being hidden under the water. But what the iceberg looks like, how it moves, how it is affected by various currents in the ocean, all these things are determined not only by the visible, but also by the invisible part. That is why I call my method of composing and notating uneconomical.[13]

DIMENSIONS OF TIME AND SPACE

Lontano was first performed by the South West German Radio Symphony Orchestra on 22 October 1967,[14] and Steinitz has described the sound of *Lontano* as:

> a study in opalescence, in slowly evolving timbral and harmonic transformation heard through polychromatic mists of sound. Within these vapourous textures, timbres and harmonies ebb and flow. Sometimes the sonic mists almost clear, to reveal for a moment tangible chordal shapes, before slowly enveloping them again as other shapes coalesce in sharper focus before they too recede [. . .] the sense of floating and voyaging is absolute.[15]

Lontano starts with a concert A-flat on the flute, a note immediately adjacent to the usual tuning note of the orchestra, conventionally a concert A. So, the very first sound of *Lontano* immediately starts slightly distant, slightly far away from conventional tonality.

The tempo is marked at 64 beats per minute, close to the human heart rate at rest. There is no sense of absolute duration and the length of the piece varies from performance to performance. In the case of the Berliner Philharmoniker with Jonathan Nott from December 2001, the performance lasted 11'37", while in the 1988 recording by the Wiener Philharmoniker with Claudio Abbado conducting, the performance lasted 12'47". Ligeti's own written instructions on the score state, 'the piece must be played with great expression; apart from the indicated rallentandos and accelerandos, other fluctuations in tempo are permissible'.[16] There is no discernible melody to this music, rather appearing and receding changing combinations of instruments, which with their individual and collective timbres and variations in volume, form the heart of the composition. Each instrument is like an individual water droplet of a cloud of sound, and like a cloud, each of these particles is not individually discernible. It is only in temporal overview that the overall form becomes more distinct. American music critic James Keller, reviewing *Lontano* for the San Francisco Symphony, describes the music this way:

> the emphasis on timbre, texture, and harmony-not-born-of-melodies yields a cloud-like effect, with the sounds moving slowly through a succession of musical shapes that are constantly coming and going, never arriving at a firm destination or even a point of real repose.[17]

The experience of *Lontano* as a listener is therefore understood cumulatively. The time of this composition is not the linear time of Baroque, Classical or Romantic music. *Lontano* does not possess the kind of kineticism of conventional tonal music that unfolds and develops towards the final destination of the tonic, the first tone of a scale. Critically, time organises the musical elements of this music, rather than pitch. Ligeti describes this by saying 'my idea was that instead of tension-resolution, dissonance-consonance, dominant-tonic, pairs of opposition in traditional tonal music. I would contrast "mistiness" with passages of "clearing up".'[18] He described the relationship between the notation and the sounds created by it, as 'polyphony is written, but harmony is heard'.[19]

As Ligeti noted, in regard to the time of his music:

> It is music that gives the impression that it could stream on continuously, as if it had no beginning and no end; what we hear is actually a section of something that has eternally begun and that will continue to sound forever. It is typical of all these pieces that there are hardly any caesuras and the music really does flow on. The formal characteristic of this music is that it seems static. The music appears to stand still, but that is merely an illusion: within this standing still, this static quality, there are gradual changes: I would think here of a surface of water in which an image is reflected; then this surface of water if gradually disturbed, and the image disappears, but very, very gradually. Subsequently the water calms down and we see a different image.[20]

So, how is time actually experienced in music? And does *Lontano* differ? Two commonly used notions of time are 'tactus' and 'rhythm', the former starting in the fifteenth century, the unit of measure of time indicated by the movements of the conductor's hand or baton. Rhythm, from the Greek for *flow*, is the variation of length and accents of a series of sounds or events, and is categorised as simple, complex, regular, irregular, rational (rhythmic elements divisible by 2) and irrational (rhythmic elements divisible by odd numbers from 3 and above). In music, there is a notion of time in which the perception of duration is, in fact, determined not by rhythm but rather by so-called Interonset Intervals, the time between the beginnings of successive notes (or events) rather than their duration. I suggest that what is happening in *Lontano* is a sense of time for the listeners derived from Interonset Intervals that replaces the regularity of a pulse created by the tempo of the music. But how can this sense of time in *Lontano*, where we feel floating in an extended present, best be categorised?

Psychologist Richard Block identifies four different kinds of contexts that may affect perceived durations in music:

1. characteristics of the observer (personality, interests, prior experience, etc.)
2. contents of the duration perceived (filled or empty, and if filled, with what kind of stimuli)
3. activities while experiencing the duration (active participation to varying degrees, passive attending, passive nonattending)
4. types of durational information demanded by the situation (estimates of absolute duration, simultaneity, successiveness, order, etc).[21]

Of these, the type of duration in number four above seems most pertinent. After all, is time in music nothing more than the sounding of Newtonian or absolute time (the time that is shared by most people in a given society and by physical processes)?[22] In order to position musical time in relationship to absolute time, Kramer distinguishes two fundamental types of time in music: linear and non-linear, defining them thus:

> linearity as the determination of some characteristics of music in accordance with implications that arise from earlier events of the piece [. . .] non-linearity is the determination of some characteristics of music in accordance with implications that arise from principles or tendencies governing an entire piece or section.[23]

These two types of musical time are not mutually exclusive and can interact and intersect in varied ways. In *Lontano*, the music lacks identifiable phases, a recognisable pulse, and a sense of momentum towards a static tonic that the long history of music has relied upon. Kramer calls this type of time in music, where phrase endings – which indicate temporal linearity – might break the temporal continuum, as 'vertical' time. Rather than phrasal structure, the:

> result is a single present stretched out into an enormous duration, a potentially infinite 'now' that nonetheless feels like an instant. In music without phrases, without temporal articulation, with tonal consistency, whatever structure is in the music exists between layers of sound, not between successive gestures.[24]

This sense of temporal continuum in which musical events take place means that rather than beginnings and endings, the music simply starts, and sometime later, ceases. Surely *Lontano* exhibits vertical time with its over 500 *pianississimo* starts and *morendo-niente* cessations, and which correlates with an experience of time in landscape space where people enter and leave at different times along a route, choosing where, and more importantly when, to leave. In our experience of landscape space, we are often in a temporal cloud of unfolding changes, not just the literal movement of clouds, but changes to views or sounds of passing wildlife, which commence without a distinct beginning, and may pause or stop without notice. The music of *Lontano* and the rich materiality of landscape space and experience embedded in an unfolding temporal field seem so strongly resonant.

THE VIEW FROM THE ROAD

To examine *Lontano*'s notation and Ligeti's notion of time in landscape architecture, we move to an existing landscape notation developed by American urbanists Appleyard, Lynch, and Myer in their publication *The View from the Road*[25] from 1965. Like Ligeti's notation in his exploration of an unfolding spatio-temporal field, *The View from the Road* also explored ways in which sequential changes could be drawn. Like Ligeti, they also used an existing symbolic language in order to develop a new notation to study and conceive this with, borrowing elements including a vertical timeline from *Labanotation* for dance or the music notation *Klavarskribo*.[26] Their book was developed in response to the post-war sprawling development of American cities. The growing role of the automobile in the experience of landscape space led the authors to question the way that road design might be indicative of 'the problem of designing visual sequences for the observer in motion'.[27] Their desire was to turn the engineering of roads into art, as 'the view from the road can be a dramatic play of space and motion, of light and texture, all on a new scale'.[28] They acknowledged that the modern car 'interposes a filter between the driver and the world he is moving through. Sounds, smells, sensations of touch and weather are all diluted in comparison with what the pedestrian experiences. Vision is framed and limited.'[29] They developed diagrammatic notations for vehicle passengers' sense of motion and space through focusing on three primary components: the apparent self-motion; the apparent motion of the visual field, and the spatial characteristics including the position of the observer. Appleyard *et al.* make the point that there is a direct connection between a visual landscape and a spatial one, stating that, 'the visual field is interpreted not only as series of remote views, or a collection of objects in motion, but also as a space, a void within which the observer can move, visually or physically'.[30] They also acknowledged that the temporal sequence of this landscape experience was not unidirectional, as vehicles could move in both directions, and could not be precisely prescribed, as individuals enter and leave at widely varying locations and distances. In similar ways to Ligeti's development of *Lontano*, a notation was needed in which this fluid time-space could be drawn. They saw that there was not a single sequence and simple forward momentum but that over extended periods of time 'these identifiable objects, motions, spaces, oriented structures, and meanings are organised at an even higher level as complex sequences'.[31] The authors saw limitations in conventional representational techniques of maps, oblique and ground photographs, and perspective sketches in the field. They noted that the disadvantages were, 'they fail to select essential elements from the mass of things potentially perceivable; they require the user to construct the third dimension; and that they present the material as a static, over-all pattern rather than as a dynamic sequence'.[32] To overcome these, they proposed a binary notation that could be applied both to the analysis of an existing highway, and also to speculate on proposals including in their study of Boston's Central Artery.[33] The notation provided a means of drawing both space-motion and orientation, with time running vertically up the page. The notation used time as the vertical scale, which together with a plan drawing, delineated a physical space travelled. Their notation relied on new symbols for each of the three fields, apparent self-motion, apparent motion of the visual field, and the notation of orientation. These symbols were relatively conventional in that they adopted, like music, a premise of one symbol one meaning. But rather than the abstract notation of musical pitch, for example, they relied on direct pictorialism: for example, apparent rotation was notated as a curving arrow, growth as expanding arrows, visual nodes as stars, proportion and scale directly denoted through the changing proportions of a rectangular box. In total, 38 symbols were used, three for apparent self-motion, six for apparent motion of the visual field, 19 for spatial characteristics, and 10 for orientation. Their own evaluation noted that:

> it has at least three parallel deficiencies. Firstly it must be read as three parallel columns. [. . .] Second, the space sections do not read as easily in sequence as do the other elements, [. . .] Third, fluctuating characteristics, such as activity and light, are not adequately handled.[34]

The authors also noted that the spatial qualities that the drivers and passengers experienced were strongly influenced by the speed of movement, that, 'where

Sequence Diagrams

Some of the visual components of this experi-
65 ence are graphically presented in Figures 65
66 and 66, drawn to a time scale, in which the
course of the road has been diagrammatically
simplified to a straight line. The time mark-
64 ings on the conventional map, Figure 64,
allow the reader to relate it to these special
65 drawings. Figure 65 is a diagram of the
passenger's sense of motion and space, while
66 Figure 66 illustrates his orientation — his
image of the total landscape. Both of these
diagrams follow the conventions developed in
the previous chapter.

4.6 Donald Appleyard, Kevin Lynch, and John
R. Myer, The View from the Road, Space-
motion diagram for Northwestern Expressway.
1965. ©Massachusetts Institute of Technology,
by permission of The MIT Press.

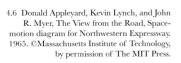

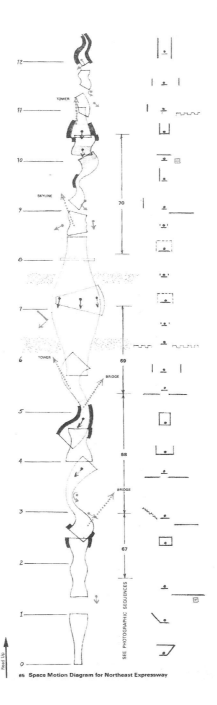

65 **Space Motion Diagram for Northeast Expressway**

Read Up

this tempo was rapid, attention was concentrated on near objects straight ahead in the road; where the tempo was slow, observers were scanning from right to left, giving more attention to far objects'.[35] In *Lontano*, the spatial effects were created by the ability to coordinate the musical materials of timbre, pitch and volume in highly complex temporal ways. Relative to Ligeti, Appleyard *et al.*'s notation, in emphasising spatial characteristics, failed to rather coordinate these with a temporal precision. Progress might have been made in the notation of the visual components of a journey against time, but time itself was no further advanced.

A CINEMATIC LANDSCAPE

Appleyard *et al.*'s exploration of the possibilities of scoring the experience of the landscape of highways accepts that the scanning of the human eye in motion can be replicated by film. They make the point that the pan, dissolve and close-up shots of film 'symbolise the scanning, selective action of the eye'.[36] There is, of course, an inherent difference between the lens of a human eye and a camera lens, which they categorise this way:

> the eye has a very small angle of acute vision, coupled with a very broad angle of hazy vision. It perceives the details of objects by searching the visual field in a quick irregular motion, while sensing the spatial relationships of the whole field by means of blurred, peripheral sight. The camera, on the other hand, is a staring eye of uniformly acute vision over an angle of moderate size. In one way, it records too much, if we want to simulate the workings of a human eye: in another way, it records too little by reducing peripheral vision. Furthermore, its center of attention does not leap from object to object as does the eye.[37]

In order to test how Ligeti's and Appleyard's *et al.*'s notation might allow us to better draw aspects of landscape temporality, I studied an 18-second section of film. The selected scenes, from 1:28':20" to 1:20':38", with their focus on motion and space rather than relationship to a particular narrative strand, are drawn from Shindo's 1964 film *Onibaba* (*Devil Woman*). This story is set in the Japanese Warring States period, which lasted just over 100 years from its start in 1467 with the Onin War in Kyoto. This 11-year battle in the then imperial capital of Japan is presumed to be the setting for the film as the protagonists make numerous references to this city in the film. Completed 13 years after Shindo's first film in 1951, which had been titled *The Story of a Beloved Wife*, *Onibaba* focuses on the relationships – sexual, emotional and economic – between the three main protagonists. A returning samurai, a young wife whose husband has disappeared, and her mother-in-law, are all struggling to survive in an expansive sea of tall swaying grass. Shindo, whose own family had gone from rich landlords through bankruptcy to farmers,[38] directed films that explored the nature of family relationships and the circumstances of those at the bottom of the social pile. In *Onibaba* the grass has a rich symbolic connotation, symbolising the protagonists' situation, as the director noted the 'lives of down-to-earth people who have to live like weeds'.[39] Shindo says of the two female characters that they are social outcasts, 'they are people totally abandoned, outside society's political protection. Amongst the outcasts I wanted to capture their immense energy for survival [. . .] an expression of the uncontrollable events which these people meet in their actual lives.'[40] Shindo says of the film's structure that 'I see film as an art of "montage" which consists of a dialectic or interaction between the movement and nonmovement of the image'.[41]

The film was shot on location in Inba Swamp (*Inba Numa*) in Chiba Prefecture, located between the current international airport at Narita, and Tokyo city proper. The open water of the swamp's lake has a surface area over 11 square kilometres, and in 1964, the year of the filming, there was a rich aquatic plant habitat with 49 species present.[42] This selection of a cinematic landscape rather than a physical one grew from two concerns. Firstly, in investigating landscape temporality the choice of one where time is embedded in the representation, where the landscape, a cinematic one, literally unfolds over time, was logical. Secondly, the 18-second section selected does not use landscape as scenery in the conventional way as a simple setting to narrative, rather, it is an encompassing field. This extract from the film creates a visual and aural experience embedded in the monotony of the grass, while the absence of a static scene encourages us to vividly experience the non-visual qualities of the landscape, the sounds of the rain and the swaying grass. It is a landscape where time and materiality dominate spatial qualities and so provides a rich field for these studies. The Israeli film critic Zvika Serper in a detailed analysis of Shindo's film notes that:

> In *Onibaba* he employs two contrasting natural objects to convey the main theme of the film, recreating the contrasting natural elements in the *noh* space [. . .] this combination reflects symbolically the *noh* ideals of longevity, sanctity and harmony. In *Onibaba* the main theme of turning the Middle-aged Woman into a demon and then vanquishing her is correlated with nature and its various components, which have

a symbolic function in addition to serving as the setting for the narrative. Shindo makes meaningful use of two contrasting natural objects: the deep pit and the dry tree trunk.[43]

The 18-second extract focuses on four temporal materials of this landscape space, the grass, rain, light, and sounds, and simulates in its five scenes through the shot selections the scanning of an observer moving through the space. It has been noted that 'films of standard length average six hundred shots'.[44] In *Onibaba* between the opening and closing credits there are fewer than 350. In the first shot we are embedded within the grass, which is being swept violently by the stormy winds and bursts of lightening. In the second shot the young widow first runs towards the camera, which then tracks alongside her when she changes direction. This is followed by a brief interlude of grass and rain, then the same person now running towards us. It is only in the final shot that we see the landscape through the eyes of the young protagonist, locating us within her experiential space. We are propelled forward towards the mother-in-law, now wearing a devil mask. Each of these five segments of film are shot from different camera angles, articulated by the changing direction of moonlight. The sense of isolation in this eighteen-second sequence is heightened by the absence of music. Instead, we hear only the sounds of the rain and wind on grass, and a single thunderclap. In simplifying the materiality of the landscape space to a single expanse, a monoculture of grass, it focuses our attention on the temporal phenomena of light, wind, and rain. The Irish film critic Ciaran Crilly has noted that while film is an audio as well as a visual medium, 'the hierarchial norm of sound in film is voice, sound effect and music, usually in that order'.[45]

In *Onibaba*, the use of extended shots without human presence foregrounds sound as a vital component in this landscape experience.

The nature of this cinematic landscape space, an endless monoculture of Susuki grass (*Miscanthus sinensis*), seems to resonate with the timelessness of *Lontano*. Lynch makes the point that 'where surrounding objects are [...] featureless, [...] then the sensation is one of floating, of no forward movement'.[46] *Onibaba* is also reminiscent of *Lontano* in that we are located in both an expanse of amorphous time: in *Onibaba* symbolised by the sea of swaying grass; in *Lontano* by the sea of appearing and disappearing sounds. In both we are in the visceral immediacy of each moment of experienced time. The sense of fear in this section of the film is heightened by the fact that we are already aware of the hidden pit within the grass,[47] and that the two female characters who use their knowledge of it in daytime to dispose of the warriors' bodies, might themselves fall victim to it in darkness.

The film is reminiscent of the ink paintings of Japanese painter Tohaku Hasegawa (1539–1619), whose own life cut across the Warring States period, and particularly his folding screens titled *Pine Trees in Moonlight*.[48] The ghostly images lose us in their abstract scale, the treetops identify their form and type, but denied by the mist their full representation, as viewers we are drawn in to complete the scene ourselves. Consisting of a pair of screens of six panels, and three and a half metres in overall length, the scale of the painting takes time to comprehend. Each detail we are drawn to focus on we somehow see through the periphery of the broader expanse of earlier views. Our attention is held simultaneously at the detail and overview. Rather than just a detached

4.7 Kaneto Shindo. The five sequences extracted from *Onibaba* for detailed study. 1964.

viewing, we feel suspended within the scale of the painting. Both *Onibaba* and *Pine Trees* prevent us from clarifying the spatial depth. In doing so, both create first a focus on the monotonous materiality, and from this we are then more strongly drawn to

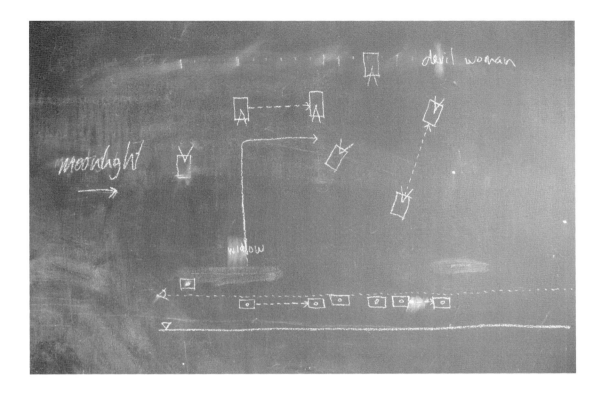

4.8 David Buck. Plan above showing the relative movement of the young widow and the respective camera angles, and section below showing the relative camera heights and actor locations. 2012.

notice the richly varied time implied by the image. Hasegawa's painting is devoid of human presence, yet we picture ourselves in the scene. *Onibaba* does depict the figures within the fiction but they seem incidental in the vastness of the landscape, which itself can be considered as the dominant 'character' of the film. By running the camera either parallel to the plane of the film's surface or perpendicular to it, Shindo echoes the experience of viewing Hasegawa's screen. The inherent flatness of the film in this way is strongly reminiscent of traditional Japanese landscape representation. We can move closer towards it or traverse along it, but we cannot enter into the spatial depth in an appreciably three-dimensional way.

LINES BURNT IN LIGHT

While Chapter 3 *Horizons* my research practice was contained within a single, static notation, in this and subsequent chapters I wanted my landscape architecture notation to bear witness to the activities that created it, and for the traces of past actions to be visible in the surface. This grew logically out of the study of the notation of longer temporal events: *Projection 1* in performance is just over two minutes, while *Lontano* is typically between 11 and 13 minutes long. The additional information contained within the correspondingly larger musical notation under investigation created the necessity to develop a notational method capable of including much more information. This was also a response to my desire to synthesise aspects of music and landscape architectural notations in the creation of the new. This new mode of working also means that like a landscape space itself, these landscape architectural notations can reveal not just lines of current activity, but past paths, and places visited. Simultaneously containing both drawing and erasure, they are like a landscape architectural space; they contain both construction and demolition. For this reason, and as a development from the previous one, the landscape architectural notation developed in *Clouds* and the following *Meadows* are constructed into films. Additionally, these notations benefit from being films by addressing the deficit of recording a moving process only through still images, which inevitably leads to a sense of time expelled. Corner noted in his own extensive studies of the American landscape that, 'the static nature of the photograph is unable to convey the temporal experience of passage, the emerging and withdrawing of phenomena, and the strange ways events unfold'.[49] Girot has said of his belief in the possibilities of digital video as an alternative mode of landscape representation that 'the actual blending of different times in space produces a new dimension',[50] and that 'it is now possible to imagine a new form of thinking that can integrate the travelling continuum of space and time, rather than present a series of immutable frames in our understanding of landscape'.[51]

This notation, *Lines Burnt In Light*, 2012, (see www.db-land.com/films/LinesBurntInLight to watch the full film), was developed on a large surface, one wall of my London apartment. Covered in three coats of blackboard paint, this surface provided the place to investigate, to test, and to develop a new landscape architectural notation, which was created from Crayola white chalk and a Holbein Bottle Green artists' coloured pencil, the chalk leaving behind remnants of the marks even when erased. The notations consist of lines, erasures, and alphanumeric marks, which were recorded photographically in 149 events that spanned a period of three months. The photos were taken with a camera mounted onto a marble shelf on the opposite wall. These digital images recorded not just each mark made, but also their partial erasure to allow further development of the subsequent phases of the notation to take place. These notations embody their own history on a single surface, the present containing and informed by traces of the past.

The notation starts with the feint impression of *4'33"* in partially erased chalk dust in homage to Cage's composition of the same name and his assertion that time, not tonality, was the central material of music. To this was added the music's early notation history, *in campo aperto* (in an open field) written in white ink (see notation N3).

Two benchmarks are added on the left hand side and lower left corner to locate this 'open field' in space. Layers of marks appear against the soundtrack of *Lontano*, some inscribing words, some temporalities, and from Appleyard *et al.*, some notions of a visual field in motion. Each new mark is located within this exploratory notational field and remains there for a period of time before being erased. The erasure is never entirely complete so that the vestiges of its contribution to the developing notation continue to remain for some time. They, therefore, inform not just the notation but are reminders of the thought processes that then develop into the subsequent drawings. They are lines burnt not just into the notation, but into the imagination as well.

The 18 seconds of cinematic landscape extracted from Shinto's film are not as in Lynch's notation shown 'in their sequential and concurrent relation to each other',[52] but rather are overlain, organised through their temporal relationships rather than their spatial ones (see notation N4).

Time builds as layers of the drawing rather than as a progression along a timeline. Spatial characteristics including edge definition are, however, added to the apparent motion of the visual field. The duration of each mark is an intuitive response to their seeming importance as the notations develop. The word *Lontano*, for example, first appears in the film at 1'43" and is not erased until after 3'39" (see notations N5, N6, N7 and N8), while the note of an 'incomplete sense of time' only exists from 2'01" to 2'12". Their individual durations echo that of a particular note in *Lontano*. Each beginning and ending is more dramatic and perhaps more important than their specific duration. Together, they build, both through their arrival and their subsequent departure, a cloud of thoughts, reflections, innovations and possibilities, through which the new landscape architectural notation appears. Only the inscription *in campo aperto* remains for the whole film as a lasting reminder that the

in campo aperto

4'33"

N3 *Lines Burnt In Light*. The beginning of the notation with *In Campo Aperto* and *4'33"* marked onto the surface. 2012.

development of temporal landscape architectural notation is, indeed, still at its commencement.

Additionally, and unexpectedly, the surface of this notational field was softly illuminated by another line of light. The changing light conditions outside through an adjacent window brought the temporality of the natural world to its surface. Suddenly at 3'49" bright sunlight shone onto the surface of the

notation. I find it fascinating to note that Ligeti had imagined the music of *Lontano* creating a similar effect, stating:

> At the moment when the high D sharp is there, forming the concentrated 'pencil' of this musical beam, suddenly there yawns an abyss, a huge distancing, a hole piercing through the music. It is a moment that has an irresistible association

N4 *Lines Burnt In Light*. Transcription of spatial experience in landscape. 2012.

for me with the wonderful painting by Altdorfer, *The Battle of Alexander* in the Alte Pinakothek in Munich, in which the clouds – these blue clouds – part and behind them is a beam of golden sunlight shining.[53]

The inscriptions, in chalk and pencil or charcoal, were filmed to form a notation. This investigative process combining drawing and erasure causes constant choices about which material is retained, and which discarded, a constant oscillation between drawing and reflecting on it. Every moment of notation, whether addition or removal, is followed by a corresponding moment of reflection, internalisation, and calm. Like landscape, the temporality of this notation is also a kind of extended present in which both the past and future co-exist. Within this new audio-visual

N5 *Lines Burnt In Light*. The first appearance of 'Lontano'. 2012.

material we are simultaneously distanced by the filter of this notation, but also immersed, complicit in its experience.

THE TIME OF LANDSCAPE

In examining the notation of a musical work and its specific approach to time Ligeti's *Lontano* reveals that the precise notation of quantities of time can lead to the creation of temporal qualities experienced in its performance. These qualities are similar to aspects of landscape temporality and experience and new notational tools for landscape can be derived from similar strategies to those contained within *Lontano*. Like in *Lontano*, these can be notated through a precise rendering of each components' relative end and beginning. Additionally, beyond this similarity

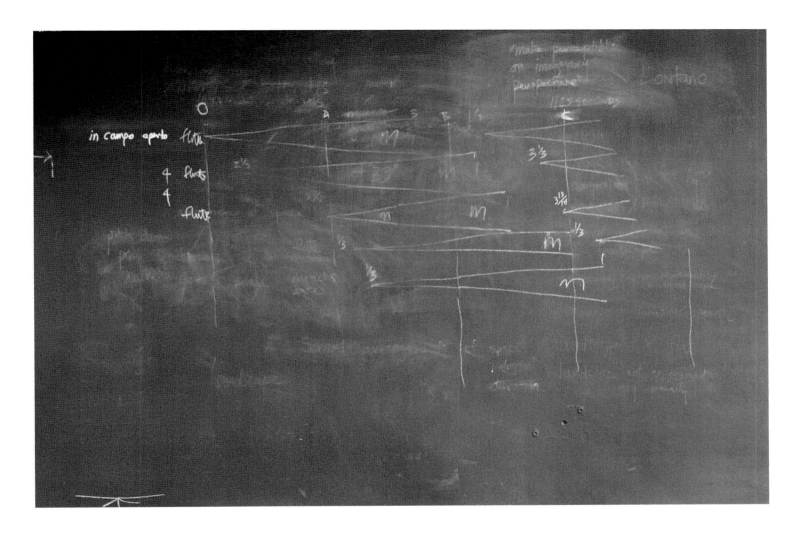

N6 *Lines Burnt In Light*. The final appearance of 'Lontano'. 2012.

between an expansive scale of time in landscape and the vertical time in music compositions as illustrated by *Lontano*, there are there other potential connections with landscape architecture. Kramer describes listening to a vertical musical composition as like looking at a piece of sculpture; we view from angles we select and from distances of our choosing. As he says, 'for each of us the temporal sequence of viewing postures has been unique. The time spent with the sculpture is structured time, but the structure is placed there by us.'[54] In other words, we make our own individual and subjective temporality, to which there can be a spatial connection. Kramer also takes up this notion of the spatiality of time again. He makes the distinction between temporalities in cases where there is not straightforward goal oriented

N7 *Lines Burnt In Light*. Initial transcription
of *Onibaba*. 2012.

linear time: multiply-directed time, moment time, and non-directed linear time. These are:

1 if the implication in every section is continually frustrated by the subsequent section but is often realised elsewhere then the musical time is multiply-directed. The multiplicity resides in the conflict between implied linearity on the foreground and realised nonlinearity on the middle-ground.

2 if despite continuity within sections there is nothing in a subsequent section that follows from a potential implication in an earlier section then the temporal mode is moment time; there is nonlinearity in the middle-ground

3 if the implied progression from one section to another is continually realised but the deeper-level implications arising from the middle-ground progressions fail to be fulfilled, then there is nonlinearity on the background level while the middle-ground linearity is non-directed.

in campo aperto

N8 *Lines Burnt In Light.* Later transcription of the landscape of *Onibaba.* 2012.

Thus three temporalities mediate between the extremes of goal-oriented linear time and vertical time.[55]

So, within the context of a vertical time as notated in *Lontano*, other temporalities may also occur between these degrees of temporal foreground, middle ground, and background. Corner, writing about landscape and temporality, states that 'there is a duration of experience [. . .] it cannot be frozen as a single moment of time'.[56] He suggests that duration in landscape space refers to linear time as we move directionally through it, but our spatial experience refers to vertical time as it also includes notions of the past and future. The notation of *Lontano* seems to describe a landscape that is spatially vast and temporally complex, where 'every present moment can make a vertical cut, as it were, across horizontal time perception'.[57] *Lontano* has additional correlations

4.10 David Buck. *Lines Burnt in Light*. Sunlight cast into the notational field from an adjacent window. 2012.

4.11 Albrecht Altdorfer. *The Battle of Alexander at Issus*. 1529. ©bpk | Bayerische Staatsgemäldesammlungen.

with time as experienced in landscape space. We are normally not conscious of precise beginnings or endings, rather we are aware of events starting and then sometime later ending. Within the rich temporality of landscape spaces we notice aspects of it, some triggered by vision, others by sound. I believe that vertical music also provides a textural density or depth that gives a spatial quality to the music. As American musicologist Robert Morgan observes of Ives's music, but which to me seems equally relevant to Ligeti's *Lontano*, 'the passages are so complex in regard to their internal relationships that the ear perceives them as totality [. . .] they must be heard simultaneously – spatially'.[58] Certainly, it seems that Ligeti was conscious of the spatial qualities of his work. In conversation with English musicologist Adrian Jack, in 1974, he describes his work as 'to

make from time a kind of sculpture. Sculpture which is empty.'[59] Perhaps the emptiness he refers to is one of harmonic momentum, the absence of a progressive movement towards a tonic resolution. We are invited to focus, then, on the temporal aspects of this plastic work, rather than the material ones. Space in *Lontano* is temporal as much as, or more than, material.

The spatial references are also clear from the word *Lontano* itself, which Griffiths notes 'owes its title to the musical marking "da lontano" (from the distance)'.[60] The distance referred to is not just confined to a sense of spatial depths and changing qualities in a performance of the music. Russian musicologist Marina Lobanova sees an imaginary historical depth in *Lontano*, too. She notes that the word *Lontano* had also occurred 'in Schumann (*Davidsbundlertanze: "Da Lontano"*), at the beginning of the fifth movement of Berlioz' *Symphonie fantastique* ("*du lointain*"), in the third movement of Mahler's *Third Symphony* [. . .] and at the end of the Debussy *Prelude*'.[61] This is acknowledged by Ligeti who in a series of conversations with musicologists discussing the essence of *Lontano*'s 'distance', stated that 'behind the music there is other music, and behind that still more.'[62] Ligeti was particularly interested in the spatiality implied by Romantic music. In reference to Mahler's *Fifth Symphony* and the end of the first movement, he noted how spatial qualities could be created by the changing sonic qualities of different orchestral instruments, and that:

> there is a trumpet-call, then suddenly silence, then the same trumpet-call can be heard, but transposed to a flute. Well, in terms of actual space, the flautist is sitting just as near or as far from the audience as the trumpeter. And yet, the sound of the flute, with the same musical outline as the trumpet had, seems to us in a purely imaginary fashion to be a trumpet-call from very far away.[63]

Lontano's expansive, floating, sense of time strongly contributes to creating a comparable sense of space: the slow morphing of time allows us to also experience a slow unfolding spatiality. The composition, appearing to grow out of a mist, develops a spatial quality, where 'temporal relations become spatial relations; interest arises from the way phenomena melt into each other'.[64] Ligeti referred in the latter third of *Lontano* to the imaginary space created through the notation, and that a 'very soft plane of sound, formed by a major second and a minor third, a gradually passing into dim, deep regions. [. . .] Now, this dark progress is suddenly lightened, as if the music had been illuminated from behind.'[65] The music of *Lontano* seems so evocative of aspects of landscape temporality: a slowly evolving cloud of changing conditions that create spatial qualities for the listener. We are conscious of time, of its changing nature, and of its endless variety, without ever experiencing it as regular, metronomic, or directional. Ligeti described musical form being replaced instead by:

> a kind of musical aura. It is music that gives the impression that it could stream on continuously, as if it had no beginning and no end; what we hear is actually a section of something that has eternally begun and will continue to sound forever.[66]

This quality is precisely that created by the notation of *Lines Burnt in Light*.

A PROXIMITY TO NOTATION

It is pertinent to question the degree to which *Lines Burnt in Light* shares common traits with music notation. The American musicologist V. A. Howard refers to Goodman's five criteria for notationality as 'the conjunction of five properties of a system: syntactic disjointedness and articulateness, unambiguity, and semantic disjointedness and articulateness. Any system lacking even one of these features thus far fails of notationality', in which case 'many modern scoring methods fall short of strict notationality (usually through violation of syntactic or semantic articulateness) and not even standard music notation is entirely "notational" inasmuch as it incorporates ambiguous symbols'.[67]

These ambiguous symbols in music include expression marks such as the *glissando* wavy line denoting an unbroken glide from one note to the next, or *sfz* (for *sforzando*), meaning an abrupt accent. Goodman himself accepted that 'the verbal language of tempos is not notational',[68] nor are, of course, dynamic markings, and their relative scale of *ppp* to *fff*, which is used for the volume of single instruments and also for whole orchestras. *Lines Burnt in Light* certainly fails Goodman's test due to the ambiguity of the symbols used in the three areas of the notation of time, the spatial quality of the cinematic landscape under examination, and the protagonists' movement through it. Goodman's requirement, of unique determination that forbids the ambiguity of inscriptions, has at its core his notion that 'one can identify the same work in each and every score-copy and performance indefinitely often'.[69] In music this is to ensure that the identity of the work is preserved in both copies of the original notation to establish authorship, and also to establish fidelity in all subsequent performances. It is interesting that Goodman's own strict criteria for a notational language, and one that he asserts music complies with, are based upon the notion of 'auxiliary directions'. Goodman needs this additional category in order to circumvent the fact that many symbols from music notation are often, indeed, vague and would fail his own test for notationality. In order to circumvent this, he defines tempo, timbre or phrasing, for example, as auxiliary directions 'whose observance or non-observance affects the quality of a performance but not the identity of the work'.[70] The American musicologist Alan Tormey has proposed an alternative answer.[71] He has suggested that in order to amend Goodman's definition to allow for the greater variation between performances in indeterminate and graphic notations, that instead of constitutive characters, notations be understood in terms of rules. So, 'rules suitably conceived might allow for a certain kind of specification not captured by traditional characters. A musical work [. . .] is a class of performances in which all the appropriate rules are followed.'[72]

Freed from the requirement of creating identical copies and performances, the notations in *Lines Burnt in Light* have been able to unpack the components of a cinematic landscape, allowing them to be better understood. These landscape architecture notations contain a close proximity to Busoni's notions of notation as the transcription of abstract ideas, and at best have 'notationality', rather than complying with Goodman's strict definition of notation, or even Tormey's more open one. Removed from the confines of strict symbolic notation (one symbol, one meaning, universally understood) *Lines Burnt in Light* has explored the unfolding attributes of time shared by both Ligeti's music and landscape architecture, attributes that conventionally have been excluded by the lack of accepted symbols. I have also incorporated sound into these landscape architecture notations, by setting them to the sounds created through Ligeti's notation for *Lontano*. The interface in the film between the appearing and erasing marks and the sound is not the coordinated accompaniment of conventional film music and image; rather, sometimes these two senses coalesce, at others they move 'far away'. *Lines Burnt in Light* brings not just the sounds of *Lontano* itself, but also the experience of landscape spaces where sound and visual experience are separate but related entities, connected by but not unified by time, that together so often provide the rich experience we recognise as integral to landscape space.

The inclusion of time through the medium of film also changes notation from a fixed object, to a temporal field, and from an allographic tool to communicate with others to an autographic

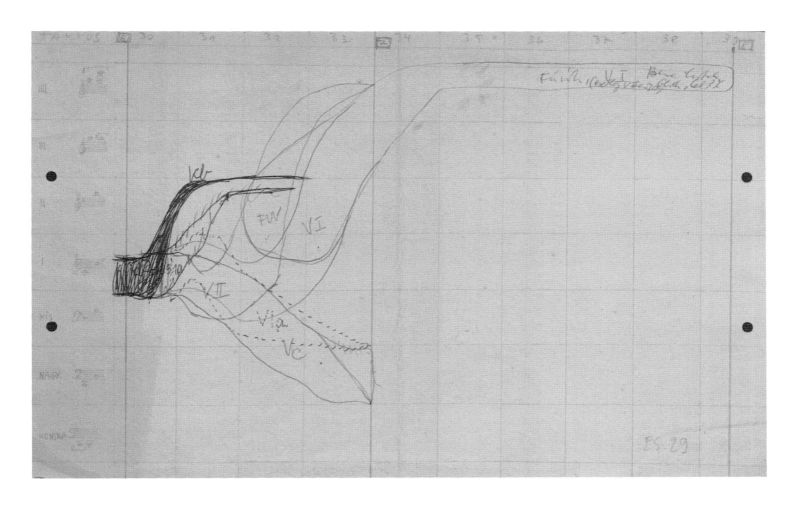

4.12 György Ligeti. Early sketch of *Atmospheres* by the composer. 1961. ©György Ligeti Collection, Paul Sacher Foundation, Basel.

personal tool to investigate the temporality of music and landscape architecture. *Lines Burnt in Light* is intriguingly similar to Ligeti's own experimentations that preceded *Lontano*. His initial notations for *Atmospheres* from 1961 show cloud-like musical forms drawn first in outline, and further explored through notating droplets of sound, that make visible the sonic particles that constitute the music. It is as though committing them to paper causes Ligeti's thoughts to condense, the music constructed from thousands of particles of notated sounds and silences. For *Atmospheres*, from 1961, an early sketch in the lower left corner showed the manner in which the sound of each instrument melted into others, while above it another showed the development of a 'cloud' of sound. The letters in pencil denoted the pitches of this composition, which utilised every note of a five octave chromatic chord, while the red pen shows the instrumentation such as Tr1 to Tr4 for four trumpets (*Trompete* in German). These

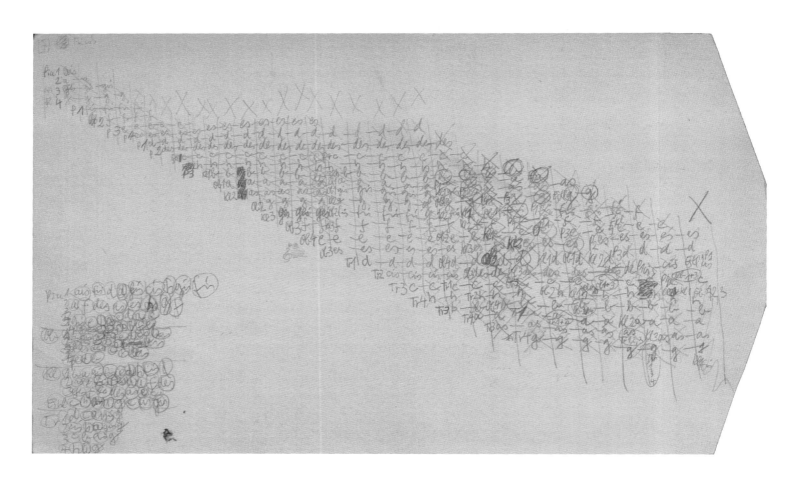

4.13 György Ligeti. Extract from the notation of *Atmospheres*. Early sketch of *Atmospheres* by the composer. 1961. ©György Ligeti Collection, Paul Sacher Foundation, Basel.

early exploratory works by Ligeti reveal notations that start as autographic, and then later becoming allographic at the point that the works are complete and require the notation to be read and then performed by others. As Cole notes, notation can function simultaneously in different ways, stating that 'in practice, however, directive, descriptive, and theoretical uses of notation cannot be neatly separated off',[73] as even conventional music notation is both a record of the composers intentions and an instruction. In this way, my notations are similar to music notation, a hybrid condition containing both a theoretical investigation of new possibilities for landscape architecture, and a record of the research process development. This lack of completeness may be an inevitable consequence of any notational system, as Cole has noted, quoting Hungarian composer Bela Bartok (1881–1945) who remarked 'the only true notations are the sound tracks of the record itself'.[74]

As American architect Stan Allen noted, 'allographic arts do not imitate or reproduce something already existing, they produce new realities, imagined by means of abstract systems of notation. By these criteria, it is obvious that architecture is neither clearly allographic or autographic.'[75] This was also acknowledged earlier by Goodman who stated that, 'insofar as its notational language has not yet acquired full authority to divorce identity of work in all cases from particular production, architecture is a mixed and transitional case'.[76] This research in exploring new notations for landscape architecture, like Ligeti's early works, uses autographic forms of notation in investigating new notational strategies. Ligeti's compositional method of a notation that changes and becomes more precise as the work progresses provides a model for my own investigations, together with Busoni and Tudor.

NOTATION OF TIME

In *Clouds* we find that metric precision in music notation can also create cloud-like, unfolding qualities of time that appear to lack the metric precision that creates them. Ligeti's *Lontano* reveals that precise drawings of time can lead us to notice temporal qualities shared in music and landscape space, unfolding changes at both the scale of temporal immediacy as well as over longer temporal spans. We discover that an understanding of complex temporal events can be aided by examining the detailed nature of their interonset intervals. Some aspects of landscape time are similar to those of *Lontano*. For example, both auditory and visual aspects of landscape do not abruptly start, but, rather, one becomes gradually conscious of their presence, and then sometime later, conscious of their absence. While absolute time is linear, time in landscape architecture is not just a vehicle of forward momentum but also allows us to travel back to places we remember. Just as films use flashbacks and flash-forwards, the time of landscape also moves us to recall and anticipate. Individual sounds can produce opposing effects. Kubrick used *Lontano*, for example, to evoke the future in *2001 A Space Odyssey*, while Ligeti saw it as drawing from earlier music, from having a historical depth as well as the spatial one created during performance. In examining landscape as a moving image in *Onibaba*, we find that devoid of spatial depth, both by the nature of a projected image and the cinematography, time expanded. Rather than a measured chronology, by tracking movement in precise increments, by focusing on detailed aspects of landscape space and experience, we can discover an expanded temporality revealing the multivalent time of landscape space.

NOTES

1 Crilly, 'The Bigger Picture' (2011), 245.

2 Steinitz, *György Ligeti* (2003), 103.

3 Ligeti, *Ligeti in Conversation* (1983), 14–15. *In Conversation: Gyorgy Ligeti in Conversation with Peter Varnai, Joseph Hausler, Claude Samuel and Himself*

4 Ligeti, *Ligeti in Conversation* (1983), 136–137.

5 Later, in 1972–3, Ligeti, inspired by an article by Karl Popper titled 'Of Clocks and Clouds', composed *Clocks and Clouds* for choir and orchestra, noting that 'the musical happening consists mainly of processes in which clocks are dissolved into clouds, and clouds condense and materialize into clocks'. Ligeti, *Ligeti in Conversation* (1983), 9. Ligeti also noted an interest from Popper in what he says about two kinds of processes in nature, one that you can measure exactly and the other that allows only for statistical approximation. The title is really the only feature of my work and his essay have in common.' Ligeti, *Ligeti in Conversation* (1983), 64.

6 Ligeti, *Ligeti in Conversation* (1983), 64.

7 Ligeti, *Ligeti in Conversation* (1983), 67.

8 Bernard, 'Rules and Regulation' (2011), 245.

9 Griffiths, *György Ligeti* (1983), 59.

10 Ligeti, *Ligeti in Conversation* (1983), 90.

11 Ligeti, *Ligeti in Conversation* (1983), 14.

12 Ligeti, *Ligeti in Conversation* (1983), 96.

13 Ligeti, *Ligeti in Conversation* (1983), 101.

14 Griffiths, *György Ligeti* (1983), 119.

15 Steinitz, *György Ligeti* (2003), 153.

16 Ligeti, *Lontano* (1967), 4.

17 Keller, *Ligeti: Lontano for Large Orchestra* (2010) http://www.sfsymphony.org/music/ProgramNotes.aspx?id=33250.

18 Ligeti, *Ligeti in Conversation* (1983), 60.

19 Ligeti, *Ligeti in Conversation* (1983), 86.

20 Ligeti, *Ligeti in Conversation* (1983), 84.

21 Block, 'Contextual Coding in Memory' (1985), 169–178.

22 Kramer, *Time of Music* (1988), 452.

23 Kramer, *Time of Music* (1988), 20.

24 Kramer, *Time of Music* (1988), 55.

25 Appleyard, Lynch and Myer, *View from the Road* (1965).

26 Klavarskribo notation was developed by Cornelius Pot in 1931, to simplify the notation of music by aligning the notes on the notation with the positions of the left and right hand on the piano, resulting in time running vertically up the page denoted by 10 vertical lines that the notes were locate onto.

27 Appleyard, Lynch and Myer, *View from the Road* (1965), 2.

28 Appleyard, Lynch and Myer, *View from the Road* (1965), 3.

29 Appleyard, Lynch and Myer, *View from the Road* (1965), 5.

30 Appleyard, Lynch and Myer, *View from the Road* (1965), 12.

31 Appleyard, Lynch and Myer, *View from the Road* (1965), 5.

32 Appleyard, Lynch and Myer, *View from the Road* (1965), 19.

33 Appleyard, Lynch and Myer, *View from the Road* (1965), 39.

34 Appleyard, Lynch and Myer, *View from the Road* (1965), 23.

35 Appleyard, Lynch and Myer, *View from the Road* (1965), 17.

36 Appleyard, Lynch and Myer, *View from the Road* (1965), 20.

37 Appleyard, Lynch and Myer, *View from the Road* (1965), 20.

38 Mellen, *Voices from Japanese Cinema* (1975), 72.

39 Mellen, *Voices from Japanese Cinema* (1975), 80.

40 Mellen, *Voices from Japanese Cinema* (1975), 82.

41 Mellen, *Voices from Japanese Cinema* (1975), 90.

42 Nakamura *et al.*, 'Restoration of Submerged Plants' in proceedings of International Lake Environment Committee Foundation, Wuhan, 2009. http://wldb.ilec.or.jp/data/ilec/WLC13_Papers/S1/s1-5.pdf.

43 Serper, 'Shindo Kaneto's films Kuroneko and Onibaba' (2005), 250.

44 Pallasmaa, *Architecture of Image* (2001), 43.

45 Crilly, 'The Bigger Picture' (2011), 250.

46 Appleyard, Lynch and Myer, *View from the Road* (1965), 8.

47 This appears in the opening credits of the film when we are shown both the overhead view of the hole and then a circle of sky from a camera looking up from the base of the pit.

48 The two screens that form *Pine Trees in Moonlight* are a pair of six-panel screens in ink and gold wash on paper. They sold at Christie's in New York for $880,000 on 20 March 2007. Each screen is 150.5 by 351 centimetres in size. http://www.christies.com/lotfinder/lot/attributed-to-hasegawa-tohaku-pine-trees-in-4870097-details.aspx?from=salesummary&intObjectID=4870097&sid=7900dac5-6dde-4930-b6f2-10a8dd0da0d7.

49 Corner, *Taking Measures* (1996), xv.

50 Girot, 'Vision in Motion' (2006), 95.

51 Girot, 'Vision in Motion' (2006), 96.

52 Appleyard, Lynch and Myer, *View from the Road* (1965), 22.

53 Ligeti, *Ligeti in Conversation* (1983), 93.

54 Kramer, *Time of Music* (1988), 57.

55 Kramer, *Time of Music* (1988), 58.

56 Corner, 'Representation and Landscape' (2002), 147–148.

57 Kramer, *Time of Music* (1988), 201.

58 Morgan, 'Spatial Forms in Ives' (1977), 155.

59 Ligeti and Jack, 'Ligeti talks to Adrian Jack' (1974), 24–30. http://www.ronsen.org/monkminkpinkpunk/9/gl2.html.

60 Griffiths, 'Invented Homelands: Ligeti's Orchestras', (2011), 266.

61 Lobanova, *György Ligeti* (2002), 155.

62 Ligeti, *Ligeti in Conversation* (1983), 98.

63 Ligeti, *Ligeti in Conversation* (1983), 92.

64 Steinitz, *György Ligeti* (2003), 94.

65 Ligeti, *Ligeti in Conversation* (1983), 92.

66 Ligeti, *In Conversation: György Ligeti in Conversation with* (1983), 84.

67 Howard, 'On Representational Music' (1972), 46.

68 Goodman, *Languages of Art* (1976), 185.

69 Goehr, *The Imaginary Museum* (2007), 23.

70 Goodman, *Languages of Art* (1976), 185.

71 Tormey, 'Indeterminacy and Identity in Art' (1974), 203–215.

72 Goehr, *The Imaginary* Museum (2007), 33.

73 Cole, Sounds and Signs (1974), 16.

74 Cole, Sounds and Signs (1974), 17.

75 Allen, Practice: Architecture (2000), 45–46.

76 Goodman, Languages of Art (1976), 221.

This chapter investigates the notation of a particular material in music and landscape architecture: sound. It commences with a detailed study of the notation of the English composer Michael Finnissy's composition, *English Country-Tunes* from 1977, focusing on the first movement within it, *Green Meadows*. I examine the strategies utilised in the composition of a notation that addresses notions of landscape in a musical work, creating a notation titled *Pink Elephants*. This is followed by an analysis of whether the notation of sound-as-music might also allow us to notate sound-as-landscape. By exploring the limitations of Western art music notation in this transposition we can question what amendments to this musical language, including those from ethnomusicology, a more complete transcription of landscape sound might require. These studies are focused on the Girraween National Park in Queensland, Australia, and include both a descriptive notation, *655*, and a prescriptive one, *923 Above*. This is followed by an examination of Kent's Rousham gardens in Oxfordshire, exploring whether sound was an aspect of the Picturesque. These studies from music and landscape architecture notations are then used to 'locate' the auditory landscape from *923 Above* within Kent's eighteenth-century landscape to examine the juxtaposition of these composed sounds into the materiality, spatiality and temporality of a historic landscape space. In relocating sound as a material of landscape space, I also question its historic absence, and propose how new landscape architecture notations might address this.

MICHAEL FINNISSY

Finnissy is extraordinarily prolific. Having composed over 325 works to date including 172 works for solo

5.1 David Buck. Memento of landscape discussions with Michael Finnissy. 2011.

english country-tunes

Michael Finnissy

For David

[signature]

Souvenir of landscape discussions
in Staynor, 3-xii-2011.

UNITED MUSIC PUBLISHERS LTD.
42 RIVINGTON STREET, LONDON EC2A 3BN

piano, 28 for duo, as well as 126 for chamber groups, 8 orchestral, 44 for solo instruments, 70 vocal, and 25 choral.[1] Early influences included the work of Ives, whose own innovations in music and notation Finnissy first encountered in childhood,[2] and drawing. Finnissy learnt penmanship at technical school and has said of his relationship with drawing, 'line is what I learnt from drawing and line is what I pursue in music [. . .] now, by analogy, I pursue the sense of line, rather than colour and texture, in my own work'.[3] Within this varied and extensive musical output, Finnissy has drawn inspiration from landscape in a wide range of contexts.

His composition *Afar* from 1966–67 looked at the tension created by the duality implicit in the widely varying scales of landscape. It 'encapsulates two extreme perceptions of an expanse of water: the ocean viewed from a distance, and the sea of water when looking in extreme close-up at an eye',[4] a polarity inviting comparisons with English artist

J. M. W. Turner's (1775–1850) *Sea and Sky*. Between 1966 and 1968 he also wrote a piano series titled *Songs 5–9*, that rather than drawing on a pictorial representation of landscape, explored transitory landscape phenomena in unexpected ways. The English musicologist Paul Driver identifies in *Song 9* periods of silence that:

> were intended as an attempt to realise in music the experience of certain phenomena in musical terms – a car passing behind a building, or the sun behind a cloud – where something is observed in one particular state, then later re-identified.[5]

These silences in the performance of this notation were part of an un-notated temporal continuum. Even the score instructions open with 'the song must start as though the pianist had already been playing for some considerable time before the first chord becomes audible – as though another person suddenly opened a door to the room where he is playing'.[6]

Finnissy returned again to a representation of landscape in his orchestral composition *Sea and Sky*, premiered in 1980. Driver reviewing the first performance four months later in September of the same year says that the work 'has a musical surface which can be fantastically intricate and ductile. The primal images "sea" and "sky" are contraposed not only with each other but with immense elaboration at the purely musical level'.[7]

Another orchestral work, *Red Earth*, commissioned by the BBC and composed in 1987–88, drew upon his experiences of the Australian landscape. The English musicologist Ian Pace wrote in 1986 that this composition is a 'reflexion on the other-worldly colourations, inhumanity and barrenness of the Australian landscape'.[8] As Finnissy himself remarks:

> when one calls a piece "red earth" and it's ostensibly about just a landscape I think it could be confusing to people that they are expecting to hear something which in some ways sounds like that landscape looks. For me there are a lot of other things involved in it, feelings, emotions, which in some ways contradict that landscape.[9]

The sonic landscape of *Red Earth* captures the impression of spaciousness of the physical landscape in sound, as well as the feelings that the experience of such a landscape evokes. He continues by saying:

> the intrusions on the landscape are sometimes a kind of artistic necessity that if one is making very long space like that, if you are not varying the sound within it, in order to create that impression of space, suddenly I felt it was necessary to have something cut through it. [. . .] and I could relate it to natural phenomena, like sudden flashes of lightning in a sky, or sudden fissures in a rock surface which certainly you see in that kind of landscape. It is difficult to say if those things again come from one's observation of natural phenomenon or whether they are something you feel is a structural necessity, to do with balance, to do with purely musical criteria. The composition of a piece of music, which is I suppose in some ways abstract, in some ways cuts right below the emotions, in some ways is purely emotional and about feelings.[10]

MELTY WATERCOLOURS WITH SAMUEL PALMER GLOOM ON TOP

Landscape has been a rich source of inspiration for English music, from English composer Edward Elgar's (1857–1934) ambulatory tempos of 72 beats per minute to the idealised landscape evoked in Hubert Parry's (1848–1918) *Jerusalem*. But it is against the backdrop of Finnissy's extensive interest in landscape that *English Country-Tunes* was selected for detailed study.[11] This solo piano composition was written for the Queen's Silver Jubilee in 1977, a year when the country was examining what it meant to be British. For Finnissy, *English Country-Tunes* 'are kind of fantasy English landscapes. They are kind of melty watercolours with a bit of Samuel Palmer gloom and doom on the top. That is how I see English landscapes really.'[12] *English Country-Tunes* resonates with this research in two specific ways. Firstly, it directly explores in musical sound, notions of a particular English landscape that expands upon the narrow conventions of scenic beauty. Finnissy, in 2011, explained his inspiration for this composition as partially a contrast to conventional ideas of how music might draw upon a landscape as inspiration, saying:

> the English pastoral is based upon a kind of set of symbols which represent the English countryside, so it is usually D minor, A minor, E minor in key, the oboe is playing, there might even be bag-pipey type noises underneath. It is slow and has that mellow mood. But it is all contrived. [. . .] not that I dislike it but I get dissatisfied as it is not mine anymore. So if I were walking through any landscape on the Downs, it's muddy, there are thorns, there are brambles everywhere. [. . .] You have to re-invent it.[13]

Secondly *English Country-Tunes* draws upon innovative notational strategies in its composition. Finnissy's work has been widely categorised as part of 'New Complexity', a term first credited to the Belgium musicologist Harry Halbreich (1931–2016). This musical movement led to the development of more complex musical notation that could draw in greater precision parameters including micro-tonality, abrupt changes in volume, and complex polyrhythmic notions of time. Finnissy himself has expressed dissatisfaction with this classification, saying that 'I wish it meant complexity of design, vision, topic [. . .] I worry it means complexity of surface detail on the page'.[14]

Finnissy likens his approach to notation and the sounds it creates this way,

> notation is about choice and degrees of exactitude, reality-unreality. [. . .] if you start from the premise of sound – when you impose the conventions of music on it, you're imposing a filter, [. . .] the filter of our understanding, or our tolerance or our prejudice.[15]

English Country-Tunes contains eight movements: *Green Meadows, Midsummer Morn, I'll give my love a garland, May and December, Lies and Marvels, The seeds of love, My bonny boy, Come beat the drums and sound the fifes.* The performance of the first, *Green Meadows*, which consists of nine sections, lasted 10'55"[16] when performed by the composer in 1990.[17] Finnissy draws a parallel between the notation and the landscape it represents, saying that,

> it looks like a landscape. Each line is like a sound landscape [. . .] there are sort of hills and it looks visually like a landscape. [. . .] The energy is pitch rather than heights and widths. It becomes transferred to pitch. [. . .] The density of movement is like walking uphill.[18]

This connotation between pitch flow and landscape form has been observed by the Czech ethnomusicologist Bruno Nettl, who, in 2005, noted that 'the content of English folk music seems to reside substantially in its melodic contour'.[19] Pace described the sound of *Green Meadows* as:

> Tempestuous yet distant surges of activity all around the keyboard erupting into split-second violence. Low rumblings, building to a peak, then calm again. Emergent shimmerings, extremely quiet, using all registers. Sudden cut off. Violent, but exhilarating traversals up and down keyboard, continually under threat of envelopment by the ascending swathes of notes. A gap in the texture, appearance of more diatonic melody in middle register. Top line dissolves, bottom line suddenly returns to rumblings. Alternation of more measured and spacious violence, now with monadic diatonic melody, accompanied first by rumblings, then by top register melody (now *ppp*). Long, timeless, exposition of serene but infinitely distant melody. Rumblings again. 'Almost motionless' continuation of melody leading to second movement.[20]

Pace then continues to describe the landscape rendered through this music: 'There is much which is dark and satanic, and a form of post-holocaust bleakness, a frightening landscape barely hospitable to man yet strangely beautiful, in the "England" that Finnissy presents; the country from which he felt deeply alienated.'[21]

LANDSCAPE DRAWN THROUGH SOUND

Finnissy's notational strategies within *Green Meadows* that allow for the complex sounds described by Pace above have been organised into three broad groups:

EXTENSIONS TO CONVENTIONAL SYMBOLIC NOTATION

Firstly, Finnissy extends traditional music notation in order to address shortcomings in its ability to specify particular qualities of sound. For example, he expands the notation of dynamics within the composition, adding additional letter '*p*'s so that even on the first page of the score we find *ppppp* notated, two further degrees of quietness from conventional *pianissimo*. The consequences of this movement from barely perceptible sound, into a territory closer to silence is to expand the spatial extent of the music as volume is closely correlated in human hearing with perceived distance of the sound source. He also extends dynamics in the opposing direction of loudness, with *fffff* appearing on page 4 of the score. By page 7 *fortissimo* has been superseded by *fffffff*. Also in the notes on performance he also develops symbols, still unusual within the norms of music, that allow sounds to be written one octave lower or higher than they actually sound and for this change to be subsequently cancelled, an idea found in the work of Kaihhosru Sorabji in the 1920s.[22] This is to aid the performer who in reading the notation during performance must relate notes in the page to their location on the instrument and the use of ledger lines above and below the stave can be more difficult to read at speed.

THE NOTATION OF TIME

Finnissy's notational innovations[23] are immediately visible in the notation, which starts with the words 'unsettled (violent and reckless)', replacing the conventional indication of a tempo articulated in beats per minute. This temporal ambiguity continues as the divisions of time are also not indicated by barlines, which in conventional notation allow for the metric division of time, facilitating the structuring of time into discrete and regular units against which the other components of the sonic material – pitch

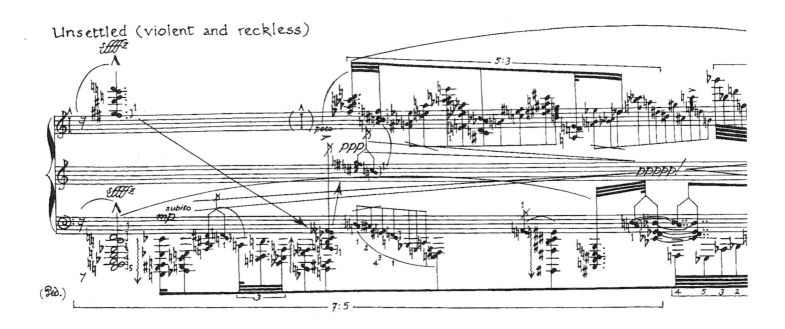

Unsettled (violent and reckless)

5.2 Michael Finnissy. Extract from the notation of *Green Meadows* with extended dynamic markings, written imperatives rather than a metronomic tempo, the absence of bars lines, and striking more than five notes with one hand. 1977. United Music Publishers.

particularly, but also volume – can be organised. In *Green Meadows* bar-lines first appear on page four to mark the division between two movements, and then again on the following page to facilitate a change of range from base to treble clef in the right hand. The time of Finnissy's music in *Green Meadows* is both personal and plastic. Each performer will approach the temporal ambiguities in different ways, both in regards to the time within the piece, and also between individual performance journeys through the notation. Finnissy also utilises words as markings in the score to express ideas that no conventional symbol denotes. On page eleven, for example, time is expressed not through a time signature but through words, in this case 'even slower (almost motionless)'. The plasticity of time created through the unconventional use of symbolic notation also

appears on pages seven and eight of the score. Here, tension is created by the simultaneous sounding of sections that are slowing down (marked *ralentando*) and their combination with complex rhythmic patterns. This section of the score is preceded by a sequence of temporal cells, each created by a slight displacement between the right and left hand sections of the composition. These include 8:5 against 17:10 (which could be re-written as 16:10 against 17:10), followed by 7:5 against 13:10 (14:10 against 13:10), and then 11:7 against 25:14.

Conventionally, the notation of temporal tension in music is through sub-divisions of the pulse, the beat providing a datum against which the detailed changes can be perceived. The tension Finnissy introduces by a sequence of smaller differences between the two components of the time are fundamentally different from this. He explains his sense of the possibilities of a more plastic approach to time this way:

> all music notation presupposes a kind of time-space canvas in which time moves from the left hand side of the page to the right hand side of the page and pitch always moves up from the bottom, so from that point of view those are the constants and any kind of graphic notation, once you have committed it to paper presupposes those ideas [. . .] a kind of grid which is superimposed on the top. So, for classical music the grid is not very interesting, mostly divided equally into fours or threes or groups, which remain constant in all parts of the music texture. For me, the first thing that was interesting about challenging this notion was if two things move at different speeds then how do you deal with that? There is a musical way of dealing with this, so that if you imagine, for example, a grid that is six squares long you can also put seven notes into that space by simply writing a bracket on top and putting seven instead of six.[24]

The plasticity of time in *Green Meadows* is also emphasised by the occasional appearance of more conventional time signatures. But even here the range indicated is unconventionally wide. Finnissy suggests a tempo of approximately 80–96 beats per minute. He also uses grace notes[25] to notate micro changes in time rather than their conventional application as melodic ornamentation. In the introductory notes on performance, he describes grace notes as like inhaling breath, interrupting the rhythmic continuity, and outside of the main tempo, while arpeggios[26] are to be performed as rapidly as possible regardless of the written duration. In *Green Meadows* there is also a three-second section of silence between the first and third section, the only interruption to the flow of sound within this section of *English Country-Tunes*,

as the notation is marked 'attacca' at the end of *Green Meadows*, moving straight into the subsequent movement. Time flows as vividly through it as through sound. Silence here connects as much as it separates, functioning as an equal structural element with sound.

NOTATION OF TECHNICAL CHALLENGES
IN THE PERFORMANCE OF THE PIECE

Finnissy introduces a number of technical challenges into the notation as obstructions to its performance. These include the sounding of more than one note by a single digit and striking seven notes simultaneously in the left hand. Later, on page nine of the score, extremely wide intervals are to be played simultaneously, the right hand playing the top two notes of the chord, from B♭ to G, an interval of a thirteenth. Each of these obstructions require the performer to make decisions regarding how to realise them in the performance, introducing areas into the notation where the degree of control the composer exerts over the performer is reduced.

PINK ELEPHANTS

As a continuation of my analysis of *Green Meadows* I developed a new notation, *Pink Elephants*, to focus and draw out aspects of Finnissy's work (see www.db-land.com/films/PinkElephants to watch the full film and to hear *Green Meadows* with it go to iTunes). My notation focuses on three critical aspects of the notation. Firstly, how the temporal movements of the composition related to real (absolute) time in minutes and seconds in order to understand the temporal structure of the composition. Secondly, what compositional strategies for duration, pitch and volume were used throughout the score in this evocation of an imagined English landscape. Thirdly, what was the relationship between the different sections of the score and what happened at the junctions between them, were they discrete and separated by silence, or linked together through gestures such as tied notes or pedals? The unfolding process of this notation was recorded with a digital SLR camera to capture each incremental development and to allow the process to be revisited later for reflection and further analysis. The notation was developed in charcoal on 320-gram white paper, started with a single pink elephant stamped onto the surface. This was in thanks to Finnissy for his riposte that while a dot between two lines on conventional manuscript paper denotes the pitch C, it could equally well have been a pink elephant: all notation is symbolic.[27] A useful reminder in the development of my own transcriptions. The next notational inscription was of duration 10'55", the length of Finnissy's own performance of the notation in 1990, and the duration of the film created for this phase of the research (see notation N9). This was followed by the addition of Finnissy's title, *Green Meadows*.

The analysis of Finnissy's notation started with plotting the real-time lengths of each movement of the score, together with the written instructions on the score for each, from the opening 'unsettled (violent and restless)' to the last verbal instruction of 'even slower (almost motionless)' at 9'37" (see notation N10).

Nine of these internal movements each has its own distinct time. They run sequentially into each other, with the exception of three seconds of silence from 3'06" and 3'09", where the absence of composed sounds created a silent continuity between the adjacent movements. Finnissy used words to notate the temporal character of each section, both as an evocation of the mood of each, as well as to move away from rigid time signatures and conventional tempos. Only briefly, at 1'56" with the words *non troppo presto* (fast but not too much) and for a brief period starting at 5'30" with the instruction *presto*, does his notation of the time of the internal movements revert to the conventional language of music notation where tempos are given in metronome markings or Italian imperatives.

Next, the analysis focused on drawing out potential connections between these broad temporal movements discussed above in order to study how different types of time within the composition were related over longer durations. Finnissy uses pedal tones[28] that extend connections both within and between sections, such as the pedal tone that starts from the beginning of *Green Meadows* and extends two-thirds of the way into this first section marked 'unsettled'. The next pedal tone links across the border between the 56 seconds of 'unsettled' and the following section titled 'much calmer'. The next pedal tone links the end of 'much calmer' to the beginning of 'very fast' at three minutes and nine seconds of the music, connecting this with the intermediate sections titled '*non troppo presto*', 'more animately' and the three seconds of silence starting at three minutes and six seconds of the music. These pedal tones create a spatial tension between the delineation of the formal sections of this score and these less pronounced areas of sound linked by the pedal tones. There is not a singular definition to the spaces of each section, but more complex and ambiguous boundaries. Like an unfolding landscape as one moves through it, rather than discrete scenes with distinct boundaries, we find

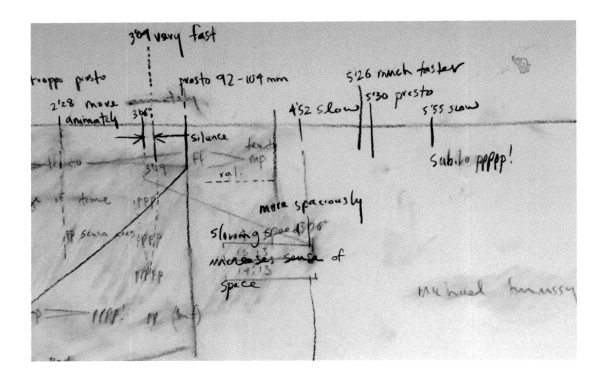

5.3 David Buck. Extract from *Pink Elephants*. 2013.

a sequence of interconnected and related spaces, in this case created through sound (see notations N11–14).

Spatial extent is also created in other ways. Midway through the section starting at 3'09", for example, the score is marked *rallentando* (slowing down) with the additional prescription 'more spaciously'. So, this change of speed from 'very fast' at 3'09" to slow at 4'52" is accompanied by an increasing sense of spaciousness as the music slows. Pedal tones are again used to connect one temporal movement with another. Just prior to the commencement at 5'55" of the penultimate movement, a pedal tone starts and extends until 9'18". A brief break before another pedal tone links into the next movement starting at 9'37". The use of these sustained notes

is also emphasised by the continuity of dynamics that traces each of the two pedal tones referred to above, firstly *ppp*, followed by *ppp sostenuto* (softest possible sustained). Other linkages are chords held across at 2'16", and individual tones sustained across the change of speed from '*presto*'[29] (very fast) to 'slow' at 5'55". Next came an analysis of the microtemporality of sections of the score. Within the 'very fast' section starting at 3'09" there is a sub-section titled *presto* (92–104MM) consisting of 15 sequential units where there are tensions between the left and right hand timings. These vary from, for example, 8:5 in the left hand against 17:10 for the right, followed by 7:5 against 13:10. Finnissy likens these as tensions that through different types of energy allow for the creation of varying moods. Within the nine

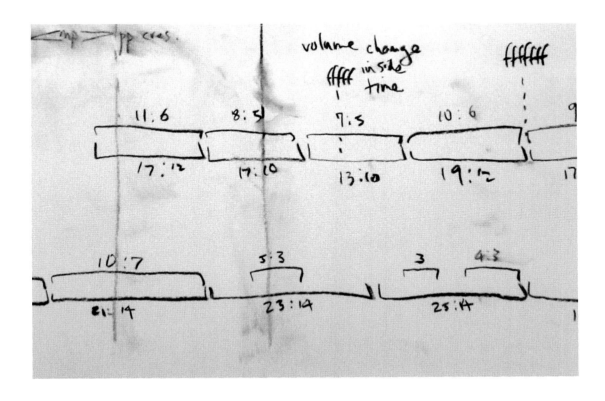

5.4 David Buck. Extract from *Pink Elephants*. 2013.

movements of this score, there are only three formal sections delineated by conventional bar lines. These occur at 3'09" ('very fast'), 4'52" ('slow'), 5'26" ('much faster'), and at 10'55", the end of the *Green Meadows* section of *English Country-Tunes*. Perhaps the first section of the composition that starts with the verbal instruction 'unsettled (violent and restless)' can be seen not as an abrupt beginning but rather connected to the preceding ambient sounds including silence of the performance space.

Finnissy's dramatic use of extended dynamics in both directions, towards silence as well as towards loudness, gives an enhanced sense of space in the composition: space is both made more intimate and also more extensive through this range of volume.

This aspect of *Green Meadows*, this expansion of the spatial envelope of his auditory landscape, connects this composition not just with an extended spatiality of Finnissy's notions of an English landscape, but also with the body of older musical works such as Gabrieli's *Sonata Piano e Forte* discussed in Chapter 3 *Horizons* earlier. As Schafer notes, 'the exaggerated dynamic plane of Western music allows the composer metaphorically to move sound anywhere from the distant horizon to the immediate foreground'.[30] Finnissy's notation uses melodic contour, complex notions of time, and the design of an expansive space through the manipulation of volume in order to create, through sound, the landscape of *Green Meadows*.

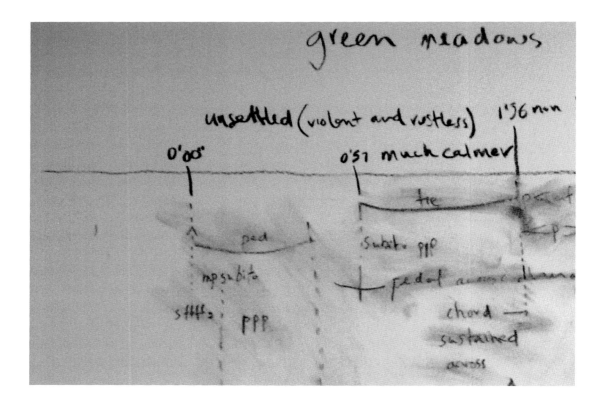

EACH BIRD IS KNOWN BY ITS SONG

In seeking to develop a new landscape architectural notation for the sounds of a landscape space, one immediately faces certain challenges in attempting to capture them through conventional music notation. Ethnomusicology is the branch of music theory most closely involved in the transcription of musical sounds that through rhythm, timbre and pitch, fall outside those of Western art music. Located in non-Western musical cultures, ethnomusicologists develop notations for musical sounds where there are no appropriate traditions or systems of notation, in order to bring them to a Western audience.

American musicologist Helen Myers has dated the academic history of ethnomusicology to 1885 and the publication *Umfang, Methode und Zeil der Musikwissenschaft* (*Scope, Method and Goal of Musicology*) by the Austrian author Guido Adler (1855–1941). A recognised term for this broad field, ethnomusicology is more generally considered to have first been 'coined in 1950 by the Dutch scholar, Jaap Kunst'[31] (1891–1960). Kunst himself saw that each culture had its own musical history, that 'each bird is known by its song',[32] and defined it as a science that 'investigates all tribal and folk music and every kind of non-Western art music'.[33] He dated the start of ethnomusicology to English philologist Alexander John Ellis's (1814–1890) publications *The History of Musical Pitch* (1881) and *Tonometrical Observations on some existing non-harmonic Scales* (1884), and his finding that 'the Musical Scale is not one, not "natural", nor even founded necessarily on the laws of the constitution of musical sound so beautifully worked out by Helmholtz, but very diverse, very artificial, and very capricious'.[34] The subsequent development of ethnomusicology was facilitated by the spread of portable recording equipment, which allowed for in-depth study and transcription of this music, together with the greater ease of travel to previously distant lands with the spread of airplanes.[35]

The American musicologist Mantle Hood (1918–2005), who founded the UCLA Institute of Ethnomusicology, writing in 1971, outlined the potential difficulties of adapting Western music notation for non-Western music, posing them in terms not just of efficiency for a Western audience, but of the nature of the music tradition itself:

> a persistent problem in transcription [. . .] how much detail is it essential to notation? [. . .]a number of related factors must also be taken into account: the nature and relative efficiency of notation in terms of the particularly musical tradition it is meant to serve, the problems of applying Western notation to the music of other traditions, and the consideration of alternative approaches to the notation of non-Western music.[36]

Swedish musicologist Ingmar Bengtsson (1920–1989), writing in 1967, lists some of the questions that an ethnomusicologist might consider when contemplating the development of a new notation:

- What are the 'essential' qualities of the material?
- What scale of calibration is appropriate to show overall structure or detail?
- How far is the notation to be generalised to represent an average or ideal performance?
- What is the nature of the unit to be separated for study?
- Who is to read the notation?[37]

At the heart of the notational challenges are differences between sound-as-music predominantly derived from diatonic scales and metronomic temporal patterns, and sound-as-landscape inevitably including non-diatonic tones and a-periodicity. These challenges include both the relative suitability of the transcription of the four parameters of sound in music (pitch, duration, timbre, and volume) covered sequentially below but also other possible sonic parameters found in landscape architecture but missing in the notation of music.

MUSICAL PARAMETERS

Pitch: the relationship between pitch is a defining quality of Western notions of song (melody), but is not dominant in the sounds of a landscape where pitch juxtapositions are largely unrelated. Some bird-calls may have identifiable pitches but these are individual and short in duration. Nothing in the sounds of landscape space is comparable to the extended pitch relationships of Western art music.

Duration: its notation in music is through symbols whose values refer to sub-divisions of a prescribed or known tempo, whereas the duration of sounds in landscape lack an identifiable durational reference. Instead, they are derived from a range of different temporalities, from the immediacy of bird song to the longer durations of weather-induced sound, such as rainfall or wind.

Timbre: the quality of sound that allows one instrument to be distinguished from another, is an important component of landscape sound, particularly given the relatively lower importance of pitch. The timbre of landscape sounds extends beyond the words used for acoustic instruments in the classical tradition.

Volume: symbolic music notation, in its conventional use of a dynamic range from *ppp* to *fff* adopts a relative scale for volume. This is capable of being extended in both directions, an approach adopted by Finnissy and other composers.

NON-MUSICAL PARAMETERS

Direction of the sound source: is not notated in music as the relationship between it and the listener is determined by the stage-to-seating arrangements of the venue, whereas in landscape the direction of the sound source is a key component of the spatial experience of it. Sounds are arriving from many directions and through a process known as sound localisation the human ear is adept at distinguishing them. Sound sources in landscape are not unidirectional but, in fact, are arriving at the listener from a 360-degree field (in plan, the azimuth) and a 180-degree field (vertically, in section).

Reverberation time: the idealised and constant reverberation time of a concert hall (1.9 seconds) is not applicable to landscape where the sound source is not a determined distance from the person hearing it, but varies. Additionally, the degree of sound reflection varies from the scale and material properties that constitute the landscape in a particular area. American acoustic architects Barry Blesser and Linda-Ruth Salter,

writing in 2007 about the complexity of an urban landscape, say:

> the environment is composed of multiple objects and numerous sound sources, some stationary, some mobile. Each traffic sign, parked automobile, or telephone pole has a surface that produces some sonic reflections when the sound source is in front of it and acoustic shadows when it is behind. A reflection can be heard as an echo if the sound is impulse-like and the surface is more than 10 metres away, or as tonal coloration if the source is continuous and the surface nearby.[38]

These reflections and alterations of the sound wave are complex, multifaceted, and unpredictable.

Motive sound source: in the case of landscape, the sound source may be moving such, as birds' calls in flight, animal sounds in motion, or a sudden breeze moving through trees.

Motive listener: the listener is far more likely to be moving through the landscape, rather than stationary in the conventional concert hall audience setting that typifies experiences of sound-as-music.

Considering these factors above while searching for new notational strategies for the auditory experience of landscape suggested the simultaneous pursuit of three lines of inquiry. Firstly, to investigate the limitations of Western art music notation for transcribing landscape sounds. Secondly, to investigate how ethnomusicology addresses the notation of pitch, types of time as well as temporal duration, timbre and volume in other musical cultures to seek to mitigate the limitations of those identified above. Thirdly, to identify what new notational strategies and techniques might need developing to address those components of landscape sound (such as changing direction of sound source) that fall outside both Western art music and ethnomusicology notation. These latter factors might simply require amendments or revisions to notation from either tradition above, such as through diacritical markings, or may necessitate the development of new approaches. Hood, writing in 1971, warns of the possible challenges in mere adaptation, stating 'no amount of pluses or minuses or similar diacritical markings added to Western notation can compensate for the inherent rigidity of the Western staff'.[39]

Hood identified three approaches towards a comprehensive solution that addressed what he described as the chronic problem of cross-cultural transcription, 'the disparity between a culturally determined system of notation and the musical sounds of some other culture it was never intended to represent'.[40] These three approaches were also linked to the immediacy of their availability, and to an author who had developed them. As Hood says:

> For the sake of simplicity I shall assign a man's name to each stage of the composite solution to the problems of notation: The one available now we shall call the (Alfred James) Hipkins Solution; available soon, the (Charles) Seeger Solution; available in the distant future, the (Rudolph) Laban Solution. The three solutions have been referred to three stages of timing or availability (now, soon, future) in the development of a Composite Solution. But we should keep in mind that each of them in itself is a valid solution for particular aspects of the notation problem and that ultimately all three are necessary as a composite.[41]

Hipkins (1826–1903), writing in 1891 in the introduction to Charles Russell Day's (1860–1900) book on Indian music,[42] supports the notion that 'the ethnomusicologist will be able to supplement the symbolic language of the indigenous notation with graphic displays of pertinent musical practice known only in the oral tradition'.[43] Hipkins' approach allowed for sounds from a wide range of cultural sources to be notated, using an existing notation where possible and supplementing it with new symbols to allow for the desired parameters to be drawn. The second of Hood's contributors to a potential composite solution was that developed by American musicologist Charles Seeger (1886–1979) whose notations were termed melographs. Produced by a mechanical transcription device, melographs show pitch (against dotted lines of the chromatic intervals of Western diatonic tuning) amplitude (representing loudness in decibels), and overtone spectrum, all recorded on 16 mm film with a horizontal scale in units of one second. A critical weakness of relying only on a Seeger-type transcription device for this research is that the new notations need not just transcribe, but also to compose. One of the reasons for Western art music notation ubiquity is that by using a common language for both descriptive notation (for the transcription of existing sounds) and prescriptive (for the composition of new ones) has led to its widespread adoption and use. The third component in Hood's trilogy quoted above, assigned at that time as an aspiration for the distant future, is to seek the adaptability of Laban's symbolic dance notation in new ethnomusicology notation. As Hood says:

> Compared to Labanotation, which approaches universal efficiency, all established manual systems of music notation are truly primitive [. . .] the system is a complex "phonetic" one made of many monomial symbols which, in various combinations, can represent detailed movements of virtually

all parts of the body. Labanotation is a scientific tool for descriptive, analytical, and comparative methods.[44]

Hood argued that Labanotation provided a potential model for a new universal music notation with a vertical staff already having been used in Klavarskribo notation, and 'basic symbols used to represent different aspects of the musical fabric might give some visual suggestion of the thing symbolised',[45] the pictorial approach used in conventional music symbols such as the trill.

655 SECONDS OF ANTIPODEAN LANDSCAPE

Girraween National Park in southern Queensland, is close to the town of Stanthorpe in the area known as the Granite Belt. This location is in the broad area colloquially termed 'the hinterland', a mix of fire-cleared meadows within areas of indigenous mixed forest with many Eucalyptus species, and a ground flora of grasses and flowers. Girraween, meaning 'place of flowers' in local indigenous languages, was described by the English botanist Allan Cunningham in his diary of 26 June 1827, as 'large detached masses of granite of every shape towering above each other, and in many instances standing in almost tottering positions, constituted a barrier before us'.[46] Forty-one threatened and endangered plant species are found within the park,[47] supported by a climate of summer rains and temperatures from 15 to over 30 degrees centigrade. Fauna is equally rich, including kookabura and red-necked wallabies, torresian crows and eastern grey kangaroos, satin bower birds and crested pigeons, and as if to emphasise its isolation, 13 species of birds of prey.[48] Staying in Australia at that time, this site was selected to test the ethnomusicological model for notation

development for twin reasons: firstly, its distance from centres of habitation and being surrounded by mountains meant that sound pollution from vehicles, a serious problem on other sites considered, could be avoided; and secondly this specific site, although fringed by forests on the granite hillsides, contained a habitat of naturally occurring grasses and flowering meadows. This combination of topography and flora resonated with Finnissy's descriptions of the landscapes he evoked in his own *Green Meadows*. This isolated location also offered greater sound fidelity that would allow the spatial extent of the auditory landscape to be examined in fine detail. In his seminal publication on soundscape from 1977, Schafer defines this difference in terms of hi-fi and low-fi, explained this way:

> A hi-fi system is one processing a favourable signal-to-noise ratio. The hi-fi soundscape is one in which discrete sounds can be heard clearly because of the low ambient noise level. The country is generally more hi-fi than the city; night more than day; ancient times more than modern. In the hi-fi soundscape, sounds overlap less frequently; there is perspective—foreground and background—[49]

The pellucid sounds of this hinterland Australian landscape, in the clarity derived from its isolation, overcome the difficulties of the loss of depth of sound one often encounters in the city. As Schafer notes, 'perspective is lost. On a downtown street corner of the modern city there is no distance; there is only presence.'[50]

The sounds were recorded on Wednesday 16 May 2012, between 8.30a.m. and 2.30p.m. As in the previous study, this notation was also formed into a film, titled *655*, (see www.db-land.com/films/655)

5.6 David Buck. Photograph of sound recording location in Girraween National Park. 2013.

with the determined duration of 10'55", selected to match the length of Finnissy's performance of *Green Meadows* (see notation N15).

This shared temporal frame allows the two sound events to be directly compared, drawing attention to the similarities and differences between Finnissy's music and the sounds of Girraween. By juxtaposing the two times, it was hoped that a structural and detailed comparison could be more clearly undertaken.

The transcription starts with a single horizontal line with an initial scale of 60 seconds to 10 0mm focusing on the most distinctive auditory aspects of the sound recording, bird-calls, starting with the conventional musical categories of duration, volume, pitch and timbre. Not all of these can be easily

recognised and in order to progress the notation, where they cannot be initially identified they are left unrecorded on the paper, to be revisited later. This process follows Hood's suggestion 'the first objective is to get on paper a phonemic outline of the piece [. . .] after a satisfactory phonemic outline has been made, the transcriber is ready to begin worrying out the phonetic details [. . .]'.[51] This ethnomusicological approach to sound transcription and its application to the four parameters of conventional Western art music is explored in more detail below.

TRANSCRIPTION OF DURATION

Perhaps the first challenge in the transcription of the temporality of landscape through drawing is that the ordering of the sounds over time is unlikely to follow an identifiable metronomic pulse. As Hood states, 'in the European tradition of music, one is inclined to think of tempo as the *governing* aspect of time, which regulates such specific divisions as meter, rhythm, density'.[52] His solution to this, for musical cultures that operate relative, rather than perfect time, was the notion of 'Density Referent' or DR. As he said:

> Although no one could say what the slowest pulse of a piece might be, everyone agreed that each piece has a fastest pulse. [. . .] If the DR for the pieces in one tradition was around 600 ppm (pulses per minute) and the DR for representative pieces from another tradition was around 200 ppm, we knew something specific about each tradition in terms of the relative density of musical events.[53]

An earlier alternative notion for the transcription of aperiodic time was developed by ethnomusicologists Dieter Christensen and Bruno Nettl in 1960 in response to the difficulties of measuring tempo by metronome where metric stability is absent. Termed 'inner tempo', it was calculated as the 'average degree or amount of rhythmic movement [. . .] investigating the relationship of the number of rhythmic impulses – i.e., the number of tones in a composition – to its total duration.'[54] While both of these methods have potential applicability to landscape temporality, given the extreme aperiodicity of these sounds the relative duration of inner tempo rather than density referent's determined reference of minutes seemed a more fruitful method to explore.

TRANSCRIPTION OF TIMBRE AND TONE

Timbre in Western art music is notated through words, such as rounded or piercing, strident or bright, and there seems to be little limitation to adapting this to the quality of landscape sounds, with the proviso that timbre is influenced not just by the material of the sound source, but like duration, is modified by attack, decay and release. Tone is more challenging. Diatonic scales, together with chromatic alterations to encompass all 12 tones of conventional music, allow for the notation of sounds that fall within this system. Those that don't are considered 'out of tune'. However, many other musical cultures do employ microtones within their own tuning system, as Hood noted:

> Perhaps the most fundamental deficiency of Western notation for purposes of transcription of non-Western music is the limitation of twelve fixed pitches within the octave. No musical culture outside of the sphere of influence of the European art tradition employs this system of tuning.[55]

Notation of pitch can be approached by mechanical transcription devices like Seeger's Melograph, or by dividing the Western tonal system into greater subdivisions to allow for non-diatonic pitches. The American musicologist Kathryn Vaughn referred in 1992 to Ellis's system of 'cents' that related 'the physical frequencies of musical sounds to the "sensation of tone"',[56] as an alternative measure. Ellis's theory, published in 1863,[57] is grounded in further subdivisions of the octave beyond those of the twelve tones of Western tempered scales. As Vaughn informs:

> the definition of one cent is 1/100 of a semitone. Ellis considered that there are 12 semitones per octave, therefore there are 1200 cents per octave [. . .] and for the sake of clarity ethnomusicologists have held with 1200 cents per octave as the standard.[58]

N9 *Pink Elephants*. The initial inscriptions of
Green Meadows, Michael Finnissy and a pink
elephant, together with a single durational line.
2013.

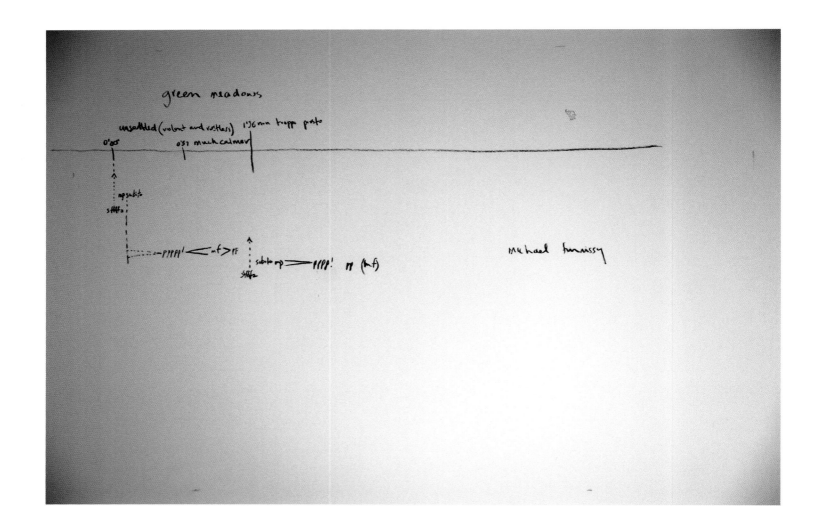

N10 *Pink Elephants*. An extract showing the early
development of the notation. 2013.

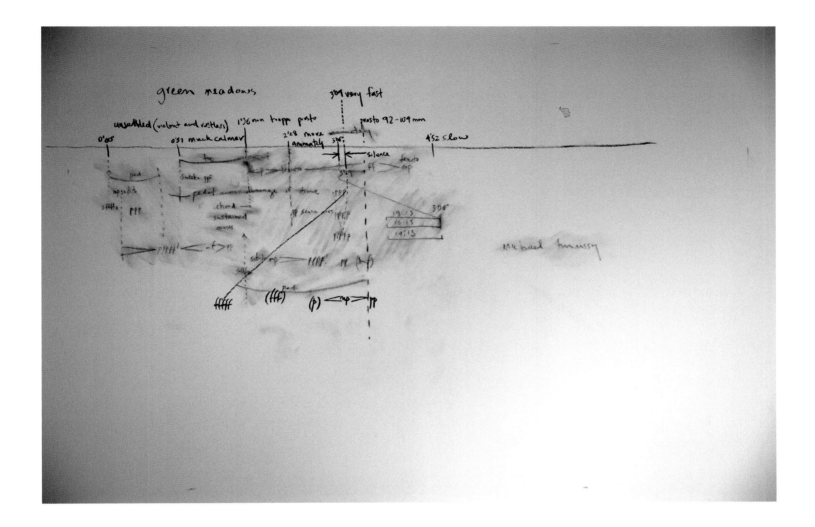

N11 *Pink Elephants*. 2013.

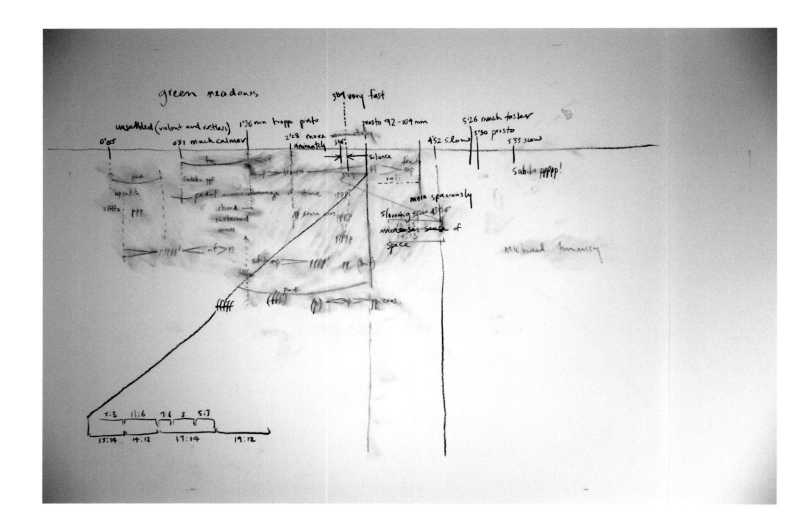

N12 *Pink Elephants.* 2013.

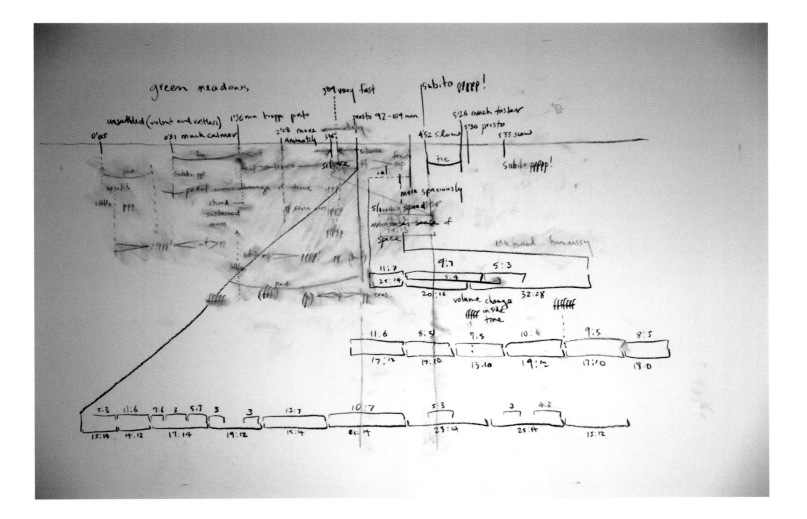

N13 *Pink Elephants.* 2013.

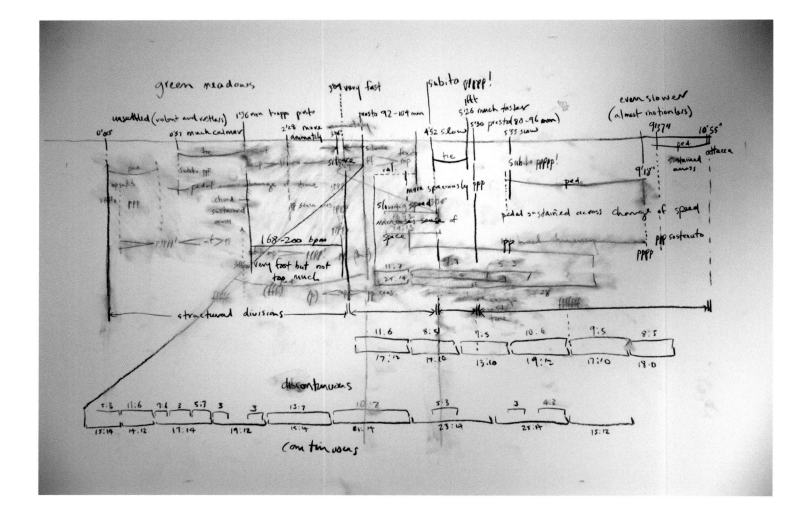

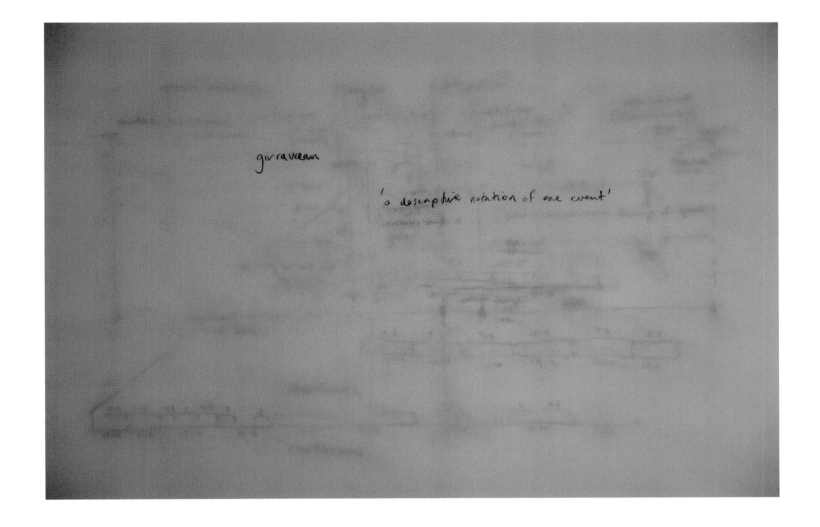

girraween

'a descriptive notation of one event'

N15 *655*. The beginning of the notation with the location of Girraween and a reminder that it was the development of a descriptive notation of one event. 2013.

should time consider attack, duration
and release

open from
previous
sounds.

148" 155"   3'33"
                    351"

non-musical parameters

① direction of sound source

② motive sound source

③ listener's movement through
     space

western art music // ethnomusicology

timbre - use words to
  describe qualities

2. volume - ppp ⟨ fff   OR   Mantle Hoods HSC
     extensions by MF to   hardness scale for loudness
     pppp ⟨ fffff   0-11db / 12-23db / ......

3. pitch - 5 line stave   OR   Seeger Melograph or
     or equidistant stave   Alexander Ellis's 1200 cents/octave

4. duration - no time   →   time space notation or
     signatures as landscape   Dieter Christensen's 'inner tempo'
     time is not metronomic

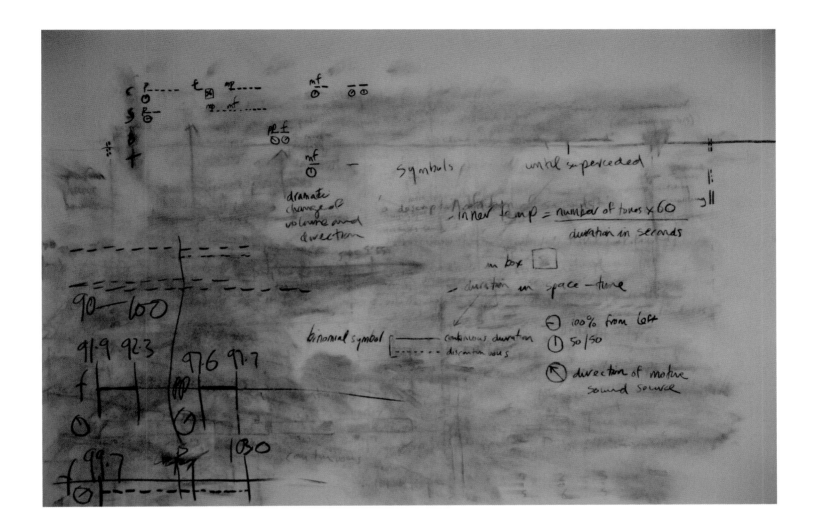

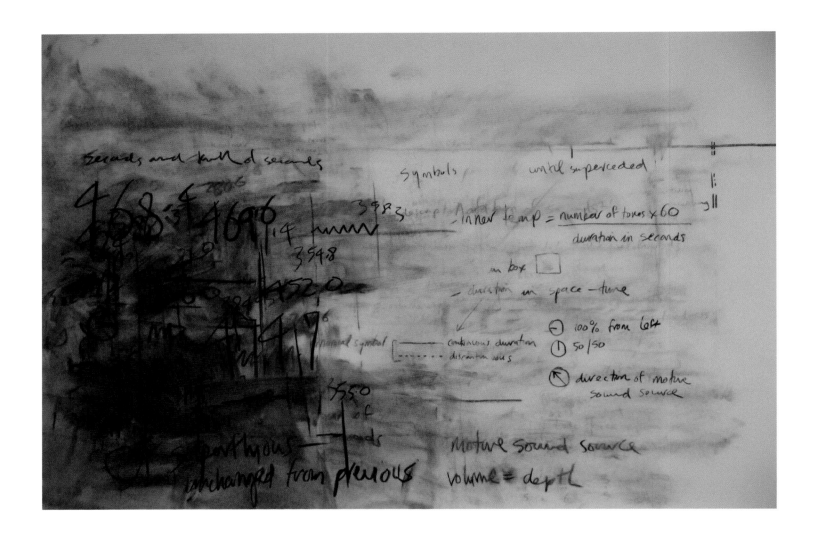

655. Overwriting and erasure as the
notation develops. 2013.

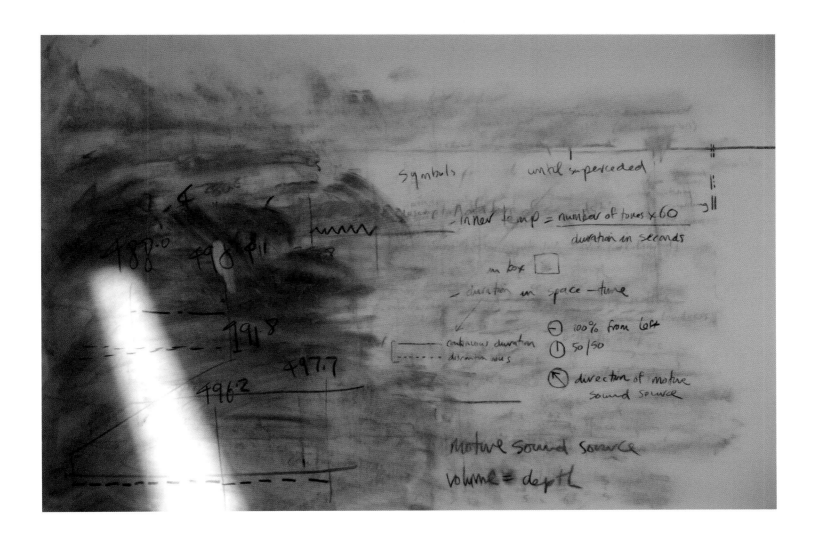

N19 *655*. Light reflected onto the notation.
2013.

tone symbols   until superceded

Inner temp = number of tones × 60
                  ————————————————
                  duration in seconds

in box ☐
= duration in space—time

——— continuous duration
- - - - discontinuous

⊖ 100% from left
① 50/50
⟳ direction of motive
     sound source

Motive sound source
volume ∗ depth

N20 *655*. An extract from the notation with
        layers of erased marks beneath. 2013.

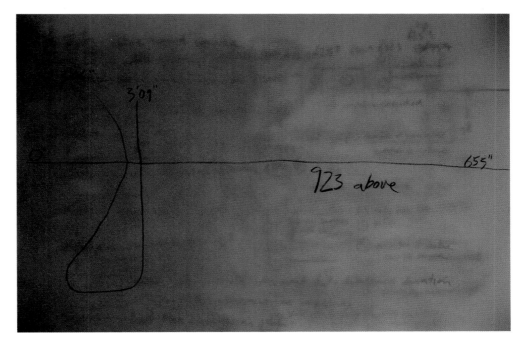

N21 *923 Above*. Three seconds of silence brought forward into this notation from Finnissy's *Green Meadows*. 2013.

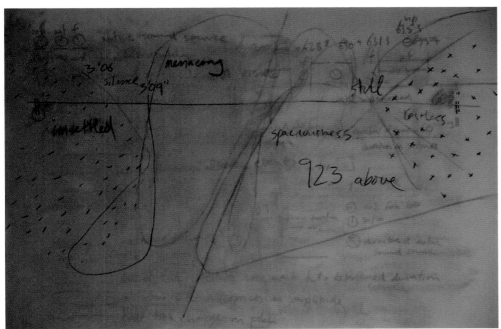

N22 *923 Above*. Areas of auditory landscape spaces outlined. 2013.

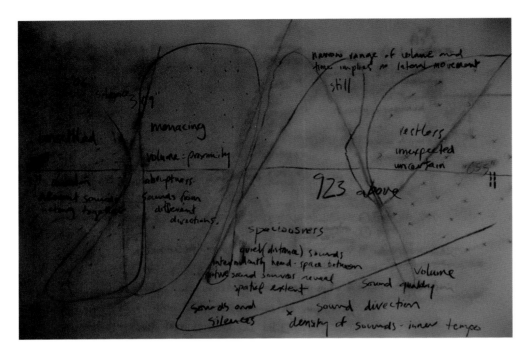

N23 *923 Above*. Qualities of landscape sounds
defined. 2013.

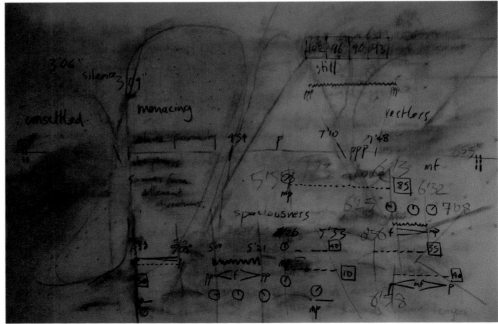

N24 *923 Above*. Detailed development of sound
qualities. 2013.

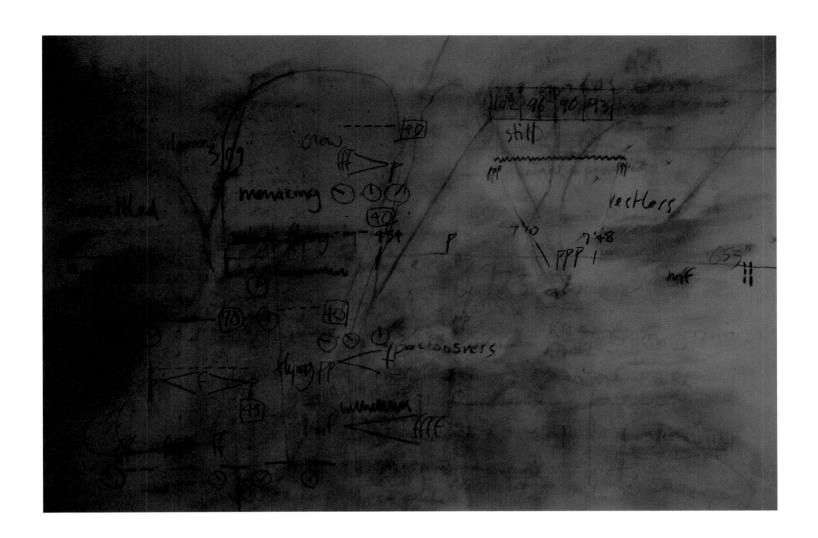

N25 *923 Above*. Further development of notation. 2013.

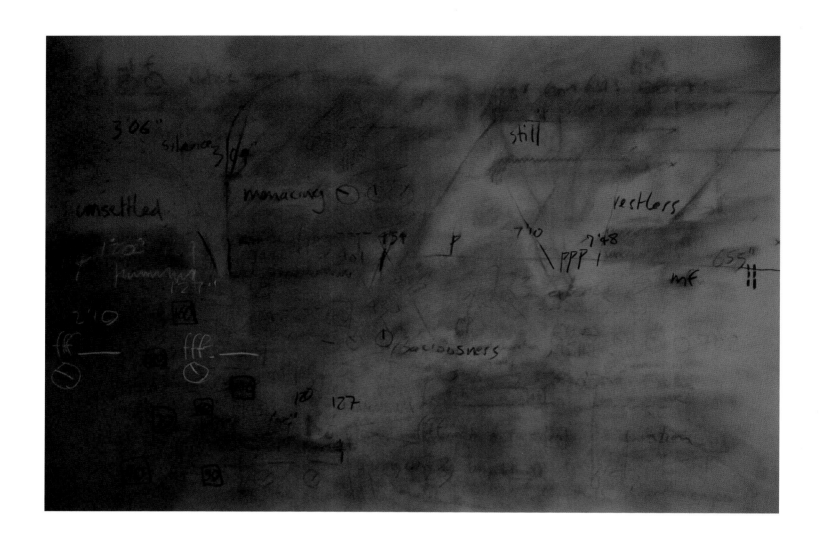

N26 *923 Above*. Layers of sound and landscape qualities. 2013.

TRANSCRIPTION OF VOLUME

Loudness in Western art music is notated through a system of relative volume denoted from *ppp* to *fff*, with six levels in-between. As Hood points out:

> The registration of loudness is subject to several variables: the size of the ensemble, the nearness or farness of the perceiver, the acoustical relationship of both these to the environment, and to some degree the climate of relative humidity and temperature.[59]

He proposed an alternative scale of absolute loudness, which he termed a Hardness Scale for Loudness (HSL), 'by dividing 120 decibels (db) into ten divisions: 1, 1–12 db; 2. 13–24db; 3, 25–36db; and so forth'.[60]

The analysis of 10'55" of the sounds of the Girraween National Park started with two reminders from ethnomusicology. Firstly, by Ter Ellingson from 1992 of the distinction between prescriptive and descriptive notations. He noted that 'Seeger introduced the distinction as that 'between a blueprint of how a specific piece of music shall be made to sound and a report of how a specific performance of any music actually did sound'.[61] By attempting to notate sounds recorded in this Australian landscape, this analysis follows the latter, that of descriptive notation. Secondly, from Hood's writing in 1971 when he stated that 'your notation won't look the way it sounds',[62] it is not expected that the developing landscape notation will appear similar to music notation, in the way we might conventionally expect sound to look like its notation, such as time flowing continuously from left to right.

This analysis took the strategic approach of Schafer from 1993 that, 'what the soundscape analyst must do first is to discover the significant features of the soundscape, those sounds which are important either because of their individuality, their numerousness or their domination'.[63] Schafer distinguished three components of landscape sounds, which he termed 'keynote sounds', 'signals', and 'soundmarks'. Using a musical connotation that connected with an idea of key or tonality of a particular composition he stated that 'the keynote sounds of a landscape are those created by its geography and climate: water, wind, forests, plains, birds, insects and animals'.[64] These he contrasted with signals defined as foreground sounds and they are 'listened to consciously [. . .] they are figure rather than ground'[65] and soundmarks, a term derived from landmark, which refer to 'a community sound which is unique or possesses qualities which make it specially regarded or noticed by the people in that community'.[66]

The sound editing software LogicPro was used in order to allow the repetitious listening to sounds that an accurate transcription required. A 50-second period of distinctive sounds from 9'18" to 10'08" was the first part of the recorded sound to be subject to detailed analysis. First, the three dominant sounds of this segment, three bird-calls, were analysed in terms of the frequency of each of them in 10-second segments. These three sounds are both derived from the geology and climate, and are also the conspicuous foreground sounds of this place, so simultaneously conforming to both Schafer's keynote sounds and signals. This analysis started with a calculation of the 'inner tempo' of each, using Christiansen's formula discussed earlier. This revealed temporal differences between the three sounds of 20 times, from an inner tempo of 2.4, to one of 44. Next, the duration of each of the three sounds were drawn as horizontal lines, denoting the beginning and ending of each part of the calls. The lines have two components, the total length of which shows the duration in seconds, and whether the line is continuous or broken, reflecting the degree of continuity within each call identified. Timbre is notated through words that describe the quality of each call, from bright and sweet, to strident, or dull whirl, an idea that resonates with the words utilised in music to describe the tonal quality of different instruments, or an individual player's sounds.

The pitch of each call was not notated at this stage, due to the difficulty of identifying both their absolute and relative pitch. This challenge of pitch location in bird song was addressed by the leading American ornithologist Aretas A. Saunders (1884–1970) in his 1951 book titled *A Guide to Birdsongs*. He identifies five characters of bird song, listed as time, pitch, loudness, quality and phonetics, acknowledging the similarity with music notation while identifying reasons why it may not be successful in actual field use. As he says, 'birds do not always sing according to human standards of pitch and time. In pitch they may use quarter-tones or even smaller intervals. In time they may vary the rhythm so irregularly that musical measures become inadequate.'[67] He goes on to add that the difficulty of notating birdsong in the dominant parameters in music, of pitch and time, may not have a deleterious effect, saying 'the *exact* pitch and time of bird songs are generally variable between individuals, and therefore not characters that would be of great help in identification'.[68] The notation system he developed uses differential scales for time and pitch, one second represented by one-half inch of horizontal movement, while a half-tone in pitch is represented by a vertical scale

of one-eighth inches. Like the clef signs in music notation that indicate a datum against which drawn pitches can be positioned, he places letters such as C or A on the left of the page to indicate the absolute pitch, with an imaginary line running horizontally from the position of the letter. Regarding the relative pitch he states that:

> in this marking middle C is C and the octaves above it C', C", C''', etc., while the few cases of pitches lower than middle C can be represented by C-1, etc. The majority of bird songs are between C''' and C''''.[69]

Saunders' system of pitch datum, his 'imaginary line' of C running across the page, seems an acknowledgement of the difficulty of attempting to recognise diatonic pitch relationships in the sounds one encounters in landscape. I include pitch only where it is clearly identifiable, instead focusing on the other auditory and spatial properties of landscape sounds.

Two additional parameters were also included in the development of this landscape notation to address other distinctive and critical aspects of these sounds. Firstly, for volume I followed the Western art musical convention of eight degrees of relative volume from *ppp* to *fff*, and that volume symbols in the score are only drawn at the beginnings of changes of volume. Secondly, the direction of the sound sources were added, following the musical prerogative that symbols are placed at the beginning of changes only, and are presumed unchanged until replaced by a following symbol. The recorded sounds of bird calls in flight, which can be from anywhere within a 360-degree direction were drawn as directional lines within a circular symbol. While considering the development of symbols for duration it became clear that a binomial symbol that would denote both duration (through length) and also the level of continuity within the sound (by the use of a continuous line, or a discontinuous one with a dash for each component) could be used. Where the sound source was static, the bisected circle symbol discussed earlier was used, where the sound source was motive an arrow was added to the line head to indicate direction. This detailed analysis, proceeding systematically through the recorded soundtrack, produced such volume of notation that it could not be recorded on a single sheet. Rather like my earlier notations, erasure of parts of previous work became necessary in order to create space to proceed. Constant choices were created about which material should be retained, and which erased. This reflective process resulted in an ongoing, and developing dialogue, working towards the formulation of an answer to Bengtsson's 1967 question of 'what are the essential qualities of the material'.[70]

AN ICONOGRAPHY OF NEW LANDSCAPE NOTATIONS

As Goodman wrote in *Languages of Art*, 'obviously anyone designing a notation will try to minimise the probability of errors [. . .] what distinguishes a genuine notation is not how easily correct judgements can be made but what their consequences are'.[71] It is also acknowledged that the precision of pitch and time in the transcription of sounds of this Australian landscape is limited by my own aural capacity. The identification of pitch and the duration of the sounds is one that might reveal as much about the limits of my own ability than an intrinsic nature of the sounds being emitted. But perhaps this is inevitable. The musicologist Richard Widdess, writing about

the challenges of transcription in ethnomusicology, says this: 'As with translation from another language, some element of interpretation is essential, and the use of a different notation system may force interpretative decisions on the transcriber',[72] before continuing, 'notation preserves those aspects of the music which the *notator* considers essential for its transmission or recall'.[73] The focus of these studies has been on drawing out through notation the 'essential' qualities of sound as a landscape material. In seeking to address how notation systems can be adapted to different musical cultures, the American ethnomusicologist Ter Ellingson sets out a series of five contrasts of emphasis that 'need to be considered both in the study of notation systems and the design of transcription systems'.[74] These are: function (prescriptive /descriptive); reference (articulatory/ acoustic); symbolic mode (iconic/abstract); encoding form (analogue/digital); and musical context (culture specific/intercultural). In regard to the second of these contrasts, this research focuses on the acoustic, not articulatory. It is not concerned with how the sounds are created, as landscape sounds are not the result of players' actions on instruments, but rather on the sounds perceivable by a listener. Ellingson's third pair of contrasting considerations is the iconic, 'relying on synaesthetic parallels with the visual (or another) sense to depict'[75] and which includes Western art music, high and low pitch position, whereas 'all number, letter, and syllabic notations are abstract'.[76] So, Western art music notation combines both, the iconic pictorialism of pitch position or turns with the abstract symbols of durational note values or clef marks. Perhaps like Western art music's pragmatic integration of both iconic and symbolic modes, new landscape notations developed here

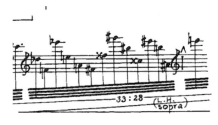

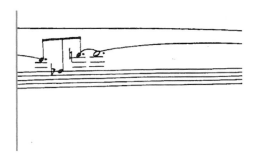

values for inner tempo, relative volume, words to denote timbre or sound quality), and the compound symbol for changing relative volume from both systems. In the transcription of sounds of this Australian landscape space there is also the question of whether analogue or digital encoding might be preferable, which also impacts upon the degree to which the notation will look the way it sounds. As Ellingson explains:

> analog encoding typically produces complex polynomial symbols which display a structural patterning that corresponds to the patterning of the original and are relatively sparse for the amount and complexity of musical information (Hood, 1971, p.76). Digital encoding produces a dense number or relatively simple monomial symbols for a similar amount and complexity of musical information.[78]

In order to examine and extract information regarding the non-musical components of the sounds of this Australian landscape, this research has focused on looking at each parameter in isolation, resolving towards the digital representation of the data, and monomial symbols. While this may lead to the notation appearing more complex as each component is drawn separately, this may be a satisfactory compromise as, unlike music notation, there is not the requirement for landscape notation to be read at speed.

923 ABOVE

To test the effectiveness of the previous studies using notation as a prescriptive tool for the composition of an auditory landscape, I next used over 170 hours of field recordings from Girraween National Park. These sounds, edited in LogicPro

in order to transcribe landscape sounds could also combine these two approaches. Where there are obvious visual parallels for the parameters being notated, iconic pictorialism has the advantage of potential ease of assimilation into the drawing culture of landscape architecture representation. Where such pre-existing connotations are absent or not obviously identifiable, perhaps abstract symbols can be selected. This research purposefully extends the notation of landscape architecture into currently unexplored terrain, where the benefits of pre-existing recognition are unlikely to apply. Having said that Ellingson argues that there might be a sensible predilection for transcriptions to look the way it sounds, saying:

> A general preference for iconic representation seems implicit in Kunst's and Hood's dictum that a transcription "should look the way it sounds". It would certainly be absurd to argue that a transcription "should look different from the way it (the music) sounds", and there is no denying that iconicity can enhance the communicative power of transcriptions.[77]

5.7 Michael Finnissy. Left: Iconic pictorialism of pitch position in Western art music notation. Right: Abstract symbols of duration in Western art music notation, both from *Green Meadows*. 1977.

New symbols developed from this study include the iconic (arrows denoting sound direction, the directionality of sound sources, the number and duration of sonic events), the abstract (numerical

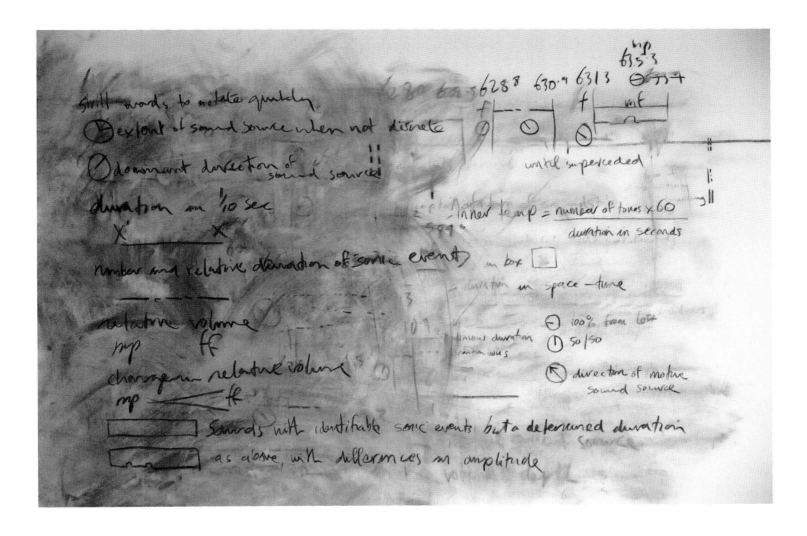

5.8 David Buck. New symbols developed for the sounds of landscape space. 2014.

software in terms of their length, volume and stereo separation, allowed for them to be reconstituted into new sonic materials, exploring how sound as a material of landscape architecture and landscape space might be notated.

Overlaid on the previous studies described earlier, this directly located this work in the temporal and spatial vestiges of the preceding work, conflating music notation, landscape sounds and compositional intent, and was titled *923 Above* (see www.db-land. com/films/923Above). The notation's title comes from the height above sea level in metres of the site where it was located, referring to the local habit of naming wine from the altitude above sea level of its production. This moves the notion of place specificity from the French *terroir* of an agrarian landscape, to that of the naturally occurring characteristics of this landscape. It also makes reference to the primacy in the Australian landscape of elevation, which because of its capacity to produce precipitation in an otherwise dry climate, is a more dominant determinant of landscape habitat than the edaphic factors or orientation of a temperate European landscape where water is not a limiting factor.

These sequential inscriptions in charcoal and colour pencil started with three simple homages to *Green Meadows*: the same determined duration of 655 seconds; three seconds of silence from 3'06" to 3'09"; and an opening in a territory defined as 'unsettled.' This first territory is superseded, by four others, defined as 'menacing', 'spacious', 'still' and 'restless'. Words are used to express these qualities in this initial sketching out as no appropriate musical symbol currently exists. This composition of five broad structures is also a way of drawing out or emphasising certain of the environmental conditions that influence the creation of the sounds: from habitat on wildlife, to rock formations on wind, to edaphic factors on plant species, and on to spatial scale and the micro-temporality of auditory events within the landscape. Each of these five movements, to use a musical term, by implication also constructs a set of physical conditions, as well as acoustic ones (see notation N21).

Each is articulated by varying volume, direction, inner tempo, timbre, and motivity of the sound sources, creating auditory 'scenes' rather than visual ones (see notation N22). Dashed vertical bar-lines begin and end the notation. These denote the structural extent, rather than the temporal one, as I consider this work as not finite, but rather an auditory landscape that will continue to sound in the listeners' imaginations. There is not a definable pulse or trace of metronomic regularity, but rather a sequence of elements of different durations with varying temporal qualities within them. The five movements composed use the following strategies towards the materiality of sound in the notation of their individual qualities:

Unsettled: duration; different sounds occurring together.
Menacing: loudness to create proximity; abruptness of attack and release of sounds; and sounds from different directions.
Spaciousness: quiet, so distant, sounds intermittently heard creating space between them; motive sounds to reveal the spatial extent.
Still: narrow range of volume and time implies no lateral movement.
Restless: unexpected and uncertain sounds (see notations N23–24).

Colours were also added as the notation progressed (see notations N25–26). Rather than the rolling melodic contour that Finnissy refers to in *Green Meadows*, here, analogous to the land in which the sounds were recorded, the overall range is flat, expansive and monotonous at the strategic level in terms of pitch. The pitch of sounds in this landscape largely occurs in the narrow octave range between C3 and C4 on the piano, similar to those identified by Saunders. This is in contrast to the range of inner tempo which varies from the extremes of two, to over 160, created from the rich temporality of the original source material. An expanded sense of spatial depth is created through the drama of this extended volume range. Where in *Green Meadows* there was a tension in places between the simultaneous occurrence of two speeds in the right and left hand, here the tension is not just regarding time, but also becomes expressed through stereo separation of the sounds. This creates an enhanced sense of space in two ways, both by spreading the auditory components over a wider horizontal range through the separation into two channels and also by increasing the sense of spatial depth through adjusting volume, which is strongly perceived as distance.

Enhanced spatial qualities, induced by a separation from sound sources resonates with landscape spaces where the direction, strength and genesis of sounds is often ambiguous. The absorptive and reflective qualities in the varied materiality and scale of landscape, the uneven extent of sound in all directions, and the effect of dynamic environmental conditions on it, from wind to temperature, create complex acoustic conditions. Such uncertainty of sound source has been termed acousmatic, 'a word of Greek origin, discovered by Jerome Peignot and theorized by Pierre Schaeffer, describes "sound one hears without seeing their originating cause"'.[79] According to the French film theorist Michel Chion, 'when we listen acousmatically to recorded sounds it takes repeated hearings of a single sound to allow us gradually to stop attending to its cause and to more accurately perceive its own inherent traits'.[80] I believe this acousmatic nature of the sounds of landscape space encourages us to linger and dwell in it, engaging us in a form of extended temporal listening. But is listening in landscapes equally acousmatic in all scales and with all degrees of familiarity? One can argue that within the field of unobstructed vision, where sight can aid the identification of sound sources, that this

'foreground' auditory landscape is less acousmatic. This mode of listening is defined by Chion as causal, consisting

> of listening to a sound in order to gather information about its cause (or source). When the cause is visible, sound can provide supplementary information about it; for example, the sound produced by an enclosed container when you tap it indicates how full it is.[81]

As the ability of the eyes to support the identification of sounds decreases with distance the listening mode changes. As Chion says, now we focus 'on the traits of the sound itself, independent of its cause and of its meaning'[82], a process termed by French composer Pierre Schaeffer (1910–1995) reduced listening. So as the scale of the landscape increases, the listening experience changes to an increasingly acousmatic one, one that

> draws our attention to sound traits normally hidden from us by the simultaneous sight of the causes – hidden because this sight reinforces the perception of certain elements of the sound and obscures others. The acousmatic truly allows sound to reveal itself in all its dimensions.[83]

Landscape is therefore largely acousmatic at the middle and far distance, less so at the near. Perhaps in landscape architecture, the visual envelope of conventional site analysis needs to be augmented with an auditory envelope, the extent of the landscape space we can perceive through sound. Blesser and Salter term this the *acoustic horizon*, 'the maximum distance between a listener and source of sound where the sonic event can still be heard [. . .] the acoustic horizon is thus the experiential boundary that delineates which sonic events are included and which are excluded'.[84]

At Girraween National Park we sense our gaze alternating between two landscape spaces, experienced simultaneously, the dust at our feet and the haze in the distance. The film *Land of Flowers* (see www.db-land.com/films/LandOfFlowers) captures a single journey across the meadows towards the distant forest and granite peaks beyond. As we navigate the unknown and uneven surface we glance down, then up towards the forest edge. We are conscious of the linearity of our journey directing our attention towards a distant point. Only occasionally do we glance around, when our movement disturbs animal, or reptilian, life in the grass. The auditory landscape is quite different. We are immediately conscious of the array of sounds, both those generated by our movement, as well as those independently occurring. A binary spatial extent in vision is now an encompassing auditory field, an open field that extends beyond the visual one, and one so richly populated. We listen as sounds fill the space from all distances: our footsteps in the grass, to wallaby calls from the forest edge, to birds in flight crying out. While the sun moves slowly over the grass, light diffused by passing clouds creates subtle changes in hues in the meadows. The investigations in *655* revealed a temporal variation between 2 and 160. Through their individual and collective nature, we are drawn towards listening to this temporal variety. Sounds generated by one's movement are affected by the materiality of the landscape spaces. As we approach the granite outcrops sounds are increasingly reflected back at us, while the forest absorbs sounds, muffling their volume and reducing their resonance. Past bush

fires have cleared the grass in places; our footsteps are made silent by the fine dust of the volcanic soil. As this film reveals, the temporality of sound is dramatic indeed.

EARLY DESIGN NOTATION

We now return to the UK, examining aspects of landscape architecture and sound, focused on studies in Rousham garden in Oxfordshire. Rousham was designed by Kent and is often considered to occupy a critical place in the formation of the Picturesque a movement described by English architecture critic Christopher Hussey (1899–1970) as providing 'the earliest means for perceiving visual qualities in nature. It consists in the education of the eye to recognise qualities that painters had previously isolated.'[85] From its long history Rousham provides three critical opportunities for this research: firstly to examine historic aspects of sound in the landscape architecture of one of England's most regarded practitioners; secondly to investigate whether the conventional reading of the Picturesque as a visual movement is correct; and thirdly to provide a landscape space to investigate sound's potential as a material of landscape space. Kent's design at Rousham built upon an earlier, more formal one, by English landscape architect Charles Bridgeman (1690–1738). We have only sparse surviving records of Kent's design for Rousham, a plan, a small sketch of Cuttle Mill, and two fuller drawings of the mill and a more distance folly, with an ink drawing for the Venus Vale. According to French landscape critic Elisabetta Cereghini, at Rousham, Kent, who had spent an earlier decade in Italy from 1709 to 1719,[86] drew upon drawing methods of the *quadratura* painters who 'used geometric devices and perspectives in order

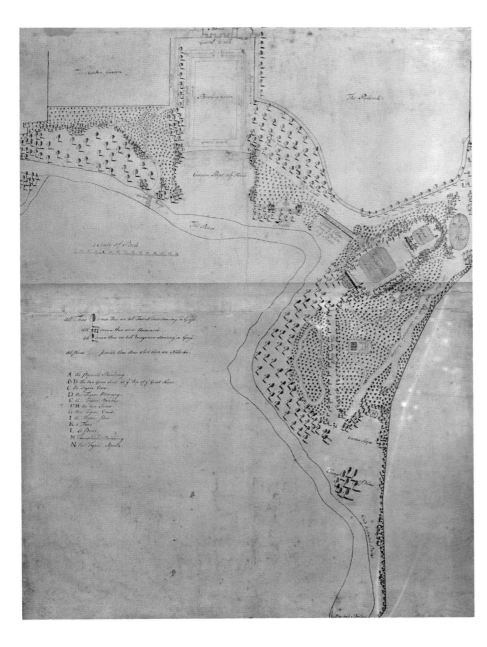

5.9 William Kent. Plan attributed to Kent.
1738. Courtesy Country Life.

to represent the spatial effects of architecture on a flat surface'.[87] These drawing devices were further developed by Italian Giovanni Paolo Pannini (1691–1765) and in his synthesis between the *quadratura* techniques and landscape painting, developed a way to 'use perspective as a means of relating real space to the space represented'.[88] This method, rather than the single visual focus of a conventional perspective drawing, focused on the interconnectivity between the components of a scene. Rather than the representation of a static visual experience, it revealed the relationships between constituents and their connectivity over time. Cereghini describes its use by Kent this way:

> Kent adopted a technique based on the use of oblique perspectives comprised of two or more axial lines converging from points outside the "scene", which no longer corresponded with the line of vision of the spectator. This prompted the spectator to seek out viewpoints independently rather than be confined to any single perspective prescribed by the architect.[89]

On page 25 of Kent's notebook from his Italian travels, he makes reference to two books on perspective. First he mentions 'books of perspective brought into light' (i.e. made public) by Italian painter Giulio Troili (1613–1683) and sold in Bologna by Italian Gioseffo Longi (1620–1691) in 1683 (original title: *Paradossi per praticare la Prospettiva senza saperla, Fiori, per facilitare l'intelligenza, Frutti, per non operare alla cieca. Cognitioni necessarie a Pittori, Scultori, Architetti, ed a qualunque si diletta di Disegno)*[90] and then further mentions a book 'about practical perspective' by Italian author and architect Pietro Accolti (1570–1642), fully titled *Lo Inganno de*

Gl'occhi Prospettiva Practica, published in 1625. On page 25 of Troili's book the illustration shows an iconographic view in plan (*pianta*), an orthographic view raised up (*alzato)*, and a scenographic view as a solid body (*corpo solido)*[91]. From this, Kent perhaps understood that scenography, or theatrical stage design, provided drawing tools more closely allied to the spatial richness of three-dimensional space than those of orthographic perspective. He was certainly significantly influenced by his studies in Italy as his own sketchbook reveals, indeed all of Kent's notes on page 27 of his diary are, in fact, taken directly from page 110 of Troili's text. Cereghini refers to these axial arrangements as oblique angles. But perhaps we can also understand Kent's design through the drawings from Troili's book, which shows how a scene can be simultaneously constructed as horizontal planes, vertical planes, and three-dimensional bodies. The spaces at Rousham are not solely as Cereghini implies, simple points of view, but rather created from the relationships between axes, planes and volumes, which can be simultaneously drawn, and experienced. Integral to this is the topography at Rousham, which Kent's design so skilfully incorporated. A plan view of the main visual axes does indeed show them as being oblique angles, which rarely physically cross but are linked through viewing along them to other axes. But drawing these same axes in section shows the complex spatial construction created by the changing levels. The visual axis becomes much richer for a viewer who, in response to moving through the gardens, discovers these axial arrangements exist not just in two dimensions, but in three.[92] Kent's design and use of the *quadratura* techniques developed by Pannini

as a way of relating the real spaces to the space represented provided the technique for Rousham's development. Cereghini observes in reference to Rousham's main features of Venus Vale, the Praeneste terrace and theatre, saying:

> it is impossible to take in these three features at a single glance because they are set at oblique angles to the viewpoint of the spectator. This spatial device involves the choice of at least three different points of view from to frame the scene. And it now becomes clear in what way the various features are interrelated: a scene viewed in a direct line is comprised also of aspects of those scenes placed at the margins of the spectator's vision, in which the architectural focus is set at an oblique angle to the straight perspective.[93]

Looking at the extent of the visual envelope for 10 of the garden's main features, including the Temple of Echo, Praeneste Terrace, and the sequence of Upper Cascade, Octagon Pool and Lower Cascade, we can see that rather than the spatial clarity one might expect from the axial framework designed by Kent, the spaces created at Rousham are far more amorphous. They are amended first by the topography, which unexpectedly conceals and reveals the axial structure, then further by the now mature planting, which acts as a secondary veil. Instead of axially constructed formal views the visual relationships between the pieces are actually more extensive, ambiguous in form, and interconnected than one might imagine. Kent's drawings for Rousham emphasise places of visual interconnectivity, locations where the visual axes coalesce. The landscape spaces may be structured from these nodes but there is a much broader ambiguity in the places between them.

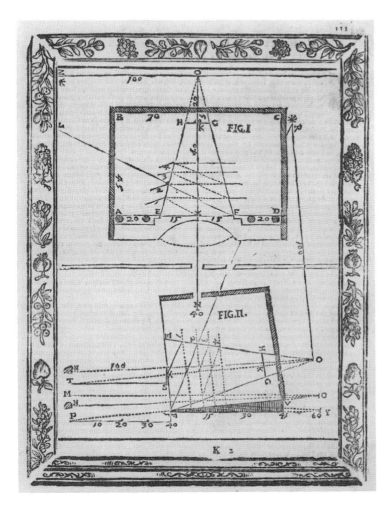

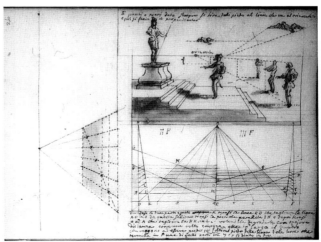

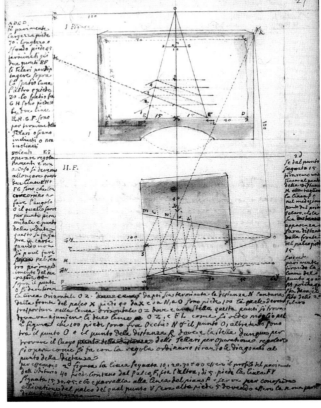

5.10 Giulio Troili. Page 111 from *The Paradox of Perspective*. 1683. ©The British Library Board, 536.l.21.(4.), 111.

5.11 William Kent. Extracts from Kent's *Italian Diary*. Courtesy The Bodleian Library, University of Oxford, *Italian Diary 1714–1715*, M.S.Rawl. D. 1162, fol.26r.

5.12 William Kent. Extracts from Kent's *Italian Diary*. Courtesy The Bodleian Library, University of Oxford, *Italian Diary 1714–1715*, M.S.Rawl. D. 1162, fol.27r.

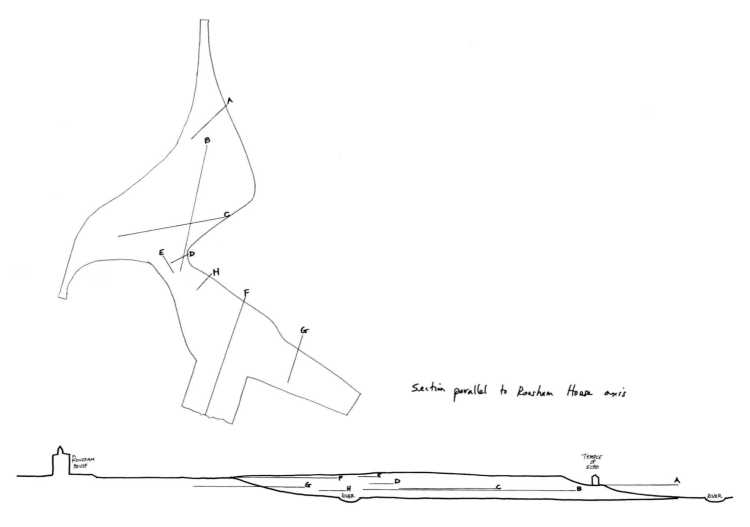

5.13 David Buck. Plan and section showing visual connections from Kent's design for Rousham. Axis – A: Temple of Echo, B: Long Walk with Statue of Apollo, C: Vale of Venus, D: Dying Gladiator, E: Praeneste Terrace, F: Rousham House with Lion and Horse, G: Pyramid. 2014. Adapted from 1:1000 sections drawn and generously provided by Hal Moggeridge.

Returning to Kent's drawings we see that the Cuttle Mill and Eye Catcher are rendered close to the actual scene. The bridge over the Cherwell, the skyline, now with more trees, and the change in agricultural practice from the field behind the Mill with the most distance field, are all in Kent's drawing. Clearly, we know from Cuttle Mill that he was able to accurately render spatial scale and arrangement

in his drawings. But, when we look more closely at Kent's drawing for the Venus Vale, we see that he distorts the scale of the three pools he inserted into the topography at this location. English landscape architect Hal Moggridge has already noted that Kent's drawing 'exaggerates the size of the cascades',[94] and together with the oblique perspective Kent adopts in this drawing, moves it away from representation

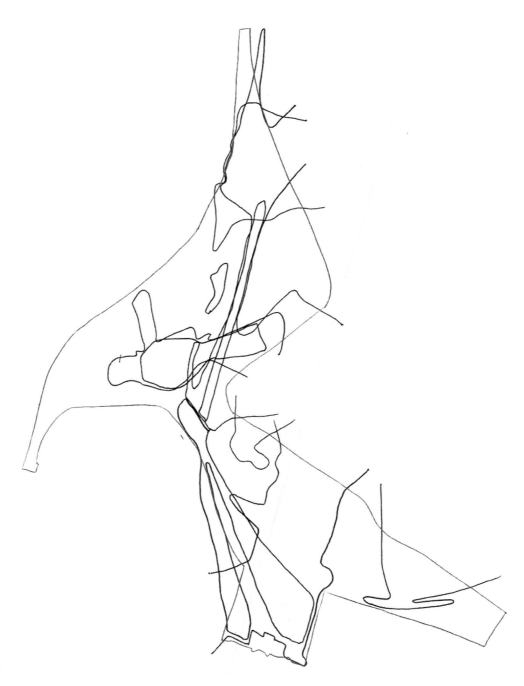

5.14 David Buck. Visual envelope at
Rousham. 2014.

The TEMPLE of the MILL and EYE CATCHER at ROUSHAM

5.15 William Kent. Drawing of *Cuttle Mill* and *Eye Catcher.* *c*.1738–40. Courtesy Country Life.

5.16 David Buck. Photograph of *Cuttle Mill* and *Eye Catcher.* 2014.

towards notation. We are now presented with a work that reveals the arrangement between elements of the design, allowing us to understand how the components of Kent's design operate at Rousham. American architect Stan Allen argues in *Practice: Architecture, Technique and Representation* that 'notations are not pictures or icons. They do not so much describe or represent specific objects, as they specific internal structure and relationship among parts'.[95] This surviving drawing for Rousham by Kent reveals the inter-relationships between fields, axes and routes and can therefore be considered a form of notation.

5.17 William Kent. *Venus Vale. c.*1738–40.
Courtesy Country Life.

5.18 David Buck. Photograph of *Venus Vale.*
2014.

5.19 David Buck. Lower cascade wide view. 2014.

And if we walk back towards the river we now find another element at Rousham, the Praeneste terrace, partially revealed, enticing us towards further exploration of these landscape spaces.

ROUSHAM'S HISTORY OF SOUND

As part of his designs for Rousham, Kent designed, and English builder William Townsend (1676–1731) constructed, a limestone ashlar Temple of Echo.[96] Completed in 1740, the octagonal plan opens out through a pedimented portico to face the River Cherwell, located on a slight rise to capture the sounds of the water at its most animated as it flows around a bend. American landscape historian John Dixon Hunt likens the scenes created by Kent to those of theatrical stages, noting:

> as on the real stage, where word aids image, visitors to Rousham may add a verbal exposition of what they see in order to apprehend the garden's themes, its *genius loci*. Inasmuch as visitors participate by interpreting these scenarios, they are actors as well as spectators in these garden theatres.[97]

Intriguingly, Hunt fails to mention sound as either a narrative strand or a critical component existing in this synthesis between the theatrical and garden stages, given that a history of theatre is hardly a history of silence. It is, of course, likely that Kent was aware of some of the properties of sound as the velocity of sound waves 'was first measured [. . .] by Mersenne in about 1636',[98] and local historian Robert Plot had written in 1677 of the nearby Woodstock Echo.[99] What might the echo at Rousham have been? As the American acoustician John Pierce (1910–2002) has noted, we can calculate the frequency of the number of echoes per second from a simple formula of dividing the speed of sound by the distance between two walls that are reflecting the sound.[100] So, in the case of the Temple of Echo at Rousham, this would be 344 divided by 3.84 metres. So, someone standing in the middle of the space would hear a frequency of 89.583 echoes per second, which if converted into musical pitch would equate to a tone close to F (87.307 for the F between C2 and C3 on the piano). There is also

5.20 David Buck. *Temple of Echo* facing the River Cherwell. 2014.

another aspect to the echoes. The Temple of Echo is located between 62 metres and 100 metres from the bend in the River Cherwell and as Pierce noted 'when we hear the same sound from two sources 20–26 meters (60–80 feet) away (a time difference of 68–80 milliseconds), we hear an echo'.[101] We may not hear these sounds as echoes when we stand inside Kent's building but rather we hear an enhanced sense of the auditory component of landscape space as sounds on three sides are screened by the walls. The Temple of Echo collects sounds and focuses our attention on them.

Is there evidence of a broader culture of sound that Kent might have been aware of when designing Rousham beyond his own Temple of Echo? If Hunt is correct in asserting that Alexander Pope's (1688–1744) poem *The Temple of Fame* (composed in 1711) 'which William Kent certainly had in his library'[102] then Kent must have been aware that this poem on its first page includes the lines:

> O'er the wide prospect as I gaz'd around
> Sudden I heard a wild promiscuous sound
> Like broken thunders that at distance roar
> Or billows murm'ring on the hollow shore[103]

Kent must also have known of the second part of this publication titled *And an Ode for Music of St Cecilia's Day*, which had been written in 1708. Lines 71 to 75 in verse five include the following:

By the streams that ever flow

By the fragrant winds that blow

O'er th' Elysian flowers

By those happy souls who dwell

In yellow meads of Asphodel.

The auditory component of the experience of Rousham was also noted in the anonymous Latin poem *Roushamius Hortus* published in 1747, shortly after the completion of the garden, in *The Museum: or, The Literary and Historical Register*, a bi-weekly publication running from 29 March 1746 to 12 September 1747, where the following lines occur:

> *et per balatus it sinuosus ovium Cherwellus* (and the bleeting of the sheep goes to the winding Cherwell)
>
> *suave ruentem undam per saxa audire sonora,* (sweet wave rushing over rocks to hear,)
>
> *aut decurrentem flumine praecipiti*[104] (the sonorous flow of the river)

This poem later makes reference to '*lasciva in luco dum Philomela canit*' (while the nightingale sings in a grove lascivious), and in additional lines denoted by letters at the end at line f of '*praecipites aquarum lapsus per saxorum*' (the headlong fall of water through rocks). Presumably, this later reference is not to the River Cherwell but to Kent's design for the upper and lower cascade. Another source of reference for the experience of Rousham's landscape comes from a contemporary source. In a letter dated 1750 to the absent family, to Clement Cottrell's wife and husband, the gardener John Macclary (subsequently known as Clary), described a clockwise walk starting from the Hall door. He noted that from the journey through the garden 'we look into four Countys, and see no less than ten parrish Churches at one time'.[105] He also mentioned that elements outside of the garden curtilage formed part of the experience of Rousham, noting that 'there is a fine Meadow, cut off from the garden only by the River Cherwell whereon is all sorts of Cattle feeding, which looks the same as if they was feeding in the garden'.[106] The only mention of sound in his letter is in reference to Townsend's building[107] where he states 'you goe in & sett down and hear a very fine Echo'.[108] It is certainly curious that Macclary, in his letter extolling the virtues of the ambulation of the gardens, fails to mention, with the exception of the Temple of Echo, the sounds one would have heard throughout the journey he describes. Hunt assigns this to the fact that 'he must equally be telling what he knows they will appreciate about Rousham' and that 'a person's prejudices, assumptions, and habits [. . .] determine discourse'.[109] So, rather than sound not being present in the experience of Rousham in 1750, Macclary was not attending to its contribution on the assumption that it would not be enticing to the estate's owners. Its absence reflects the letter's audience's presumed disinterest, rather than its actual absence. What might Macclary have heard during his walk around the landscape? From historical records we know that in 1645, 120 acres of pasture along the Cherwell was enclosed, but otherwise the open field system remained until 1775.[110] A map of 1721 shows enclosed land by the river, but otherwise the surrounding land was a mix of open fields and common meadows. Reference is also made to a number of 'leets', which are similar to the more commonly used 'leys', implying land that was seeded with grass for periods from between

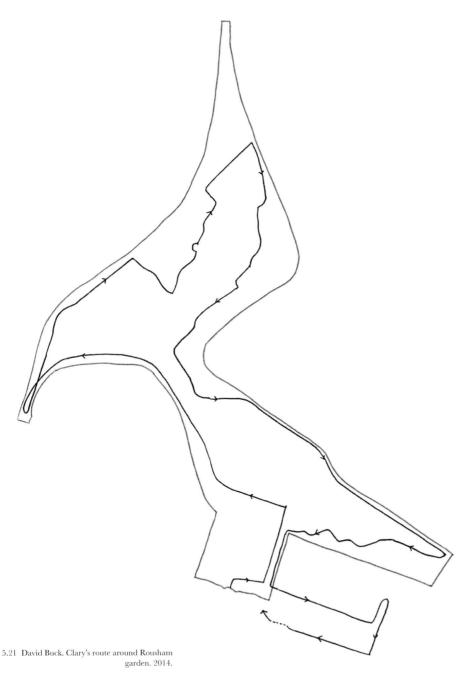

5.21 David Buck. Clary's route around Rousham garden. 2014.

one season to a limited number of years, rather than permanent pasture. This may have been part of a crop rotation system in which seeded grassland alternated with arable crops including turnips and fallow. By 1770, crops included wheat, barley, oats, ryegrass, beans, peas, while livestock (including sheep, cattle and oxen) also featured prominently. He would not have heard children enjoying break-time play as the school at Rousham was not opened until 1785.[111] By 1801, the 1039 acres of Rousham Parish was divided into 59% arable land, 35% permanent grassland, with the remaining 5% woodland.[112] Tree and shrub planting inside Rousham was likely to have been then, as it is now, a rich habitat for birds, including the nightingales mentioned in the poem *Roushamius Hortus*, with their habitat requirements[113] of tree canopy with low dense planting underneath.

As a corollary to Clary's 1750 letter, my description below follows the same clockwise route but instead focuses on the auditory experience of the landscape one January morning in 2014:

Water trickling into the ha-ha, bird song from the Yew hedge. The river Cherwell is silent, only your footsteps on the gravel. Songbirds singing and crows cawing. A prop plane drones, a car drives by. Blackbirds call from high up in the canopy of the Larch tree. A small tickle of water. Birds call again. Louder now as you walk. There is no sound from the rill as the water is so shallow. Bird calls again from the tree canopy. Blackbirds startled by your movement call out warning cries. A quiet murmur as water flows into the Cold Bath. Traffic passes. The Temple of Echo. We hear echoes, reflected sounds, of muffled birdsong, periods of vehicles passing controlled by the traffic lights on the bridge, and in quieter times, the water flowing in front of you in the River

Cherwell. The sounds from the river are loudest as the water flows past tree branches that trail in the water. Crows call from deep woodland. Crows above the Arcade are cawing. Sounds of crows and the running river water from a wide angle in front of you. A bird calls from the tree canopy directly in front. Bird song behind. A wood pigeon in the tree above calls out. Occasional bird song emanates from the Laurel, Holly and Yew. Pigeons' wings clatter. Doves circle from the dovecot, their wings cutting through the air as they circle in groups.

What is striking on this journey is that sounds are amended at a dramatic range of scales. Simply walking behind a tree stem near the Praeneste Terrace causes the sound from the water flowing into the octagon pond from the rill to be perceptibly reduced. Undulations in the topography function in the same way. Standing in front of the upper cascade with one's back to it, one can hear the sounds of water falling behind you, whereas the lower cascade is silent. All one sees are the octagon pond and river beyond. The period of Rousham's completion marked the end of the era of natural sound dominance, to be replaced by an increasing mechanisation. Exactly one hundred years after Clary's letter, in 1850, the opening of Heyford station on the Oxford to Banbury train line permanently changed the sounds experienced at Rousham.

The visual experience of Rousham is time interrupted or suspended – both through the time of the journey with its places to pause, and through the references to the past. Hunt writing about Rousham's visual references notes that 'now it is also worth asking what the contemporary literature does *not* mention, or at least what it seems either to take for granted or else not bother to spell out',[114]

strikingly, sound would seem to be first on this particular list. Clary's description of a series of views gives a sense of time interrupted, whereas my response to Clary, with thanks, through the description following in his footsteps emphasises the temporal continuity of the experience of landscape sounds. Unlike vision we cannot avert our ears or direct our hearing at will, but rather sense sound continuously. Our movement through the landscape, echoing Clary's route, also creates sound in two different ways. Firstly, our footsteps change with the material qualities we are walking over, at Rousham from grass to gravel, from leaves to sawn stone. We are investigating the spatial and material qualities of landscape spaces as we move through them. Secondly, our movement generates sound through the movement of wildlife that our progress creates, both by fleeing our arrival, and conversely drawn towards us. We are not just passive recipients of sound, but also active generators of it. We may not have records of Kent describing the sounds of Rousham per se, but we can be confident that he was aware of the auditory component of landscape experience and its significant presence in the literary sources to which Rousham draws and to which Kent was aware.

FIVE OVER ELEVEN

Intriguingly, what appears largely overlooked in conventional landscape architecture discourse is that at the same time that the understanding of landscape as a visual construct was becoming embedded – Wiley's landscape as 'a unit of visual space'[115] – that English writers Pope (1688–1744), William Gilpin (1724–1804), and Kent, all held as so influential in the formation of the Picturesque, were also designing and writing about the auditory component of landscape. Pope for example, in a letter to his friend Martha Blount (1690–1762) in 1724 when describing the landscape at Sherborne, wrote 'you lose your eyes upon the glimmering of the Waters under the wood, & your ears in the constant dashing of the waves'.[116] While Gilpin describing his observations on the mountains and lakes of Cumberland and Westmorland in 1772, wrote this:

> Often too the road would appear to dive into some dark abyss, a cataract roaring at the bottom: while the mountain-torrents on every side rushed down the hills in notes of various cadence, as their quantities of water, the declivities of their fall, their distances, or the intermission of the blast, brought the sound fuller, or fainter to the ear; which organ became now more alert, as the imagination depended rather on it, than on the eye, for information.[117]

Beyond a mere description of its auditory nature, Gilpin also understood that sound provided a method to investigate the material and spatial properties of landscape, and to reveal different qualities from those attended to by vision. He reminded travellers to the Lake District of the differences in sounds of Derwentwater and Windermere. He informed visitors that 'every lake, being surrounded by rocks and mountains of a structure peculiar to itself, forms a variety of instruments; and of course, a variety of sounds. The echoes of no two lakes are alike.'[118] These differences in sound were so distinctive, he noted, that the Duke of Portland, who had properties in the area, had a boat with brass guns fitted for the purposes of exciting these echoes. Gilpin proposed that 'instead of cannon, let a few French-horns and clarionets be introduced'[119] so that the material and spatial properties of these landscapes, even down to individual rocks, could be appreciated.[120]

Apart from its Temple of Echo and rich auditory profile, Rousham's design is also distinctive in the broad references that Kent himself used included those beyond the physical edge of the garden or the historical allegory. A drawing in the collection in Chatsworth in Derbyshire includes a sketch elevation and partial plan of Cuttle Mill, which was, in fact, a building on the far side of the river and as Hunt notes 'by giving it a gothick front; this heightening of an indigenous building, making it participate in the overall scheme at Rousham',[121] and shows this landscape open to spatial connections as well as literary or allegorical ones. Developing earlier designs by Bridgeman, Kent's proposals were considered with strong reference to the existing conditions of the site, his landscape designs developed not through imposition, but through intervention. The site was re-worked by Kent through small insertions of new material rather, than wholesale reconfiguration. As Hunt has noted, Rousham's history draws upon a disparate range of sources, saying 'it is the juxtapositions already noticed, ancient and modern, classical and gothick, natural and artificial, foreign and English, that constitutes its "subject"'.[122] Rousham contains a number of focal nodes created by Kent through the importation of visual references from another culture. Peter Scheemaker's (1691–1781) statue of a lion attacking a horse refers to a similar one at Villa D'Este; Rousham's Praenestre Terrace references the Temple of Fortune overlooking Palestrina, here surveying not a city but the River Cherwell; the Vale of Venus refers to the Villa Aldobrandini in Frascati with its famous water theatre.[123] Hunt refers to the possibility for material absences to also be a constituent part of Rousham's design, saying

> like those old gaps which Alexander Pope left in the parallel texts of his *Imitations of Horace* to signal what could not be duplicated or what needed extrapolation from the Latin. At Rousham, antique and Renaissance Rome are there but not there, implied but eloquently absent.[124]

This research supplements the visual allegories and connections of Kent's design with a new series of auditory materials, materials that in a sense are also there but not there, exploring the introduction of auditory stimuli from another culture.

I decided to transpose the sounds I composed from the Girraween National Park described earlier in *923 Above* into an English landscape to explore how the explicit introduction of sound might resonate with the thinking of Gilpin, Pope, and Kent. As Gilpin noted, sound can both reveal different properties of landscape space than vision, and in doing so can emphasise the temporality of landscape. While the Duke of Portland fired canons, I less-intrusively brought the five movements composed in *923 Above* through digital means to Rousham garden. Each of these five composed sounds from another place (unsettled, menacing, spaciousness, still, restless) were treated as separate sonic events so that they could be individually placed within the space of Kent's Rousham, additions to 11 sound sources created by Kent's design. These five sounds are 'located' in the landscape spaces through the use of augmented aurality software that allows us when visiting Rousham to listen to them via the GPS signal of an Android phone. Each of the sounds is located as a circular auditory space with

a specified diameter. Entering the space is detected by the device, which then plays the specified sound until one leaves, restarting if you re-enter. Fading in and out depending upon your proximity to the centre of the circle, the device operates as a live sound source, the closer one approaches, the greater the volume. Both in-situ and introduced sounds are heard simultaneously as you walk.

Positioned within the existing sounds of the site, this new auditory material was connected not by axial visual arrangements or the unidirectional linear temporality of a timeline, by the temporality of an individual's movement through the landscape. This is a form of through-composition where each journey creates a new work. This ability to construct one's own landscape space – through sound – directly resonates with Kent's design at Rousham. As Moggridge in his studies of Rousham from 1986 noted, there are over a thousand variations of routes through this landscape space with 'none passing along the same walk twice and each leaving

5.22 David Buck. The introduced sounds located on a plan of Rousham garden denoted by white circles, the grey ones are recordings of the existing sounds added during the project development. 2013.

a significant level in the northern part of the garden unvisited, temptation for another day'.[125]

When we compare the acoustic horizons for Rousham with the visual envelopes, this reveals both the inter-connectivity between the complementary senses of vision and sound, while also potential differences in scale between these two sensory worlds. There are a number of discrete permanent sound sources within Kent's design: the water outfall from the Octagon Pond, the water flowing into it from the rill in the Watery Walk, water from the same rill into the Cold Bath, the Upper Cascade with Venus and Cupids, the Lower Cascade, and, of course, the River Cherwell itself. Additionally, varied sounds emanate from a much larger area, from the transport systems of train, road and air; from farming activities; from the habitats created from Kent's design as well as the wider agrarian landscape; and from the inhabitation of spaces within the garden. Using this hand-held device in order to focus attention on the sounds of Rousham has echoes with the use of the Black Mirror (or Claude Glass) by artists in the eighteenth century. Claude Mirrors were hand-held square, rectangular, circular or oval,[126] with a convex mirrored surface used to modify the views of landscape spaces in order to draw out tonal ranges and emphasise painterly qualities. The digital equivalent also provides an instrument to measure qualities of landscape space in-situ, drawing our attention to aspects of auditory experience and emphasising their qualities. While the polished glass with black backing or the polished obsidian that was used in Black Mirrors stimulated one's imagination through reflected light rays, the digital device supplements this through emitted sound waves.

Walking in the landscape of Rousham we are able to listen simultaneously to the live in-situ sounds together with those composed from *923 Above*. As Hunt noted in his studies of the Picturesque, 'further, throughout the relatively small garden Kent emphasized both the old and the new, classical and Gothick, often side by side; by these juxtapositions our attention is drawn to the new English location of classical ideas and forms'.[127] The same is true for these sound interventions at Rousham. They focus attention on the Englishness of the ambient sounds through their relationship with the imported ones. While some of the sounds from Australia are place specific, others share common sources: crows can be heard cawing in both. Bringing together these two landscape spaces acoustically, we are drawn to notice the rich variety of sound, from the varied locations of Rousham as well as those from Girraween heard through the headphones. Our movement through the historic landscape spaces is given new delight by this experience. In synthesising a landscape space through sound, its vivid contribution to our experience of it is made manifest.

UT PICTURA SONITU

The notion of *ut pictura sonitu* takes the meaning of exploring a sisterhood between the arts of sound and painting as influences on landscape architecture, rather than a strict definition implied by a more direct referencing of *ut pictura poesis* as a translation of classical texts into image. The eighteenth-century Picturesque drew references from a proximity to *ut pictura poesis*, which as Hunt noted was not a singular reference direction but included a two-way interaction, 'as in picture, so in a poem, and vice versa'.[128] But sound surely might also function as

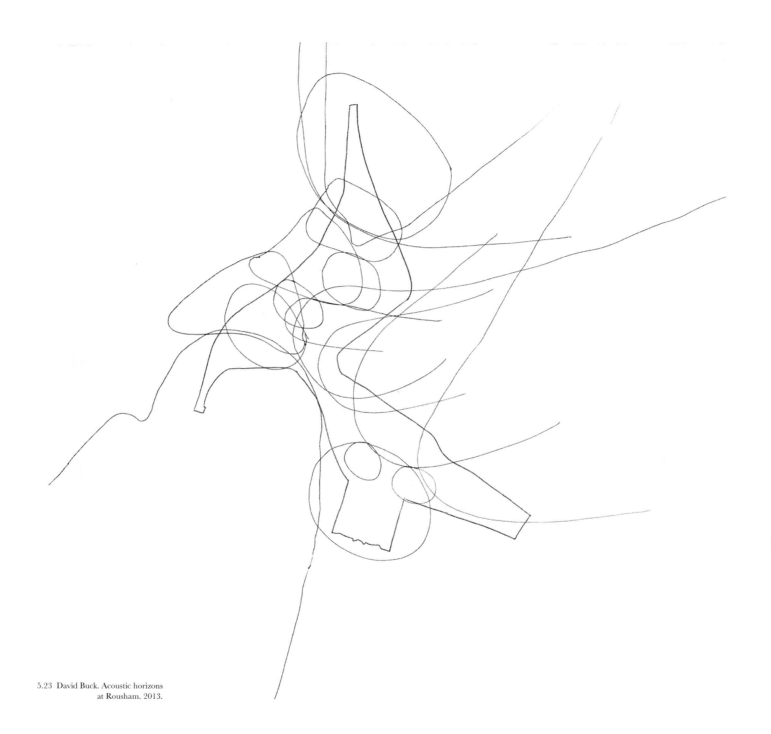

5.23 David Buck. Acoustic horizons
at Rousham. 2013.

proxies for pictures and that landscape architecture might refer to what I term *ut pictura sonitu*. Like literature, sound also can provide a narrative source and a sensory stimulus, and can also connect us to historic ideals. As Goodman noted, 'objects and events, visual and nonvisual, can be represented by either visual or nonvisual symbols'.[129] At Rousham's garden scenes, Kent made the visitor complicit in the stories that linked across time to a broader history. Conscious of the ability of sound as an equal evocator with vision, as part of this he designed the Temple of Echo, still standing in the landscape today. This research adds to this history. Rather than just ancient texts giving gravitas to garden designs, sound also evokes places and past histories. But, in doing

so it builds upon more universal links that cut across cultural ranges and time spans much more than the simple idolatry of ancient Rome. Perhaps Kent understood this ubiquity when he referenced sound at Rousham.

I wished to see whether the broadening of landscape materiality to include sound might also allow a re-interpretation of the Picturesque itself, addressing a previously omitted aspect of it. After all, if Gilpin, writing in 1772, wrote expansively on the auditory component of landscape, wouldn't it be valuable to see if this connection still resonated? If Hill is correct when he states that 'working in conjunction rather than competition, the hybridisation of historical and geographical references within a building and garden is characteristic of the picturesque',[130] then by introducing sounds into the experience of the landscape at Rousham this research directly connects with the Picturesque. In doing so this research ennobles sound in the sensory appreciation of landscape.

Rousham can certainly seem an appropriate choice for examining the introduction of alternative sensory sources. Walpole describes Rousham as 'by Kent, a half kind of gothick',[131] and so by implication from its design origins, open to other sources and combinations of influences. Hunt sees these comparative influences as part of the eighteenth century's 'growing search for new "natural" styles in the arts'.[132] So the addition of new 'natural' sounds, albeit from non-native sources (of course, like the Italian references in Kent's design), and arranged and then synthesised into new sounds, connects this new auditory landscape space at Rousham, to the eighteenth-century notions of what nature meant in garden art. Landscape architecture itself is a synthetic construct, appropriating from ideas of 'nature' in order to allow us to conceive and construct it.

Hunt writing about the decline of the universal language of *ut pictura poesis*, notes that 'Lockean psychology and the rise of sentiment fostered individual responses, which in their turn neglected the universal languages of *ut pictura poesis*'.[133] I would argue that our response to sound is more universal than culturally defined, and so connects us back to the beginnings of the Picturesque, rather than those of the latter half of the eighteenth century that Hunt describes above.

Intriguingly, Kent's use of visual references from both real places and idealised ones resonates with Finnissy's use of equivalent sources for his evocation of landscape in *Green Meadows*. Finnissy brought emotions from the experience of English landscape space as well as interpreting musical notions from its topography and time, while Kent brought the experience of Italian landscape architectural spaces to Rousham, interweaving it into the existing. While the use of these visual cues in Kent's design required a classical education or experience of the Grand Tour, sound permits a more open, intuitive, and individual response to place. If the Picturesque of the eighteenth century needed an external stimulus – painted or poetic – then the new landscape architecture conceived and constructed in this research through the materiality of sound at Rousham provides a new possible source. From this research an auditory landscape can be considered more pluralistic, timeless, and individual, as each of us experiences it differently. The ear will come to the world of landscape space without the long history of reinforcement that the eye would bring. Hunt, in 1992 discussing visual and verbal meanings in garden history, states that:

> to label buildings classical or *gothick*, let alone to say that a pavilion is "built in the Tuscan order," as a Rousham steward does in 1750, or to name the mythological figure which a statue is supposed to represent, or to call a terrace, as has already had to be done, Praeneste, is to encode these objects with meaning. And we can only fully understand such meanings if we can, in the first place, share the literary or verbal language that articulates them.[134]

Sound requires no such pre-existing history or a narrowly prescribed culture. Removed of this necessity, it connects us directly to the experience of places. The sound of wind rushing through tree tops, for example, does not require a cultural reading but immediately reveals spatial extent and micro temporal changes of the weather. Sound, unlike vision, connects us directly to experience of landscape spaces without cultural veils.

Linda Cabe Halpern notes that:

> Composition, viewpoint, and other details of a picture can be used as evidence of a prevailing attitude at the time when a view was painted. The format of a painting, in addition to being a response to the topography of an actual garden, includes clues as to the ideology lying behind certain kinds of garden design. Most garden views do not show us what a viewer could have seen, but are instead *characteristic*—concentrating and encapsulating what were considered the most important aspects of the design of a garden.[135]

So, pictures both guide as well as describe how we understand and experience landscapes. Perhaps the absence of an equal auditory history of gardens is due to the fact that the methods in which they can be described, and so guide and nurture this aspect of landscape appreciation, has been missing. There is of course, in music, exactly such a history, where sounds from and evocative of landscape are recorded in notation, providing precisely such a historic record that in the visual field is so amply provided by painted and drawn representations. This research directly addresses this, providing direct tools and guides to aid appreciation of the sounds of designed landscapes spaces. As Goodman commented, the mode of representation helps to define the field itself, noting that 'the making of a picture commonly participates in making what is to be pictured'.[136] Halpern notes that in the early eighteenth century 'sets of painted views of parts of gardens began to be produced in addition to single house portraits that included gardens',[137] and that these paintings showed the variety of scenes, emphasising the varied constituents that made up the garden's composition. They also:

> allowed an observer of the pictures to seem to discover a garden in an experiential way rather than to know its form at a single glance, as one does with a bird's-eye view. This gradual discovery of the garden through paintings conformed both to the way in which a viewer would visit the actual garden and also to current ideas about the importance of learning about the world through experiment—gradually accumulating knowledge of the parts to construct a mental image of the whole.[138]

Halpern goes on to assert the importance of a drawn record to guide taste and provide an education in how landscapes might be designed, noting that 'Picturesque tourists approached particular views by searching for correspondences with the compositional principles associated with Italianate landscape painters'.[139]

CONCLUDING THE PICTURESQUE

The philosophical background to the Picturesque[140] can be traced to the writings of English philosopher John Locke whose seminal 1689 publication titled *An Essay Concerning Human Understanding* provided new thoughts on how the senses operated. Locke's central thesis was that both knowledge and reason were derived from experience. He saw two equal sources of the ideas that humans could develop through observation. The first of these was from external objects, termed 'sensations', and secondly from an internal sense of perception and thought, which he termed 'reflection'. For Locke, all of the senses operated in perception and they entered our minds simply, directly, and unmixed, while acknowledging that they produced different responses:

> For, though the sight and touch often take in from the same object, at the same time, different ideas; – as a man sees at once motion and colour; the hand feels softness and warmth in the same piece of wax; yet the simple ideas thus united in the same subject, are as perfectly distinct as those that come in by different senses.[141]

Locke noted that what may be said of colour and smell, could also be said of taste and sounds, as the qualities that we perceive were not intrinsic to the objects themselves but rather through the sensations they elucidated. Considered central to the development of the Picturesque in the early eighteenth century, however, was Locke's belief that although all senses operated in our observation of the world around us, that they did so unequally. For him, sight was 'the most comprehensive of all our senses, conveying to our minds the ideas of light and colours, [. . .] and also the far different ideas of space, figure, and motion'.[142] As Hill notes, conventional understandings of the Picturesque are that it 'draws attention to the pleasures and problems of seeing'.[143] But there is an alternative reading of the Picturesque that Locke's thesis implies. Although he believed vision to be the dominant sense, he also proposed that all of our other senses could operate in similar ways. If hearing as well as vision could create 'sensations' and 'reflections' to use Locke's terms, surely it is possible for sound also to be Picturesque, if we understand it as being the pleasure brought forth from our perception of the natural world.

By the end of the eighteenth century, these ideas had been further developed in the writings of English author Uvedale Price (1747–1828) in his *Essays on the Picturesque, as Compared with the Sublime and Beautiful, and on the Use of Studying Pictures, for the Purpose of Improving Real Landscape*, published in 1810. Explaining in the preface of his belief in the inter-relationship between pictures and picturesque scenery, he stated 'this Essay, undertaken to treat of two subjects, distinct, but intimately, connected; and which, as I conceive, throw a reciprocal light on each other'.[144] He believed that a study of pictures would free one from both just a fashionable arrangement of objects and equally from the dangers of looking at nature alone, without, as he noted, 'having acquired any just principles of selection'.[145] Certainly, he saw one advantage of studying pictures of nature, in spite of having the real thing in front of us, was that we would benefit from the accumulated experiences of history. Acknowledging that these representations of landscape excluded some aspects of time, he noted that 'the great change which the growth and decay of trees must produce in the original work of the artist'[146] would be missing if one revisited the landscape rendered in paintings. The absence of time was certainly a weakness of the pictorial representation of landscape. He saw that the absence of a long history of designed landscapes, which might have led to an accepted canon of works, required us out of necessity to look instead at paintings. Now, 200 years later, it is particularly ironic that in spite of a much enhanced canon of designed landscapes, the legacy of pictorialised nature still too often leads to time being excluded, together with sound. Price argued for the inclusion of two overlooked sources of human pleasure, variety 'the power of which is independent of beauty, but without which even beauty itself soon ceases to please' and intricacy, 'a quality which, though distinct from variety [...] might be defined that *disposition of objects, which by a partial and uncertain concealment, excites and nourishes curiosity*'.[147] His description of the visual qualities of places is intense. He criticises the tameness of plantation trees, for example, by contrasting them with old neglected pollards, which:

> stretch out their limbs across these hollow roads, in every wild and irregular direction: on some, the large knots and protuberances, add to the ruggedness of their twisted trunks; in others, the deep hollow of the inside, the mosses on the bark, the rich-yellow of the touch-wood, with the blackness of the more decayed substance, afford such variety of tints, of brilliant and mellow lights, with deep and peculiar shades.[148]

Price's book was written as a critique of the manicured lawns and lines of the landscapes epitomised by 'Capability' Brown. He refers to Gilpin's definition of *Picturesque objects* as those 'which please from some quality, capable of being *illustrated in painting*',[149] while finding it both too vague and confined, arguing for Picturesque characteristics to be as distinct as the sublime or beautiful. Price, while acknowledging the implication that the Picturesque might refer only to visual objects, was convinced that:

> the name and reference only are limited and uncertain, and that the qualities which make objects picturesque, are not only as distinct as those which make them beautiful or sublime, but are equally extended to all our sensations by whatever organs they are received; and that music (though it appears like a solecism) may be as truly picturesque, according to the general principles of picturesqueness, as it may be beautiful or sublime.[150]

Price noted the aural landscape could also be Picturesque, that discords in music could be analogous to sharp and angular objects in vision. He saw no reason why music by Italian composer Giuseppe Domenico Scarlatti (1685–1757) or English composer Joseph Hadyn (1732–1809) could not be Picturesque as

> a movement, from its sudden, unexpected, and abrupt transitions, from a certain playful wildness of character and appearance of irregularity, is no less analogous to similar scenery in nature, than the concerto or the chorus, to what is grand or beautiful to the eye.[151]

He went on to say that 'there is, indeed, a general harmony and correspondence in all our sensations when they arise from similar causes, though they affect us by means of different senses'.[152] Price summarised his Picturesque as roughness, sudden variation, and irregularity, locating it between the sublime and beautiful. He argued that the Picturesque was a process that worked with both natural and artificial objects, creating the possibility for composed sounds to be as effective as found ones. Critically, he saw that while beauty belonged to freshness, time created Picturesque qualities, again supporting sounds inclusion. Price argued that an essential quality of pictures, but not of other arts, was wholeness, noting:

> if there is one thing in the universal range of the arts peculiarly required to be a whole, it is a picture. In pieces of music, particular movements may without injury be separated from the whole; in every species of poetry, detached scenes, episodes, stanzas, &c. may be considered and enjoyed by themselves; but in a picture, the forms, tints, lights and

shadows, all their combinations, effects, agreements, and oppositions, are at once subjected to the eye [. . .] the picture wants it's [sic] most essential quality.[153]

So vision, rather than the other senses, requires completeness in its apprehension. He went on to say that the visual elements that might be contained within a picture can also bring pleasure without being pictorialised, noting that the charms of spring are universally felt. In doing so, he opened the way for landscapes to be made beautiful or picturesque through design,[154] and that a representation of landscape might guide us towards these design improvements. Although commonly understood as an exclusive insistence on the visual, Price, in fact, willingly accepted the contribution towards the experience of a place through other senses, merely suggesting that pictures were – amongst the arts – particularly suited as a media to understand the differences between beauty, the sublime, and his new category of the Picturesque. He noted that 'though picturesqueness and deformity are by their etymology so strictly confined to the sense of seeing, yet there is in the other senses a most exact resemblance to their effects'.[155] Eighteenth-century discussions in music theory also drew upon the similarities between poetry and music. The English composer John Potter (1754–1804), writing in 1762, noted that:

> we shall find, that a mind rightly qualified for the study of the sublime science of music, should be capable of taking the representations and images of things set before it by the variety of sounds, as in lively, distinct, and exact a manner, as a mirror of fine glass reflects the objects presented to it, simply as they are, without alteration.[156]

Like Locke, he saw that our first conceptions of sound might be simple and small in number, but that these could by considered attention, be noticeably increased. Composers' great ability he saw as 'to be able to perform the same wonders by sounds, that a delicate poet commands by words'.[157] Beyond this, he believed that:

> for this reason the musician unquestionably claims preheminence [sic] over the poet. For musical description (if I may be allowed the expression) is more difficult than poetical, and requires a stronger faculty of imagining, and a juster manner of conception. Let the poet, give a description of a tempest, or a sky enrag'd with storms, flashing out lightening, and clouds bursting with thunder [. . .] But music's thunder shakes the very soul, and raises each tumultuous passion in the breast![158]

For Potter, music might not directly represent in the way that painting could, but excited the same feelings in the listener as vision did in an observer, and was an equal awakener of the senses. Locke's idea was that the senses could be trained. The ready availability of pictures was a perfect tool for this in the visual construction of landscape. Perhaps the reason for the paucity of sound in landscape architecture was not its absence from the experience of places (as writings from Potter, Gilpin and Price readily acknowledged) but rather the means to train the sense of hearing in the absence of readily observable, or readily available, tools to do so. Knowledge of vision could be obtained through pictures but how could an equal knowledge of sound? This historic deficit still continues and consequently informs this research, which in providing tools for a priori study could, be thought of as a conclusion of the Picturesque movement. The notation *923 Above* developed five new compositions of sounds for Rousham and provides this framework to allow for the development of the auditory component of landscape. If as Gilpin suggests Picturesque objects contain qualities capable of being illustrated in painting, then why cannot Picturesque objects include sound, now that through this research, the qualities of inner tempo, spatial extent, volume and direction, are capable of being pictorialised in notation.

Locke's ideas were developed further by the middle of the eighteenth century. Swiss philosopher Jean-Jacque Rousseau (1712–1778) wrote that 'the effect of colours is due to their permanence and that of sounds to their succession',[159] while earlier German writer Gotthold Ephraim Lessing (1728–1781) in his 1766 publication *Laokoon, oder Über die Grenzen der Maleri und Poesis* had expressed similar ideas. The English musicologist Stephen Rumpf notes in reference to Lessing's arguments that 'painting and sculpture inhabit space, he explained, while poetry operates through time. The visual arts should therefore represent the single "pregnant" moment, while poetry should represent narrative sequences.'[160] If poetry and pictures respectively occupy both time and space, then why cannot sound substitute for pictures as it also exists spatially? But, moreover, as sound is of both time and space, can we not argue that it is the quintessential material for *ut pictura poesis* in a new Picturesque? Sound can function both sequentially as well as spatially. Sound can represent both time and space.

So, why is it that conventional readings of the Picturesque fail to see the possibilities of sound as a valid basis for it? Certainly, one influence was Locke's hypothesis that vision was the dominant sense. But it can also be traced to the relationship between the representation of landscapes' visual qualities in paintings, and the paucity of their equivalents for the representation of sound. To return to Price's idea that representations allow us to draw upon the accumulated experiences of history, the sounds of landscape were not available in representations in the same way that the visual qualities were and yet the advantages of a representational language were clear. As Price noted, 'the chief object I had in view, that of recommending the study of pictures and of the principles of painting, as the best guide to that of nature, and to the improvement of real landscape'.[161] So Price articulated a four-way interaction. We could learn both from representational objects – the painting themselves – but also from the related theories of representation. In doing so, it would allow us both to better appreciate the qualities studied earlier when we found them in nature, and would also permit their use in design. Transcribing this to listening, does studying notation and principles of music composition guide us towards the study and design of aural landscapes? Like pictures, notation provides a means of study and a way to acquire *a priori* knowledge of sound, which can be used both in the appreciation of sounds we discover as *objets trouvés* in the natural world, while also providing a means to compose sounds in the landscapes we design.

There is no reason why sound cannot function in similar ways to vision does in conventional readings of the Picturesque. As Goodman noted 'nothing is intrinsically a representation; status as representation is relative to symbol system',[162] continuing, 'representation is frequent in some arts, such as painting, and infrequent in others, such as music'.[163] He also noted that 'pictures [. . .] have to be read; and the ability to read has to be acquired'.[164] The notations developed in this research provide the means for the ability to listen to sounds to be acquired, acquired through studying them in notation.

NOTATION OF MATERIAL

In *Meadows* we see that landscape can spark musical compositions through reference to aspects of topography, ambulation, speed of movement, and the emotions of being in a particular landscape space. Landscape as a musical inspiration can be real or idealised, experiential or imagined. In examining Finnissy's *Green Meadows* in the film *Pink Elephants* we find that new and complex forms of musical time, far beyond those of pre-twentieth-century music, can, in fact, be notated. The film *655* from 2013, examines landscape through the prism of the natural world, the Girraween National Park in Queensland, Australia. In this Australian landscape sounds became a vivid material enabling it to join commonly considered landscape materials such as vegetation, topography or water. Sound, as well as being a material in its own right, reveals different properties from vision including an enhanced temporality. In bringing together the music of Finnissy, the notation of Kent, and the landscapes of Girraween and Rousham garden, this study foregrounds sound as a material of landscape architecture and space, connecting it both to the music of Finnissy's *Green Meadows* and to the eighteenth-century development of the Picturesque. As my work shows in *Pink Elephants*, *655*, and *923 Above*, notation can be applied both to the description and composition of the sounds of landscape space. This reveals methods to notate the richness

of landscape temporality, including its complex inner tempo, developed through the application of ethnomusicology to landscape architecture. In addition to creating tools for the notation of landscape temporality, my work also provides evidence of sound as a material of landscape architecture in the work of Kent at Rousham garden, re-imagining it through the introduction of new sounds. If music is 'humanly organised sound' as Blacking suggests, then these sounds introduced into the landscape space at Rousham are also music, just in the way that Kent's own design introduced them. He utilised the placement of water fountains and rills, sculpted topography and tree planting, designing the sounds we still experience visiting Rousham today. My research, in organising the pitch, timbre, volume, and spatial array of sounds described in *Five over Eleven*, is I believe as musical a composition as Finnissy's own *Green Meadows*.

NOTES

1 http://www.michaelfinnissy.info/works/full_list.php.

2 The childhood inspiration for Finnissy's interest in musical composition was from coming into contact in 1958 with the music, via a radio broadcast, of the American composer Charles Ives, and particularly his Second Piano Sonata titled *Concord, Mass., 1840–60*, better known as the *Concord Sonata* for solo piano. As Finnissy says: 'I was absolutely captivated, partly by the sound. It is quite extraordinarily dissonant. And it has everything, tone clusters, bits of C Major, bitonality, atonality, you name it, it's got it. [. . .] So that was it. Ives was my main model.' Ives's composition is not a direct interpretation of a physical landscape but an interpretation of the landscape of Concord seen through the prism of its influence on the writings of the Transcendentalists and their thoughts on nature and landscape. Ives's score for *Concord Sonata* contains a number of innovative notational possibilities for his compositions, including many that came to later be found adapted in the notation of *English Country-Tunes*. These included volume extended to *pppp*, two adjacent tone clusters played with the palm or clenched fist, bar lines largely absent, on page 21 of the score Ives instructs that 'it is not intended that the relation 2:1 between the 32nd and 16th notes here, be held too literally', and he also uses extensive written notes in the score as detailed clarifications of time, he created

new symbols such as the triangle, which align chords with rhythmic note groupings to be played below, and lastly he used conventional symbols in new ways including bar-lines not for temporal divisions but solely for changes of key signature alone. Quotations above are from the author's interview with Michael Finnissy on 3 December 2011.

3 Brougham, Fox and Pace, *Uncommon Ground* (1997), 2.

4 Pace, 'Panorama of Michael Finnissy (I)' (Apr., 1996), 26.

5 Brougham, Fox and Pace, *Uncommon Ground* (1997), 48.

6 Finnissy, *Song 9* (1968), 2.

7 Driver, 'Michael Finnissy's "Sea and Sky"' (Sept., 1980), 82.

8 Pace, 'The Panorama of Michael Finnissy (II)' (Apr., 1996), 11.

9 Finnissy, discussing the work prior to its first public performance, http://www.youtube.com/watch?v=9W8cYK5RxwY [Accessed 21.11.2011]

10 Finnissy, discussing the work prior to its first public performance, http://www.youtube.com/watch?v=9W8cYK5RxwY [Accessed 21.11.2011]

11 I am indebted to Professor Neil Heyde, RAM, for suggesting this work to me.

12 Finnissy, interview with the author (2011).

13 Finnissy, interview with the author (2011).

14 Finnissy, public lecture at the Institute of Contemporary Art (London: November 2011).

15 Brougham, Fox and Pace, *Uncommon Ground* (1997), 32–33.

16 Finnissy, *English Country-Tunes* (1990).

17 The first performance of *Green Meadows* was on 19 January 1978 at Leeds Polytechnic by Alexander Abercrombie. Brougham, Fox and Pace, *Uncommon Ground* (1997), 365.

18 Finnissy, interview with the author (2011).

19 Nettl, *Study of Ethnomusicology* (2005), 294–295.

20 Brougham, Fox and Pace, *Uncommon Ground* (1997), 66–67.

21 Brougham, Fox and Pace, *Uncommon Ground* (1997), 71.

22 I am indebted to Michael Finnissy for bringing this earlier history to my attention.

23 Finnissy acknowledges the precedents for these in the work of Luciano Berio (in *Tempi Concertati*), Sylvano Bussotti (in *Pour Clavier*), Karlheinz Stockhausen (in *Klavierstücke VI and X*), and many other composers working with 'graphic notation' and 'time-space notation' post-1950.

24 Finnissy, interview with the author (2011).

25 Grace notes are notated by smaller note heads and occur before regular notes to indicate their role as melodic ornamentation and are without a specific duration with the implication they are to be played fast.

26 Arpeggios are when the notes of a chord are played sequentially, rather than simultaneously

27 Finnissy, interview with the author (2011).

28 Pedal tones were originally a feature of organ music when a pedal was depressed with the foot in order to create a tone that spanned a number of harmonic changes.

29 Presto is normally very fast and a tempo of 180–200 beats per minutes

30 Schafer, *The Soundscape* (1993), 156.

31 Myer, 'Ethnomusicology' (1992), 3.

32 Kunst, *Ethnomusicology* (1974), 2.

33 Kunst, *Ethnomusicology* (1974), 1.

34 Ellis, 'On the Musical Scales of Various Nations' (1885), 526.

35 The Czech ethnomusicologist Bruno Nettl gave a four-part definition of the term as the study of music in culture; the study of the world's music from a comparative and relativistic perspective; study with the use of fieldwork; and a study of all the musical manifestations of a society, in Nettl, *Study of Ethnomusicology* (2005), 12–13.

36 Hood, *The Ethnomusicologist* (1971), 55.

37 Cole, *Sounds and Signs* (1974), 111.

38 Blesser and Salter, *Spaces Speak* (2007), 42.

39 Hood, *The Ethnomusicologist* (1971), 86.

40 Hood, *The Ethnomusicologist* (1971), 89–90.

41 Hood, *The Ethnomusicologist* (1971), 89–90.

42 Day, *Music and Musical Instruments of Southern India* (1891), xii.

43 Hood, *The Ethnomusicologist* (1971), 96.

44 Hood, *The Ethnomusicologist* (1971), 102.

45 Hood, *The Ethnomusicologist* (1971), 121.

46 Robbins and Ryan, *Vegetation of Girraween National Park* (2011), 9. http://www.rymich.com/girraween/downloads/GRWN_Booklet_20110802.pdf.

47 Robbins and Ryan, *Vegetation of Girraween National Park* (2011), 9. http://www.rymich.com/girraween/downloads/GRWN_Booklet_20110802.pdf.

48 http://www.rymich.com/girraween/downloads/girraween_bird_species_list.pdfp.2.

49 Schafer, *The Soundscape* (1993), 43.

50 Schafer, *The Soundscape* (1993), 43.

51 Hood, *The Ethnomusicologist* (1971), 59.

52 Hood, *The Ethnomusicologist* (1971), 114.

53 Hood, *The Ethnomusicologist* (1971), 114.

54 Christiansen and Nettl, 'Inner Tempo and Melodic Tempo' (Jan., 1960), 10.

55 Hood, *The Ethnomusicologist* (1971), 86.

56 Vaughn, 'Pitch Measurement' (1992), 464.

57 Ellis, 'On the Calculation of Cents from Interval Ratios' (1863).

58 Vaughn, 'Pitch Measurement' (1992), 465.

59 Hood, *The Ethnomusicologist* (1971), 117.

60 Hood, *The Ethnomusicologist* (1971), 118.

61 Ellingson, 'Transcription' (1992), 111.

62 Hood, *The Ethnomusicologist* (1971), 54.

63 Schafer, *The Soundscape* (1993), 9.

64 Schafer, *The Soundscape* (1993), 9–10.

65 Schafer, *The Soundscape* (1993), 10.

66 Schafer, *The Soundscape* (1993), 10.

67 Saunders, *A Guide to Bird Songs* (1951), 3.

68 Saunders, *A Guide to Bird Songs* (1951), 14–15.

69 Saunders, *A Guide to Bird Songs* (1951), 15.

70 Cole, *Sounds and Signs* (1974), 111.

71 Goodman, *Languages of Art* (1976), 134.

72 Widdess, 'Notation' (1992), 224.

73 Widdess, 'Notation' (1992), 226.

74 Ellingson, 'Transcription' (1992), 157.

75 Ellingson, 'Transcription' (1992), 159.

76 Ellingson, 'Transcription' (1992), 159.

77 Ellingson, 'Notation' (1992), 162.

78 Ellingson, 'Notation' (1992), 159.

79 Chion, *Audio-vision* (1994), 71.

80 Chion, *Audio-vision* (1994), 32.

81 Chion, *Audio-vision* (1994), 25–26.

82 Chion, *Audio-vision* (1994), 29.

83 Chion, *Audio-vision* (1994), 32.

84 Blesser and Salter, *Spaces Speak* (2007), 22.

85 Hussey, *The Picturesque* (1967), 17.

86 Cereghini, 'The Italian Origins of Rousham' (1991), 320.

87 Cereghini, 'The Italian Origins of Rousham' (1991), 320.

88 Cereghini, 'The Italian Origins of Rousham' (1991), 320.

89 Cereghini, 'The Italian Origins of Rousham' (1991), 320.

90 http://www.chelseabookfair.com/index.pl?isa=Metadot::SystemApp::BookSearch;op=detail;book=39606;image=264272.

91 Reference is also found to the same Troili text in 'diagram of a cube in perspective, after Giulio Troili' in J. M. W. Turner's perspective sketchbook of 1809, currently in the Tate collection as part of the Turner Bequest.

92 I am indebted to Hal Moggridge, OBE, PPLI, for kindly providing me with his own original source studies.

93 Cereghini, 'The Italian Origins of Rousham' (1991), 320.

94 Moggeridge, 'Notes on Kent's Garden at Rousham' (1986), 200.

95 Allen, *Practice: Architecture* (2000), 42.

96 This garden building is also known as Townsend's Building, but appears in The National Heritage List for England as entry number 1052956 as the Temple of Echo. http://list.english-heritage.org.uk/resultsingle.aspx?uid=1052956.

97 Hunt, 'Verbal versus Visual Meanings' (1992), 176.

98 Pierce, *Science of Musical Sound* (1983), 29.

99 The town of Woodstock is only 6 miles from Rousham and Plot's extensive account of echoes included his observation that 'as for polysyllabical articulate echoes, the strongest and best I have met with here, is in the park at Woodstock, which in the day time, little wind being stirring, returns distinctly seventeen syllables, and in the night twenty.' Plot, *Natural History* (1677), 7. I am indebted to Professor Jonathan Hill, UCL, for bringing this to my attention.

100 Pierce, *Science of Musical Sound* (1983), 32.

101 Pierce, *Science of Musical Sound* (1983), 135.

102 Hunt, 'Verbal versus Visual Meanings' (1992), 159.

103 Pope, *The Temple of Fame* (1758), A2.

104 Anonymous, *The Museum: or, The Literary and Historical Register* (1747), 205.

105 Batey, 'Way to View Rousham' (1983), 131.

106 Batey, 'Way to View Rousham' (1983), 128.

107 Batey, 'Way to View Rousham' (1983), 127. Batey noted that on the 1738 Rousham Estate Plan it is referred to as 'Townshend's Temple', although it was actually designed by Kent himself.

108 Batey, 'Way to View Rousham' (1983), 129.

109 Hunt, 'Verbal versus Visual Meanings' (1992), 162.

110 http://www.british-history.ac.uk/report.aspx?compid=101859#n9.

111 http://www.british-history.ac.uk/report.aspx?compid=101859#n9.

112 http://www.british-history.ac.uk/report.aspx?compid=101859#n9.

113 http://www.birdwatching.co.uk/Articles/BTO-Report/Nightingale.

114 Hunt, 'Verbal versus Visual Meanings' (1992), 161.

115 Wyley, *Landscape* (2007), 91.

116 Hunt and Willis, *Genius of the Place* (2000), 210.

117 Gilpin, *Observations, on Several Parts of England* (1808), 21.

118 Gilpin, *Observations, on Several Parts of England* (1808), 60–61.

119 Gilpin, *Observations, on Several Parts of England* (1808), 62.

120 Henry David Thoreau had written in 1854 that 'the echo is, to some extent, an original sound, and therein is the magic and charm of it. It is not merely a repetition of what was worth repeating in the bell, but partly the voice of the wood'. Thoreau, *Walden, Or Life in the Woods* (1854), 193.

121 Hunt, *William Kent: Landscape Garden Designer* (1987), 116.

122 Hunt, *William Kent: Landscape Garden Designer* (1987), 86.

123 Hunt, 'Verbal versus Visual Meanings' (1992), 167.

124 Hunt, *William Kent: Landscape Garden Designer* (1987), 84.

125 Moggeridge, 'Notes on Kent's Garden at Rousham' (1986), 191.

126 Maillet, *Claude Glass* (2004), 19.

127 Hunt, *Gardens and the Picturesque* (1992), 11.

128 Hunt, 'Ut Pictura Poesis' (1991), 231.

129 Goodman, *Languages of Art* (1976), 231.

130 Hill, *Weather Architecture* (2012), 51.

131 Hunt, 'Verbal versus Visual Meanings' (1992), 160.

132 Hunt, 'Verbal versus Visual Meanings' (1992), 161.

133 Hunt, 'Ut Pictura Poesis' (1991), 106.

134 Hunt, 'Verbal versus Visual Meanings' (1992), 157.

135 Halpern, 'Use of Paintings in Garden History' (1992), 184.

136 Goodman, *Languages of Art* (1976), 32.

137 Halpern, 'Use of Paintings in Garden History' (1992), 187.

138 Halpern, 'Use of Paintings in Garden History' (1992), 188–9.

139 Halpern, 'Use of Paintings in Garden History' (1992), 190.

140 Price noted the differences in etymology between the Italian, *pittoresco*, 'which marks the relation to the painter [. . .] while the English use the word *picturesque*, as related to the production.' Price, *Essays on the Picturesque* (1810), 218. In passing, via France, from Italy to England, the meaning moved from the subject to the object, and in doing so 'the picturesque may justly claim a title taken from the art of painting, without having exclusive reference to it.' Price, *Essays on the Picturesque* (1810), 219.

141 https://oregonstate.edu/instruct/ph302/texts/locke/locke1/Book2a.html#Chapter XIV, 10.

142 https://oregonstate.edu/instruct/ph302/texts/locke/locke1/Book2a.html#Chapter XIV, 27.

143 Hill, *Weather Architecture* (2012), 37.

144 Price, *Essays on the Picturesque* (1810), vi.

145 Price, *Essays on the Picturesque* (1810), ix.

146 Price, *Essays on the Picturesque* (1810), 7.

147 Price, *Essays on the Picturesque* (1810), 21–22.

148 Price, *Essays on the Picturesque* (1810), 26.

149 Gilpin, *Three Essays: on Picturesque Beauty* (1792), 3.

150 Price, *Essays on the Picturesque* (1810), 43–44.

151 Price, *Essays on the Picturesque* (1810), 46.

152 Price, *Essays on the Picturesque* (1810), 46.

153 Price, *Essays on the Picturesque* (1810), 176.

154 Price believed only the sublime could not be created by man.

155 Price, *Essays on the Picturesque* (1810), 208.

156 Potter, *Observations on the Present State of Music* (1762), 17.

157 Potter, *Observations on the Present State of Music* (1762), 30.

158 Potter, *Observations on the Present State of Music* (1762), 32.

159 Rousseau, 'Essays on the Origin of Languages' (1998), 325.

160 Rump, 'Beethoven and the Ut Pictura Poesis Tradition' (2005), 128.

161 Price, *Essays on the Picturesque* (1810), 368.

162 Goodman, *Languages of Art* (1976), 226.

163 Goodman, *Languages of Art* (1976), 3.

164 Goodman, *Languages of Art* (1976), 14.

BUSONI'S GARDEN

This *Musicology for Landscape* set out to investigate afresh the potential for contemporary music notation to provide ways of rethinking the representation of landscape architecture temporality. The aim was to search for alternative models for landscape architectural notation in contemporary music and its notation, and to ask whether the rich temporality of landscape architecture can be better notated by referring to musical precedents unexamined by others to date.

I began by arguing that both music and landscape architecture, sharing an allographic nature, of necessity require a visible means of representation between their conception and realisation. Although this has been the focus of some studies by others, they have persistently deferred to historic modes of music notation and musical time, ignoring the possibilities that contemporary music might hold. The central focus has been to address this, while simultaneously creating the opportunity for the proper inclusion of the under-researched and under-theorised aspect of sound in landscape architecture, a reflection of the historic absence of representational tools to properly incorporate it. By examining landscape architectural aspects of music and musical aspects of landscape architecture, a reciprocal light has been shone on both fields.

HORIZONS, CLOUDS, MEADOWS

In deference to the musical structures of sonata and triad, this book has examined three themes, space in *Horizons*, time in *Clouds*, materiality in *Meadows*, looking at them in seeming isolation, while simultaneously open to potential interconnections. As anticipated in the introduction in the words of Machado, this has been an exploratory journey: the path has been amended by the discovery of unforeseen aspects of music and landscape architecture along the way.

In examining the notational strategies of three contemporary music scores in fine detail, Feldman's *Projection I* (1950), Ligeti's *Lontano* (1967), and Finnissy's *Green Meadows* (1977), time runs chronologically through the book. The developments in these music notations with the passage of time have informed the developing study of landscape architecture temporality. The notation for varied landscapes, designed in New York City, cinematic in *Onibaba*, natural at Girraween National Park, and historic at Rousham garden, has been deliberately focused through the prism and possibilities of music notation. Accepting English composer Cornelius Cardew's assertion that notation and composition determine each other, emphasis has been given both to the role of notation in the composition of landscape, but also vice versa, the role of composition in landscape notation.

The notations described here, encompassing the analytical, the descriptive, and the prescriptive, are each a form of creative transcription that draw out aspects of the precedents examined. They are analogous to the ideas of Busoni and the works of Tudor, using notation as a method of creating new works through the detailed study and transcription of others. My analysis of these music and landscape architect notations is not just to draw them out but also to create new readings of them: *Projection I* and *MT1*; *Lontano* and *View from the Road*; *Green Meadows* and Kent's drawings for Rousham.

My notations are like the contemporary scores studied in that through their open nature they invite speculation and consequently can be interpreted in varying ways. No two performances of *Projection I*, for example, will ever be identical, nor indeed of *Lontano*, nor *Green Meadows*. These new landscape notations fall within the category described by Cole as implicit notations, providing a stimulus 'in which no defined end-result or type of activity is foreseeable [. . .] no detailed instructions for realization are given'.[1] In fact, they form a research method. Cole questions whether we should think of implicit notations 'as instruction books or as works of art? Perhaps as both.'[2] These notations are both autographic and allographic.

I hope this book reveals not just that music and landscape architecture share qualities that can be notated, but that they also share, in their composition and design, a musicality that is largely overlooked. Bringing examples of contemporary music to a design audience through these descriptive and prescriptive notations, demonstrates that contemporary music holds as vivid a possibility for contemporary design notations as the Baroque, Classical and Romantic music notations that design notations by Tschumi, Appleyard *et al.*, and others have so persistently referred to. By focusing on contemporary music scores from a period of particular musical innovation – 1950 to 1977 – and the work of three musical innovators – Feldman, Ligeti, Finnissy – no longer need studies of the intersection of music and landscape architecture be confined to music's earlier history. The design precedents by others focused on historic notions of musical time and its notation, and the notations they developed from their musical studies seem overly concerned with simply borrowing graphic techniques from music as well as a focus on rigid approaches to time. The method developed here, of films as notation, has allowed these investigations to actively engage with issues of time in ways that

earlier studies did not, bringing an unprecedented in-depth analysis of issues of temporality in music and landscape architecture.

Beyond this, the book vividly brings to landscape architecture a new ability to better notate aspects of landscape time, space and material, including the vital element of sound, so curiously omitted by others.

A NEW RELATIONSHIP TO NOTATION

Busoni emphasised the process of notation over the artefact. In challenging Goodman's notion of a rigid and fixed field, Busoni argued notations are a means of understanding, a means of analysing, and a means of composing materials, space and time: notation as temporal act rather than an object. This notion of notation as transcription of an abstract idea, proposed in his *The Essence of Music and Other Papers*, stated his belief that despite its imprecisions and limitations, notation is intrinsic to music in that it allows for the study of past works in the creation of the new. He saw that the history of the transcriptions of others' work as a tool for detailed study, in his case of Romantic music, could also be applied more broadly to the creative process. For Busoni, transcription was a process that also described the development of new works, and he asserted that the act of writing down thoughts was as musical a transcription as re-writing an earlier work by Beethoven or Bach in the composition of the new. While each new landscape architecture notation contained in this book starts at a point close to abstract speculation, it does this with the aim of bringing a focused empiricism to these investigations of landscape architecture time. By creating notations as films this allows me – through the process of capturing the landscape architecture notation's development – to observe both the notation, and the notated (time, space, material, and sound itself) becoming more precise. Notation as proposed in this book has not been an object, a 'score', a printed paper or a manuscript, but an action with time centrally located. As Cole noted in considering the future of notation, what we do with new notations may matter less than the very fact of their existence. For him, this situation

> has arisen twice in the history of Western music; in the late fourteenth century [. . .] and in our own day, when we have once more woken up to the fact that a notation is not a part of the inevitable order, but is a tool that we ourselves can modify, replace, and develop in any one of many directions.[3]

Are these new landscape architecture notations also excitingly reminiscent of the developments of the *Ars Nova* in the fourteenth century, and also the radical experiments of contemporary music including those subject to detailed study in this thesis: open, exploratory, suggestive, provocative?

As Allen noted, 'the primary variables in a notational schema—time and intangible effects—are not necessarily visual'.[4] My notations allow me to reflect back on past ideas of landscape and music – my own and others – through the prism of current action. It is a reflective process that allows me to travel through time. Although this book's opening quotation states that music in passing from the mental to the physical world must past through a process of visualisation alienating it from pure sound, it is precisely this distance that notation creates that allows me to look and indeed listen to ideas that form this musicology for landscape. Alienation as Griffiths describes it is also a process of liberation that creates

the space and time for this investigation to take place. Notation in this research is not a barrier, but a conduit, a space of invention. My studies in *Meadows* are like a condensed history of aspects of the development of music notation, synthesised into new works that allow for the shared exploration of music and landscape architecture. The temporal nature of these new works means they are intermediary between music and music notation. Rather than conforming to a strict definition of notation for landscape architecture, they are, in fact, pieces of landscape architecture. These new notations are creative works created from this research and their main purpose is to organise thoughts and to allow me to 'realise' this thinking through the act of notation. They are also, I hope, gifts to the reader to allow you to better understand the research themes.

My notation is primarily a research method that brings together music, notation, and a place, so that they can be simultaneously studied. The result, played in time and thus becoming a film, has an aesthetic value and is a means of communicating the findings, but primarily is a temporal structure. The designed temporarily within the films makes them not just notations but also landscape spaces. Cole notes that the original function of notation to preserve the composer's intention for later performance has 'today be taken over by the recording. Notation is therefore set free to assume any form.'[5] No longer need notation be to conserve and to communicate to performers, removing the barrier that historically has prevented notation from functioning as a private language. Cardew, who noted that composition and notation determine each other, explicitly saw advantages for new notations to start as private languages, stating that new works 'need camouflage to protect them from hostile forces in the early days of their life. One kind of protection is provided by the novelty and uniqueness of the notation.'[6] While not, I hope, in need of protection, the development of *Pink Elephants*, *655*, and *923 Above* as new landscape notations that are close to autographic works, has allowed for the diverse range of topics in this reciprocal examination of music and landscape architecture to be explored.

As Thiel noted 50 years ago, regarding the potentiality of the cinematic image,

> the motion-picture camera is, of course, a possibility, but reasons of cost and lack of an objective *rationale* for its use in this service limit its usefulness [. . .] although it may have a place as a recording instrument, it is not adaptable for use as a tool for conceptualising.[7]

His historic concerns have been overcome by advances in technology. In music, conventional notation represents sounds but does not include them as auditory aspects of the notation itself. By adding sound, the films developed in this research have created a new relationship between landscape notation and landscape architecture itself, as the notation now includes both auditory and visual information. This changes the role of the observer from viewer to a multi-sensory experience. Notation can now become a field for what Pallasmaa terms 'the polyphony of the senses'.[8] If notation is a filter between composition and performance, then the filter of the films is thinner than a static representation, we are brought closer through the inclusion of sound and time.

This book has drawn out a number of ways in which notation can function in design research. Nettl suggested that 'that one value of transcription may lie in the concentrated and disciplined attention to music that it brings'.[9] Notation in this research has provided the means to bring a fine focus to the study of landscape temporality and shared qualities of music and landscape architecture, enabling the detailed study of both. As Cole noted, a special quality of music notation is to 'provide both a graphical sketch map and a detailed symbolic representation of the music simultaneously',[10] to examine plural possibilities at the same time. This has been an important aspect of this research, a plurality in investigating both music and landscape architecture through the shared prism of notation, and in examining both larger issues within the constellation of topics in landscape architecture and music while bringing a focused study to particular aspects of both.

Notation has also been a record of the research processes, tracking the investigations over a four-year period. It has been like time-lapse photography, a means of recording individual incidents in isolation but activated and operative when conflated into film. It is a record of the research, conserving it for the future, and so fixing a period of fluid practice for future reference and use. Notation has also brought forth a new materiality. The notations in *655* and *923 Above* both successfully create the means to transcribe and compose sounds of landscape space. Through importing aspects of ethnomusicology and combining them with music notation, this research makes available to a design audience the critical material of sound within landscape space. Through the use of inner tempo applied to landscape, greater precision to the temporality of landscape sounds can now be notated, allowing for the design of sound within landscape architecture in ways not previously possible.

Notation has also been a language for communication. As Widdess notes 'the purposes of transcription [. . .] are first to test an interpretation of the original, and second, to make the results of that interpretation accessible to others.'[11] There is an inherent tension at times in notation between its broader accessibility and its specific accuracy. As Ellingson noted, 'the best transcription, which conveys the most essential features of the music, may be the most difficult to read'.[12] Although these notations were developed as a tool for personal research, they are also, as in music, a language for communication with others as well as oneself. They may contain difficulties of legibility, and may need studied time to acquire, but nevertheless can allow for new ideas of landscape architecture to spread.

Much contemporary music has explored the layering of different types of time from the determined to the aperiodic within a single work. The films as notations developed in this research echo this, the time of contemplative thought, the time of action in drawing, and the time of composition in their development. All are contained within each film. They offer both a transcript of the research process and also a frame-by-frame account of each moment of individual research action. Incorporating time into these notations allows them to be read both as unfolding scenes with transitory changes evoking aspects of landscape temporality, but also containing detailed information encoded within them. These films are like automated page turns of a music notation, time flows continuously through them. And in the same way that Griffiths

noted regarding the development of notation in the eleventh century including Guido of Arezzo's *Micrologus*, 'notation seems to have promoted musical composition',[13] I also hope that notation will function as a compositional prompt for others, expanding its exploration, vitality and spread within design.

TOUCHING AT A DISTANCE

I believe that sound connects us to the spatiality, temporality and materiality of landscape in entirely different ways form vision. Firstly, as the studies at Rousham support, the scale of the auditory landscape often extends far beyond that of the visual one. As Schafer rather beautifully describes this expansive acoustic horizon, 'hearing is a way of touching at a distance'.[14] Secondly, time courses through our experience of landscape spaces. As Pallasmaa identifies, 'we are not normally aware of the significance of hearing in spatial experience, although sounds often provide the temporal continuum in which visual impressions are embedded'.[15] Blesser and Salter go further, stating that 'hearing is orders of magnitude more sensitive to temporal changes. In a very real sense, sound is time.'[16] Thirdly, as sound waves travel at a speed one million times slower than light, they resonate and reverberate in space and materials in an entirely different perceptible way. The temporality of the auditory landscape, like the vertical time of music mentioned by Kramer, is a form of extended present, where past and future simultaneously occur.

Including sound in the definition of landscape presciently draws our attention and provides tools to the auditory experience of the city. In human history sound had always revealed aspects of landscape that vision could not, from a 360-degree field to the ability to operate outside of diurnal limits on vision. Historically, sound was a more dominant sensory experience in human settlement. It was only in the eighteenth century that sound produced through human activity changed as a consequence of industrialisation and started to drown out sounds that had existed for the vast history of human experience – the beginning of Schafer's 'lo-fi'. There has been a second period of noise, since 1945 we might say, created by the expansion of the combustion engine. The popularisation of motor vehicles has drowned out so much of the sounds of cities. As Armenian landscape architect Anet Gharankhanian-Siraki noted in her experiments of the sound fields of London, vehicle noise fills the urban space in the critical range between 61 and 82 decibels, the aural space at which depth and definition is critical. And yet this current dominance of the car as sound creator is set to change as vehicles move from combustion to electric motors. In the next 20 or even 10 years, sound will reappear in the life and experience of the city: people and places, like the Cockneys and Bow Bells,[17] reaffirm each other and sound is restored to its critical value. City life, in its auditory qualities, may become closer to rural life. In fact, as populations become increasingly urban, and the increasing density of cities reduces our ability to see distant views, sound will open opportunities for landscape experience that will be denied to vision: the acoustic horizon will extend well beyond the visual envelope. As Schafer notes, 'the definition of space by acoustic means is much more ancient than the establishment of property lines and fences'.[18] In urban spaces of future cities, our connection with the natural world will be maintained through sound, to augment its loss through vision.

Griffiths suggests that:

> music, being immaterial, touches on the immaterial – on the drift of thought and feeling, on divinity and death. Music, as sound, can represent the auditory world: the moan of wind, the repeated whispers of calm waves, the calls of birds. Music, as idealised voice [. . .] can sing or sigh, laugh or weep. Music, as rhythm, can keep place with our contemplative rest and our racing activity. Music, in preceding through time, can resemble our lives.[19]

Landscape is also an idealised voice, projecting our desire for an understanding of the world around us, a recognition of our transitory existence within a wider and more complex dynamic world. The English philosopher Jonathan Ree states that 'you can use your voice to populate your auditory world at will, and nothing remotely comparable applies to the other senses'.[20] So, landscape as a voice aiding us in determining our relationship with the world strongly benefits from including sound, which as Ree suggests, might allow us to actively engage with landscape space at will, and to discover aspects of it that our sense of vision cannot do.

But there is something more than simply an ability to go out and mingle with sounds. As Ree suggests, we can use the sound of our voice to go out and explore. While he reminds us that vision is a sense that allows us to explore the surface properties of materials in the landscape, sound as an investigative tool has additional possibilities. Not only does sound allow us to investigate the auditory properties of materials but those properties include both surface, through its ability to reflect sound waves, but also substantive ones such as density which amend reverberation times and degrees of

6.1 Anet Gharankhanian-Siraki. *Urban Acoustic Range.* 2014

sound absorption. Sound as an investigative tool for landscape allows us to understand material, spatial and temporal properties of landscape that vision cannot. Sound may augment vision, or at other times supplant it, but this book argues for sound to be ennobled in the sensory appreciation of landscape.

SOUND PLUS VISION

Sound has not always been ignored in the experience of landscape space as the writings by English authors Pope, Gilpin and Price clearly demonstrate – rather, they have been absent from landscape architecture, located in the dearth of tools in which to represent it. Designs in the seventeenth and eighteenth century were often organised through written instructions as much as drawings, as illustrated by the few produced by William Kent for Rousham garden.

As contemporary landscape architecture practice has become increasingly reliant on drawings, their limitations have come to act more strongly on the field, excluding the non-visible, the intangible and the auditory. It is with some irony that the tools to draw the auditory aspects of landscape space have, in fact, existed all along in music notation.

Rediscovering and re-emphasising landscape architecture as a vividly revealed and rich interplay between sound and vision, unfolding over time, has resonated with my own experiences of landscape space. At Osaka City University Library Plaza in Japan, this single landscape space, only 42 by 55 metres in extent, contained a surprising range of overlaid times, noticed through both senses. In the shallow water of the reflecting pool fountain jets operate on a 60-minute cycle, the lighting on a cycle from dusk to midnight, while clouds move with micro-temporal changes across the sky. While the flowering period of the Japanese Crepe Myrtle trees (*Lagerstroemia fauriei*) lasts from July to September, individual pink and white flowers drop into the water in indeterminate intervals, and the trees shed bark from the stem throughout the year. According to Tuan, 'with deafness life seems frozen and time lacks progression. Space itself contracts, for our experience of space is greatly extended by the auditory sense which provides information of the world beyond the visual field.'[21] The timing of human movement across this landscape space has four distinct peaks, the library opening brings flurries of footsteps, visitors for lunch arriving and departing, and the last rush prior to closing. The impromptu also occurs; we hear children splash as we watch them play in the water after school in summer, or fireworks burst into the indigo calm of mid-August night skies in celebration of the *O-bon* festivals of souls, remembering the dead. Revisiting this landscape space in early summer 2014, 18 years after its completion, we notice the effect of time. The cast aluminium bridge has resisted the white bloom of oxidation, but the water quality has faded and now contains traces of algae. Words from ecology texts from the library were cast into aluminium 'name plates', their pitted surface, designed to improve slip resistance, are now filled with dust. Looking into the site towards the building entrance the crepe myrtle trees have been pruned to restrict their height and benches have been replaced by vigorous under-storey planting. In the pool the changes to the maintenance of water quality has allowed water lilies to prosper and spread. Pedestrians have now been replaced by cyclists and scooters. The sound of warning bells and revving engines interrupts the bird songs and salutations. Some trees have out-competed others in a process of habitat succession. The natural and the man-made, the regular and the a-periodic, in sounds and in sights, are superimposed and experienced simultaneously in this landscape space. If sounds exist most vividly in an extended present, here vision provides a record of an extended past. In revisiting this space one better understands that landscape temporality exists implicitly in landscape architecture. The new modes of landscape notation presented in this book will, I hope, now allow time to be made more explicit in landscape architecture, in its understanding and conception, as well as its experience.

Recently, landscape architecture has declined to express sound as a vital component of landscape. Of the five senses humans use to interact with their environment, the primary faculty is so frequently stated as sight. According to Tuan, man is 'predominantly a visual animal. A larger world is open to him, and far more information that is detailed and specific spatially reaches him through the eyes than through the sensory systems of hearing, smell, taste and touch.'[22] I disagree with Tuan's assertion and instead argue that sound, in being an equal component of landscape space, must also be an equal component of landscape architecture. Landscape space, as a combination of sights and sounds, experienced in richly changing temporal variety, is a far richer sensual experience than a visual or auditory one alone.

NOTATION AS LANDSCAPE, LANDSCAPE AS NOTATION

To return to the very first OED reference in 1605, landscape was defined as a picture, representing natural inland scenery. If one aspect of landscape is its role as a representation, then it seems pertinent

6.2 David Buck. Photographs of Osaka City University Media Center plaza, from 1996 on the left, 2014 on the right.

to question whether a landscape is being created through the notation developed in this book. There is an implied precedent in the work of Cozens, whose 'blot drawings' published in his 1785 *New Method of Assisting the Invention in Drawing Original Compositions of Landscape* were made from smudges of ink. The accidental shapes would suggest natural features that he then elaborated and painted over. Rather than drawings of actual places, Cozens's landscapes were thus invented compositions, vividly developed in the imagination as Addison suggests. Devoid of people, they provoked personal responses in the viewer, feelings from surprise to awe, melancholy to delight. His works were evocative of being in landscape spaces, rather than pictorial representations.

While developing the notation *655*, as discussed in Chapter 5 *Meadows*, suddenly light was reflected through an adjacent window onto the drawing surface. It reminded me of English artist J. M. W.'s Turner's 1812 painting at the Tate gallery in London of *Snow Storm: Hannibal and his Army Crossing the Alps*. This was the third and final painting in a series of catastrophes starting with *The Tenth Plague of Egypt* from 1802, *The Destruction of Sodom* first exhibited in the 1805, and *Snow Storm*, where the clouds appear to break and sunlight pours onto the surface. As English art critic John Ruskin (1819–1900) writing in *Modern Painters* says of Turner, 'first he receives a true impression from the place itself [. . .] and then he sets himself as far as possible to reproduce that impression in the mind of the spectator'.[23] The notations in *Meadows* also convey the experience within the Australian landscape, the absence of a visual focus, the almost imperceptible motion, and instead the dominance of the sounds. I believe the abstract qualities of my notations also allow us to conceive 'landscapes' through them. If landscape can be formed through creating the same experience of a place through another medium, if representation through painting can be landscape, then surely notation can be also. If the origin of landscape was not a place but a drawing, then these notations are also landscape. So what started out as a study, through notation, of landscape, has, in fact, also created them.

A corollary exists in the opposing direction, that landscape is a notation. This book opens with a quotation by Griffiths arguing that notation in music is not a neutral code, that communication from composer to performer is not direct. He notes that music passes through a process of visualisation, alienating itself from pure sound. We can similarly argue that landscape is not a neutral code, and that in the process of visualising it, it is alienated from pure

nature. Landscape, in fact, is never nature or natural but is always synthetic. As Austrian art historian Ernst Gombrich (1909–2001) noted, 'there is no innocent eye. The eye comes always ancient to its work, obsessed by its own past and by old and new insinuations of the ear, nose, tongue, fingers, heart and brain.'[24] In developing our notions of landscape we extract aspects of the world around us, we synthesise landscape from them. American cultural geographer J. B. Jackson notes that the syllable scape, in addition to the common understanding as a visual field, 'could also indicate something like an organisation or a system'.[25] Landscape is constructed through our perception as well as our activity. In 1605 landscape might have been defined simply as a representation, but landscape now is not just a representation but is a representational system. As Goodman noted, 'nothing is intrinsically a representation; status as representation is relative to a symbol system'.[26] The landscape of notation, not just the notation of landscape, is a critical finding of this book.

BUSONI'S GARDEN

At the beginning of the book, I referred to Ligeti's assertion that new ideas can be created from combining two known but different fields; the approach of this book has identified something qualitatively new by uniting the known disciplines of music and landscape architecture. Casting light onto both music and landscape architecture has revealed the rich shared temporality of music and landscape architecture – if music has helped to reveal this in landscape architecture then perhaps landscape architecture might also reveal rich new possibilities for the time of music, in addition to those of landscape space and art which already inspire it.

6.3 David Buck. Extract from *655*
notation. 2013.

6.4 J. M. W. Turner. *Snow Storm: Hannibal and
his Army Crossing the Alps*. 1812. Image © Tate,
London. 2016.

Perhaps like Cozens's eighteenth-century unpublished treatise of drawings, *The Various Species of Composition of Landscape, in Nature* (consisting of 16 'Compositions', fourteen 'Objects' and 27 'Circumstances'), the three focused investigations contained in this book – *Horizons, Clouds, Meadows* – explore themes not just concerning new ways of representation, but critically new ways of thinking about landscape architecture and music as well. Investigating new forms of landscape, architectural notation has provided a reflective window through which to consider new ways of conceiving, understanding, and constructing landscape, suggesting new possibilities for landscape notation, including providing alternative ways of contemplating and representing landscape temporality. As in music, landscape architecture notation, including the more autographic notations developed in my own work, allows us to comprehend, to conceive, and to compose, opening up a window to contribute to knowledge, and future investigations by others.

I started out guided by Goodman's distinction between autographic and allographic works, but in studying aspects of music notation with the intention of producing new landscape architecture notations, the new notations created from it are, in fact, closer to autographic works. The studies contained here make available to a wider design audience the works of three influential composers of the latter half of the twentieth century, presenting a critical evaluation of their work within music, as well as a means in which they might be used in landscape architecture research. Although the focus has been on landscape architecture, I hope this book also holds potential for other design fields concerned with temporality, including architecture and urban design. As Cole noted, 'areas of interest in a musical culture are reflected in its notation'.[27] I believe the converse is also true, that notation can act as a catalyst for creating new areas of interest in landscape culture. The history of the relationship between landscape representation and landscape architecture certainly reflects this. Pictures after all, influenced the development of the Picturesque in practical and philosophical ways. The new approaches contained here might work in both directions, reflecting a growing interest in landscape's rich temporality, but also conversely, sparking an interest in an oft-forgotten aspect of landscape space, its auditory component.

As Kramer reminds us, 'music [. . .] makes time audible'.[28] Whether preserving time through references to the past, or animating the present through the materials used, landscape architecture makes time visible as well as audible. This book grew out of a very personal, abstract speculation on the connection between two temporal fields, and has journeyed from the creation of new notations to new ideas of landscape. It has moved from an open field, to concluding the Picturesque. In deference to the primary role of music in developing this work I end with Busoni. His notion of creative transcription in the development of new works has been so prescient, but also his acknowledgement below that music, even more than landscape, continues to offer ever wider, more open fields for further discovery:

> To me, a composer is like a gardener to whom a small portion of a large piece of ground has been allotted for cultivation; it falls to me to gather what grows on his soil, to arrange it, to make a bouquet of it; and if he is very ambitious, to develop it as a garden. It devolves on this gardener to collect and form that which is in reach of his eyes, his arms—his power of differentiation. In the same way a mighty one, an anointed one, a Bach, a Mozart, can only survey, manipulate and reveal a portion of the whole flora of the earth [. . .] yet the comparison is weak and insufficient because the flora only covers the earth, while music, invisible and unheard, pervades and permeates a whole universe.[29]

NOTES

1 Cole, *Sounds and Signs* (1974), 143.

2 Cole, *Sounds and Signs* (1974), 146.

3 Cole, *Sounds and Signs* (1974), 151.

4 Allen, *Practice: Architecture* (2000), 52.

5 Cole, *Sounds and Signs* (1974), 147.

6 Cole, *Sounds and Signs* (1974), 148.

7 Thiel, 'A Sequence-Experience Notation' (1961), 34.

8 Bachelard, *The Poetics of Reverie* (1971), 6.

9 Ellingson, 'Transcription' (1992), 147.

10 Cole, *Sounds and Signs* (1974), 26.

11 Widdess, 'Notation' (1992), 224.

12 Ellingson, 'Notation' (1992), 146.

13 Griffiths, *A Concise History of Western Music* (2006), 14.

14 Schafer, *The Soundscape* (1993), 11.

15 Pallasmaa, *Eyes of the Skin* (2005), 49.

16 Blesser and Salter, *Spaces Speak* (2007), 17.

17 Historically, the definition of London's Cockney population was to be born within hearing distance of the bells of St Mary-le-Bow church in east London.

18 Schafer, *The Soundscape* (1993), 33.

19 Griffiths, *Concise History of Western Music* (2006), 3–4.

20 Rée, *I See a Voice* (1999), 55.

21 Tuan, *Topophilia* (1974), 9.

22 Tuan, *Topophilia* (1974), 6.

23 Ruskin, *Modern Painters* (1904), 21–22.

24 Gombrich, *Art and Illusion* (1960), 297–298.

25 Jackson, *Discovering the Vernacular Landscape* (1984), 7.

26 Goodman, *Languages of Art* (1976), 226.

27 Cole, *Sounds and Signs* (1974), 8.

28 Kramer, *The Time of Music* (1988), 1.

29 Busoni, *The Essence of Music* (1957), 197.

Bibliography

Abraham, Gerald, *The Concise Oxford History of Music* (Oxford: Oxford University Press, 1979).

Addison, Joseph, 'Pleasures of Imagination', in *Spectator*. No.411 June 21, 1712.

Addison, Joseph, 'Pleasures of Imagination', in *Spectator*. No.414 June 25, 1712.

Alberti, Leon Battista, *On Painting* (trans.) John R. Spencer (New Haven: Yale University Press, 1970).

Allen, Stan, *Practice: Architecture, Technique and Representation* (Abingdon: Routledge, 2000).

Anonymous, *The Museum: or, The Literary and Historical Register* (Jun. 6, 1747).

Apel, Willi, *The Notation of Polyphonic Music 900–1600* (Cambridge, MA: The Mediaeval Academy of America, 1942).

Appleyard, Donald, Lynch, Kevin, and Myer, John R., *The View from the Road* (Cambridge, MA: The MIT Press, 1965).

Batey, Mavis, 'The Way to View Rousham by Kent's Gardener', in *Garden History*, 11/2 (Autumn, 1983), 125–132.

Bernard, Jonathan W. 'Feldman's Painters', in Steven Johnson (ed.), *The New York Schools of Music and Visual Art* (New York: Routledge, 2002).

Bernard, Jonathan, 'Rules and Regulation: Lessons from Ligeti's Compositional Sketches' in Louise Duchesneau and Wolfgang Marx (eds) *György Ligeti of Foreign Lands and Strange Sounds* (Woodbridge: The Boydell Press, 2011).

Blacking, John, *How Musical is Man?* (Seattle: University of Washington Press, 1973).

Blesser, Barry, and Salter, Linda-Ruth, *Spaces Speak, Are You Listening?: Experiencing Aural Architecture* (Cambridge: MIT Press, 2007).

Block, Richard, 'Contextual Coding in Memory: Studies of Remembered Duration', in John A. Michon and Janet L. Jackson (eds), *Time, Mind and Behaviour* (Berlin: Springer-Verlag, 1985), 169–178.

Boretz, Benjamin, and Cone, Edward T. (eds), *Perspectives on Notation and Performance* (New York: W.W. Norton and Company, 1976).

Brougham, Henrietta, Fox, Christopher, and Pace, Ian (eds), *Uncommon Ground The Music of Michael Finnissy* (Aldershot: Ashgate Publishing Limited, 1997).

Brown, Earle, 'Notation and Performance of New Music' in *The Musical Quarterley*, 72 (1986), 180–201.

Busoni, Ferruccio, *Sketch of a New Esthetic of Music* (New York: Schirmer, 1911).

Busoni, Ferruccio, *The Essence of Music and Other Papers* (London: The Rockcliff Publishing Corporation, 1957).

Busoni, Ferruccio, *Selected Letters* (trans., ed.), Antony Beaumont (London: Faber and Faber, 1987).

Butt, John, 'Bach's Passions and the Textures of Time', in Sean Gallagher and Thomas Forrest Kelly (eds), *The Century of Bach and Mozart* (Boston: Isham Library Papers 7, 2008).

Cage, John, *Silence: Lectures and Writings by John Cage* (Hanover, NH: Wesleyan University Press, 1961).

Cardew, Cornelius, 'Notation: Interpretation, etc.', in *Tempo*, 58 (1961), 21–33.

Cereghini, Elisabetta, 'The Italian Origins of Rousham', in Monique Mosser and Georges Teyssot (eds), *The History of Garden Design: The Western Tradition from the Renaissance to the Present Day* (London: Thames and Hudson, 1991).

Chion, Michel, *Audio-vision: Sound on Screen* (New York: Columbia University Press, 1994).

Christiansen, Dieter, and Nettl, Bruno, 'Inner Tempo and Melodic Tempo', in *Ethnomusicology*, 4/1 (Jan., 1960), 9–14.

Cole, Hugo, *Sounds and Signs: Aspects of Musical Notation* (London: Oxford University Press, 1974).

Corner, James, *Taking Measures across the American Landscape* (New Haven: Yale University Press, 1996).

Corner, James, 'Representation and Landscape', in Simon R. Swaffield (ed.), *Theory in Landscape Architecture: A Reader* (Philadelphia: University of Pennsylvania Press, 2002).

Cosgrove, Denis, 'Prospect, Perspective and the Evolution of the Landscape Idea', in *Transactions of the Institute of British Geographers*, 10/1 (1985), 45–62.

Cosgrove, Denis, and Daniels, Stephen, *The Iconography of Landscape: Essays on the Symbolic Representation, Design and Use of Past Environments* (Cambridge: Cambridge University Press, 1988).

Crilly, Ciaran, 'The Bigger Picture: Ligeti's Music and the Films of Stanley Kubrick', in Louise Duchesneau and Wolfgang Marx (eds), *György Ligeti Of Foreign Lands and Strange Sounds* (Woodbridge: The Boydell Press, 2011).

Damisch, Hubert, *A Theory of /Cloud/: Toward a History of Painting* (Stanford: Stanford University Press, 2002).

Darwin, Charles, *On the Origin of Species by Means of Natural Selection, or the Preservation of Favoured Races in the Struggle for Life* (London: John Murray, 1859).

Day, Charles Russell, *The Music and Musical Instruments of Southern India and the Deccan* (London and New York: Novello, Ewer and Co., 1891).

Deriu, Davide, and Kamvasinou, Krystallia, 'Critical Perspectives on Landscape', in *The Journal of Architecture: Introduction*, 17/1 (2012), 1–9.

Driver, Paul, 'Michael Finnissy's "Sea and Sky"', in *Tempo*, 133/134 (Sept., 1980), 82–83.

Eisenstein, Sergei, *Film Form: Essays in Film Theory* (New York: Harcourt Press Jovanovich, 1949).

Ellis, Alexander J., 'On the calculation of cents from interval ratios', in H. L. F. Helmholtz, *Die Lehre von den Tonempfindung als physiologische Grundlage fur die Theorie der Music* (Braunschweig: Friedrich Vieweg, 1863).

Ellis, Alexander J., 'On the Musical Scales of Various Nations', in *Journal of the Society of Arts* 33/1699 (27 March, 1885), 485–527.

Ellingson, Ter, 'Notation', in Helen Myers (ed.), *Ethnomusicology An Introduction* (New York: Norton, 1992).

Ellingson, Ter, 'Transcription', in Helen Myers (ed.), *Ethnomusicology An Introduction* (New York: Norton, 1992).

Evans, Robin, *The Projective Cast: Architecture and its Three Geometries* (Cambridge, MA: The MIT Press, 2000).

Feldman, Morton, *Sketchbook* (unknown date). Morton Feldman Collection, Paul Sacher Foundation, Basel.

Feldman, Morton, *Projection I for Solo Cello* (New York: C.F. Peters Corporation, 1962).

Feldman, Morton, *Morton Feldman – Earle Brown*, record liner notes, Mainstream Records (MS/5007). Compact disk. 1970.

Feldman, Morton, *Essays* (Kerpen: Beginner Press, 1985).

Feldman, Morton, 'Between Categories', in *Contemporary Music Review*, 2/2 (1988), 1–5.

Feldman, Morton, *Give My Regards to Eighth Street* (Cambridge: Exact Change, 2000).

Feldman, Morton, *Composing by Numbers – The Graphic Scores 1950–67*. Mode 146. Compact disc. 2005.

Finnissy, Michael, *Song 9* (London: International Music Company, 1968).

Finnissy, Michael, *English Country Tunes: Part One – Green Meadows* (Etcetera Records B.V., KTC1091, 1990).

Gilpin, William, *Three Essays: on Picturesque Beauty; on Picturesque Travel; and on Sketching Landscape: to which is added a poem, on Landscape Painting* (London: R. Blamire, 1792).

Gilpin, William, *Observations, on Several Parts of England, Particularly the Mountains and Lakes of Cumberland and Westmorland, Relative Chiefly to Picturesque Beauty, Made in the Year 1772 Vol 2.* (London: Cadell and Davis, 1808).

Girot, Christophe, 'Vision in Motion: Representing Landscape in Time', in Charles Waldheim (ed.) *The Landscape Urbanism Reader* (New York: Princeton Architectural Press, 2006).

Goehr, Lydia, *The Imaginary Museum of Musical Works* (New York: Oxford University Press, 2007).

Gombrich, Ernst, *Art and Illusion* (New York: Pantheon Books, 1960).

Goodman, Nelson, *Languages of Art: An Approach to a Theory of Symbol* (Indianapolis: Hackett Publishing Company, 1976).

Griffiths, Paul, *György Ligeti* (London: Robson Books, 1983).

Griffiths, Paul, 'Sound-Code-Image', in Arts Council (ed.) *Eye Music: The Graphic Art of New Musical Notation* (London: Arts Council of Great Britain, 1986).

Griffiths, Paul, *A Concise History of Western Music* (Cambridge: Cambridge University Press, 2006).

Griffiths, Paul, *Modern Music and After* (Oxford: Oxford University Press, 2010).

Griffiths, Paul, 'Invented Homelands: Ligeti's Orchestras', in Louise Duchesneau and Wolfgang Marx (eds), *György Ligeti Of Foreign Lands and Strange Sounds* (Woodbridge: The Boydell Press, 2011).

Halpern, Linda Cabe, 'The Use of Paintings in Garden History', in John Dixon Hunt (ed.) *Garden History: Issues, Approaches, Methods* (Washington: Dumbarton Oaks, 1992).

Halprin, Lawrence, *RSVP Cycles: Creative Processes in the Human Environment* (New York: Brazillier, 1969).

Hanoch-Roe, Galia, 'Linear Sequences in Music and Space', in (eds) Mikesch Muecke and Miriam Zach, *Resonance: Essays on the Intersection of Music and Architecture* (Ames, IA: Culicidae Architectural Press, 2007).

Hill, Jonathan, *Weather Architecture* (Abingdon: Routledge, 2012).

Holzaepfel, John, 'Cage and Tudor', in (ed.), David Nicholls, *The Cambridge Companion to John Cage* (Cambridge: Cambridge University Press, 2002).

Holzaepfel, John, 'Painting by Numbers', in (ed.), Steven Johnson, *The New York Schools of Music and Visual Arts* (New York: Routledge, 2002).

Hood, Mantle, *The Ethnomusicologist* (Los Angeles: McGraw-Hill Book Company, 1971).

Hood, Walter J., *Blues & Jazz Landscape Improvisations* (Berkeley, CA: Poltroon Press, 1993).

Hood, Walter J., *Dooryard Blues and Green Jazz*, (Berkeley, CA: University of California Press, 1994).

Howard, Luke, *Essay on the Modifications of Clouds* (London: John Churchill and Sons, 1865).

Howard, V. A., 'On Representational Music', in *Nous*, 6/1 (1972), 41–53.

Hunt, John Dixon, 'Ut Pictura Poesis, Ut Pictura Hortus, and the Picturesque', in *Word & Image: A Journal of Verbal/Visual Enquiry*, 1/1 (1985), 87–107.

Hunt, John Dixon, *William Kent: Landscape Garden Designer* (London: Zwemmer, 1987).

Hunt, John Dixon, '"Ut Pictura Poesis": The Garden and the Picturesque in England (1710–1750)', in Monique Mosser and Georges Teyssot (eds), *The Architecture of Western Gardens: A Design History from the Renaissance to the Present Day* (London: Thames and Hudson, 1991).

Hunt, John Dixon, *Gardens and the Picturesque: Studies in the History of the Picturesque* (Cambridge, MA: MIT Press, 1992).

Hunt, John Dixon, 'Verbal versus Visual Meanings in Garden History: The Case for Rousham', in John Dixon Hunt (ed.), *Garden History: Issues, Approaches, Methods* (Washington: Dumbarton Oaks, 1992).

Hunt, John Dixon, and Willis, Peter (eds), *The Genius of the Place* (The MIT Press: Cambridge MA, 2000).

Hussey, Christopher, *The Picturesque* (Frank Cass and Company, London: 1967).

Hutchinson, Ann, *Labanotation* (Norfolk, CN: New Directions, 1961).

Ingold, Tim, 'The Temporality of the Landscape' in *World Archaeology*, 25/2 (Oct., 1993), 152–174.

Ives, Charles, *Piano Sonata No.2 'Concord, Mass., 1840–60'* (New York: Knickerbocker Press, 1921?).

Jackson, J.B., in 'Concluding with Landscapes', in J.B. Jackson (ed.), *Discovering the Vernacular Landscape* (New Haven, Yale University Press, 1984).

Kamvasinou, Krystallia, 'Notation Timelines and the Aesthetics of Disappearance', in *The Journal of Architecture*, 15, 4 (2010), 397–423.

Knight, Richard Payne, 'The Landscape, A Didactic Poem', in John Dixon Hunt and Peter Willis (eds), *The Genius of the Place The English Landscape Garden 1620–1820* (London: Paul Elek, 1975).

Kramer, Jonathan, *The Time of Music* (New York: Schirmer Books, 1988).

Kregor, Jonathan, *Liszt as Transcriber* (Cambridge: Cambridge University Press, 2010).

Krog, Stephen, 'Creative Risk Taking', in Simon R. Swaffield (ed.), *Theory in Landscape Architecture: A Reader* (Philadelphia: University of Pennsylvania Press, 2002).

Kunst, Jaap, *Ethnomusicology* (The Hague: Martinus Nijhoff, 1974).

Kynt, E., '"How I Compose": Ferruccio Busoni's Views about Invention, Quotation, and the Compositional Process', in *The Journal of Musicology*, 27/2 (Spring, 2010), 224–264.

Ligeti, György, *Lontano* (Mainz: Schott, 1967).

Ligeti, György, *In Conversation: György Ligeti in Conversation with Peter Varnai, Joseph Hausler, Claude Samuel and Himself* (London: Da Capo Press, 1983).

Ligeti, György, *Ligeti in Conversation* (London: Eulenburg, 1983).

Ligeti, György, 'On my Etudes for Piano', in Sid McLauchlin (trans.), *Sonus*, 9/1 (Fall, 1988), 3–7.

Lobanova, Marina, *György Ligeti: Style, Ideas, Poetics* (Berlin: Verlag Ernst Kuhn, 2002).

Lynch, Kevin, *What Time is this Place?* (Cambridge, MA: The MIT Press, 1972).

McHarg, Ian, *Design with Nature* (New York: Wiley, 1992).

Machado, Antonio, *Selected Poems* (Cambridge, MA: Harvard University Press, 1982).

Maillet, Arnaud, *The Claude Glass: Use and Meaning of the Black Mirror in Western Art* (New York: Zone Books, 2004).

Mellen, Joan, *Voices from the Japanese Cinema* (New York: Liveright, 1975).

Morgan, Robert P., 'Spatial Forms in Ives', in H. Wiley Hitchcock and Vivian Perlis (eds), *An Ives Celebration* (Urbana: University of Illinois Press, 1977).

Moggeridge, Hal, 'Notes on Kent's Garden at Rousham', in *Journal of Garden History*, 6/3 (1986), 187–226.

Myer, Helen, 'Ethnomusicology', in Helen Myers (ed.), *Ethnomusicology An Introduction* (New York: Norton, 1992).

Nettl, Bruno, *The Study of Ethnomusicology* (Nov., 2005).

Pace, Ian, 'The Panorama of Michael Finnissy (I)', in *Tempo*, 196 (Apr., 1996), 25–35.

Pace, Ian, 'The Panorama of Michael Finnissy (II)', in *Tempo*, 201 (July, 1997), 7–16.

Pallasmaa, Juhani, *The Architecture of Image: Existential Space in Cinema* (Helsinki: Building Information Limited, 2001).

Pallasmaa, Juhani, *The Eyes of the Skin* (Chichester: Wiley-Academy, 2005).

Parrish, Carl, *The Notation of Medieval Music* (New York: Pendragon Press, 1978).

Partch, Harry, 'Experiments in Notation' in Elliot Schwartz, Barney Childs and Jim Fox (eds), *Contemporary Composers on Contemporary Music* (New York: Da Capo Press, 1998).

Pierce, John R., *The Science of Musical Sound* (New York: Scientific American Books, 1983).

Plot, Robert, *The Natural History of Oxfordshire Being an Essay Towards the Natural History of England* (London: S. Millers, 1677).

Pope, Alexander, *The Temple of Fame. And an Ode for Music of St Cecilia's Day* (London: T. Daniel, W. Thompson, J. Stefle, A. Todd, 1758).

Price, Uvedale, *Essays on the Picturesque, as Compared with the Sublime and Beautiful, and on the Use of Studying Pictures, for the Purpose of Improving Real Landscape Vol.1* (London: J. Mawman, 1810).

Potter, John, *Observations on the Present State of Music and Musicians* (London: C. Henderson, 1762).

Rastall, Richard, *The Notation of Western Music* (London: J.M. Dent and Sons, 1983).

Rée, Jonathan, *I See a Voice* (London: HarperCollins Publishers, 1999).

Reed, Thomas S., *Directory of Music Notation Proposals* (Kirksville, MO: Notation Music Press, 1997).

Roberge, Marc-Andre, 'The Busoni Network and the Art of Creative Transcription', in *Canadian University Music Review*, 11/1 (1991), 68–88.

Rogger, Andre, *Landscapes of Taste The Art of Humphry Repton's Red Books* (Abingdon: Routledge, 2007).

Rousseau, Jean-Jacques, 'Essays on the Origin of Languages and Writings Related to Music', in John T. Scott (ed., trans.), *The Collected Writings of Rousseau Vol.7* (Hanover: UP of New England, 1998).

Rump, Stephen, 'Beethoven and the Ut Pictura Poesis Tradition', in *Beethoven Forum*, 12/2 (Fall 2005), 113–150.

Ruskin, John, *Modern Painters Vol. 4* (London: George Allen, 1904).

Sabbe, Herman, in Thomas DeLio (ed.), *The Music of Morton Feldman* (New York: Excelsior Music Publishing Company, 1996).

Saunders, Aretas A., *A Guide to Bird Songs* (New York: Doubleday & Company, 1951).

Schafer, R. Murray, *The Soundscape: Our Sonic Environment and the Tuning of the World* (Rochester VT: Destiny Books, 1993).

Serper, Zvika, 'Shindo Kaneto's films Kuroneko and Onibaba: Traditional and Innovative Manifestations of Demonic Embodiments', in *Japan Forum*, 17/2 (2005), 231–256.

Shaw-Miller, Simon, 'Thinking Through Construction: Notation-Composition-Event, the Architecture of Music', in *AA Files: The Journal of the Architectural Association School of Architecture*, 53 (Spring, 2006), 38–47.

Sisto, Antonella, *Film Sound in Italy Listening to the Screen* (New York: Palgrave MacMillan, 2014).

Steinitz, Richard, *György Ligeti* (London: Faber and Faber, 2003).

Strunk, Oliver, *Source Readings in Music History Antiquity and the Middle Ages* (New York: W.W. Norton and Company, 1965).

Strunk, Oliver, *Source Readings in Music History* (New York: W.W Norton and Company, 1998).

Temple, Nicholas, *Disclosing Horizons* (Abingdon, Oxon: Routledge, 2007).

Tilley, Christopher, *A Phenomenology of Landscape* (Oxford: Berg Publishers, 1994).

Tschumi, Bernard, *Manhattan Transcripts* (London: Academy Editions, 1994).

Thiel, Philip, 'A Sequence-Experience Notation: For Architectural and Urban Spaces', in *The Town Planning Review*, 32/1 (April 1961), 33–52.

Thoreau, David Henry, *Walden, or, Life in the Woods* (Cambridge, MA: The Riverside Press, 1854).

Thoreau, Henry David, *Walden, or, Life in the Woods* (Boston MA: Houghton, Mifflin and Company, 1882).

Tormey, Alan, 'Indeterminacy and Identity in Art', in *Monist*, 58 (1974), 203–215.

Tuan, Yi-Fi, *Topophilia* (New Jersey: Prentice-Hall, 1974).

Vaughn, Kathryn, 'Pitch Measurement', in Helen Myers (ed.), *Ethnomusicology An Introduction* (New York: Norton, 1992).

Walker, Enrique, 'Avant-propos: Bernard Tschumi in Conversation with Enrique Walker', in *Grey Room*, 17 (2004), 118–126.

Walpole, Horace, *Anecdotes of Painting in England, with Some Account of the Principal Artists vol.III* (London: Horace Walpole, 1849).

Widdess, Richard, 'Notation', in Helen Myers (ed.), *Ethnomusicology An Introduction* (New York: Norton, 1992).

Wylie, John, *Landscape* (Abingdon: Routledge, 2007).

WEBSITES

Cage, John, interview with Robin White at Crown Point Press, Oakland California, 1978. http://writings.heatherodonnell.info/Messiaen_and_Thoreau.html#_ftn7. (Accessed on 25.08.2014).

Clement, Gilles, *The Third Landscape*. http://www.gillesclement.com/cat-tierspaysage-tit-le-Tiers-Paysage (Accessed on 25.08.2014).

Keller, James M., Ligeti: Lontano for Large Orchestra (2010) http://www.sfsymphony.org/music/ProgramNotes.aspx?id=33250 (Accessed 28.01.2011).

Ligeti, György, and Jack, Adrian, 'Ligeti talks to Adrian Jack', in *Music and Musicians*, 22/11 (1974), 24–30. http://www.ronsen.org/monkminkpinkpunk/9/gl2.html. (Accessed on 08.03.2014).

Nakamura, Shogo, Hayashi, Kaoru, Yuasa, Takashi, Musiake, Katumi, Ono, Fumio, Kubota, Hajime and Shoji, Taro, *Restoration of Submerged Plants for Water Quality Improvement of Lake Inba-Numa*, in proceedings of International Lake Environment Committee Foundation, Wuhan, 2009. http://wldb.ilec.or.jp/data/ilec/WLC13_Papers/S1/s1-5.pdf.

Robbins, Craig, and Ryan, Vanessa (eds), *Vegetation of Girraween National Park* (2011), http://www.rymich.com/girraween/downloads/GRWN_Booklet_20110802.pdf

Swafford, Jan, *A Question is Better than an Answer*, http://www.charlesives.org/ives_essay/

http://www.allmusic.com/composition/fantasia-nach-j-s-bach-for-piano-kiv-253-mc0002358702.

http://www.birdwatching.co.uk/Articles/BTO-Report/Nightingale.

http://bldgblog.blogspot.co.uk/2007/07/new-york-city-in-sound.html. (Accessed on 23.01.2014).

http://www.british-history.ac.uk/report.aspx?compid=101859#n9.

www.cengage.com Franco of Cologne, Art of Measured Song. (Accessed 10.08.2013).

http://www.chelseabookfair.com/index.pl?isa=Metadot::SystemApp::BookSearch;op=detail;book=39606;image=264272

http://www.christies.com/lotfinder/lot/attributed-to-hasegawa-tohaku-pine-trees-in-4870097-details.aspx?from=salesummary&intObjectID=4870097&sid=7900dac5-6dde-4930-b6f2-10a8dd0da0d7. (Accessed on 12.04.2014).

http://www.cnvill.net/mfworks.pdf (Accessed on 09.10.2013).

http://list.english-heritage.org.uk/resultsingle.aspx?uid=1052956

http://www.michaelfinnissy.info/works/full_list.php

http://www.newmusicbox.org/articles/cage-tudor-concert-for-piano-and-orchestra/ (Accessed on 21.09.2013).

http://www.oed.com.libproxy.ucl.ac.uk/view/Entry/124108?rskey=pevggP&result=1&isAdvanced=false#eid.

http://www.oed.com/view/Entry/105515?p=emailAacUGlP2BEXFI&d=105515.

https://oregonstate.edu/instruct/ph302/texts/locke/locke1/Book2a.html#Chapter XIV.10

https://oregonstate.edu/instruct/ph302/texts/locke/locke1/Book2a.html#Chapter XIV.27

http://www.rymich.com/girraween/downloads/girraween_bird_species_list.pdfp.2

http://whc.unesco.org/documents/publi_wh_papers_26_en.pdf (Accessed on 27.05.2014).

http://www.youtube.com/watch?v=9W8cYK5RxwY (Accessed 21.11.2011).

Index